The Art and Politics of Science

HAROLD VARMUS

—

W. W. NORTON & COMPANY

New York London

For information about permission to reproduce selections from this book,
write to Permissions, W. W. Norton & Company, Inc.,
500 Fifth Avenue, New York, NY 10110

For information about special discounts for bulk purchases, please contact
W. W. Norton Special Sales at specialsales@wwnorton.com or 800-233-4830

Manufacturing by RR Donnelley, Bloomsburg
Book design by Barbara Bachman
Production manager: Julia Druskin

Library of Congress Cataloging-in-Publication Data

Varmus, Harold.
The art and politics of science / Harold Varmus. — 1st ed.
p. ; cm.
Includes bibliographical references and index.
ISBN 978-0-393-06128-4 (hardcover)
1. Varmus, Harold. 2. Medical scientists—United States—Biography
3. Nobel Prize winners—United States—Biography
4. National Institutes of Health (U.S.) I. Title.
[DNLM: 1. Varmus, Harold. 2. National Institutes of Health (U.S.)
3. Science—United States—Personal Narratives. 4. Health Policy—United
States—Personal Narratives. 5. Neoplasms—therapy—United
States—Personal Narratives. WZ 100 V316a 2009]
R154.V47.A3 2009
610.92—dc22
[B]
2008042963

ISBN 978-0-393-30453-4 pbk.

W. W. Norton & Company, Inc.
500 Fifth Avenue, New York, N.Y. 10110
www.wwnorton.com

W. W. Norton & Company Ltd.
Castle House, 75/76 Wells Street, London W1T 3QT

1 2 3 4 5 6 7 8 9 0

Praise for *The Art and Politics of Science*

"*The Art and Politics of Science* is a unique work by a remarkable global leader: a brilliant scientist with the sensibilities of an artist and the leadership skills of a consummate politician. Harold Varmus has done it all—Nobel Prize–winning breakthroughs in cancer biology, masterful leadership of the National Institutes of Health (NIH) during its period of greatest expansion, statesmanship of the highest order in global health, and cheerful trench warfare to bring biomedical publications to the open-source Internet age. This book is captivating, fascinating, and ever instructive. It will be read the world over with enormous delight and benefit."

—Jeffrey D. Sachs, director, The Earth Institute

"Harold Varmus's new book, *The Art and Politics of Science*, is a timely memoir of a remarkable career. . . . Let us hope that this is just the first of two volumes." —Robert Cook-Deegan, *American Scientist*

"Through an artful melding of science and policy, Harold Varmus conveys not only the excitement of forefront research but the richly textured human dramas that swirl around pivotal discoveries."

—Brian Greene, author of *The Elegant Universe*

"Varmus is one of our leading scientific figures, a Nobel Prize–winning cancer researcher who advises President Obama. . . . He has also written a perceptive book about science and its civic value, arriving as the White House renews its acquaintance with empiricism."

—Peter Dizikes, *New York Times*

"If you've ever wondered about the early life of a budding scientist, the experience of doing cutting-edge research, or the translation of brilliant work into public service, read the account of this passionate, politically engaged, deeply humane scientist and marvel at the richness of a life well spent."

—Andrea Barrett, National Book Award–winning author of *Ship Fever*

"Varmus provides an entertaining exposition of what it takes to be a successful scientist and of how science is really done, as well as illuminating insights into the worlds of politics and science policy.... Varmus not only has a strong underlying conviction that science can and should be used to do good, but also knows how to make things happen and is committed to making the effort."   —Richard O'Hynes, *New England Journal of Medicine*

"Varmus makes this era's revolution in biological knowledge as comprehensible as it possibly can be. Varmus's broad abilities in scientific, literary, and political realms are evident in this graceful and often gently humorous book."
                —James Fallows, author of *Blind into Baghdad: America's War in Iraq*

"This is a book to read and then pass on to others with an earnest hope that they will enjoy it as much and learn as much from it as you have."
                                —Richard Goldsby, *Amherst Magazine*

"Harold Varmus is a person of legendary charm and limitless vision who has put his gifted mind to the service of science, health, and above all . . . the people of the world. I loved this book."
                —Donna E. Shalala, president, University of Miami,
                        and former secretary, Health and Human Services

"Any time any one of us has a cancer scare, or worse, we can be grateful to Harold Varmus and his extraordinary life in science. We are all lucky that Dr. Varmus left literature for medicine. And now, reading this book, we can be grateful that he is so very gifted in both."
—Jonathan Weiner, Pulitzer Prize–winning author of *The Beak of the Finch*

For my parents, Bea and Frank,
who missed so much of it

Contents

—

Preface

—

THIS SMALL BOOK OWES ITS EXISTENCE IN LARGE PART TO JEAN STROUSE. Late in 2003, when she was still the freshly appointed director of The New York Public Library's Cullman Center for Scholars and Writers, Jean asked me to give a series of three lectures the following fall, an annual event sponsored by W. W. Norton & Company, hoping that I would speak about some aspects of the relationship between the sciences and the humanities. This notion was inspired, in part, by her long-range goal of using her new position to promote a greater interest in and knowledge about science among her colleagues in the humanities. I was asked because she knew that I had studied literature in earlier years and continue to read widely in realms beyond the science that I practice.

At first, she suggested that I revisit the concept of two cultures, which is generally traced to the 1959 Rede Lecture delivered by C. P. Snow, who had achieved prominence as a scientist, a novelist, and a government official. Snow's description of the two cultures, the arts and the sciences, separated by a gulf of language and thought, met with both hearty acclaim and strident criticism, and the subsequent debates attracted enormous attention.[1] (I recall an evening given over to an American version of the debate at a fraternity house at Amherst College in 1960, when I was an undergraduate there.)

But on rereading both the original lecture and Snow's responses to his critics, I found (and Jean did too) that the idea of two cultures now appeared too simplistic, however accurate, to bear a lengthy reexamination. So, after a series of lunches and email exchanges, we agreed that I would endeavor to explain what it means to be a scientist—or, anyhow, what it has meant for me to be a scientist. That seemed to be a way to fulfill at least part of her original purpose, since I came to science through an education in the humanities, and my career as a scientist has included significant forays into politics, administration, publishing, and international issues. By defining my purpose in this manner, I hoped to make some aspects of the life and thoughts of one scientist intelligible and possibly interesting to even the most entrenched members of the "other" culture.

To do this, I intended to use my three lectures to describe three things: first, how I became a scientist; then, something about the work my colleagues and I have done and its significance for the control of cancer; and, finally, examples of my experience in government and policy-making, to offer a view of a scientist in a larger world that includes politics and the arts. The assignment encouraged me to think more than I would otherwise have done about the shape of my career, which revealed to me how meandering and unexpected it has been. This theme—with implicit course changes and serendipities—became a dominant one in the lectures and even more so in this volume.

Still, the "two cultures" also remained a recurring theme. In the first lecture, I described myself veering from one culture to the other, while seeking a career. In the second, I tried to make my scientific work comprehensible, in what seemed to be a very short hour, to listeners accustomed to talks on the humanities. In the course of the final lecture, one dealing with the intersections of science and politics, I recalled the real purpose of Snow's lectures: to ask which element in our culture was most likely to help those countries struggling with poverty.

To undertake the Norton lectures, I also had to agree to turn them into a book, happily to be published by the sponsor and edited by its president, Drake McFeely. I have taken advantage of the less restrained format of a book to describe some of my scientific work in greater detail than was possible in the second lecture and to expand on the political and social themes of the final lecture.

Despite the inclusion of additional material, this book is certainly very far from being a full autobiography; it does not pretend to be a comprehensive account of my work either as a scientist in a laboratory or as a scientist engaged in politics. I have tried to select aspects of my scientific work and of my life as a leader of institutions that would interest a general reader, without concern for any sense of completeness. Still, the process of selection has been difficult and anxiety provoking. In writing about my scientific work, I have followed only a couple of threads in the fabric of what my research group has tried to achieve. In doing so, I have omitted several topics—and, more awkwardly, many people—central to my experience as a scientist. At the same time, while trying to convey a coherent story about the field of modern cancer research, and hoping to illustrate the kinds of experience that science offers as well as some of its intellectual rewards, I have left out significant aspects of our field and many people whose work has been extraordinary. Happily, more inclusive treatments of recent progress in cancer research can be found elsewhere; some are cited in the bibliography. I hope that those who feel that they have been sidelined or that crucial topics have been ignored will have some sympathy for my plight and some affinity for my objectives.

The process of writing about myself, for the lectures or the book, has been awkward and slow. In July of 2004, a few months before my lectures, I happened to be in Paris on the occasion of a popular exhibition entitled "Moi!"—a collection of self-portraits by twentieth-century painters and photographers, housed in the Luxembourg Palace. Such portraits are not hard to find; artists appear to be attracted to themselves as subjects. Self-portraits by scientists, however, are uncommon. An exceptional few, like François Jacob's *The Statue Within*, are intensely personal and emotionally revealing.[2] But most tend to emphasize the objective conclusions of a scientist's work rather than the subjective experiences of the scientist who has done it. The reverse seems generally to be true in the self-representations of artists, in which the emotional content is often paramount. In one notable exception (which happened to be the work depicted on the poster advertising "Moi!"), a self-portrait by the American painter Norman Rockwell, the working methods of the painter, his efforts at objectivity, are the focal point of the portrait. Rockwell has, in fact, portrayed himself as a kind of scientist, using a technical device, a mirror, to observe and measure, and thus to help record his appearance in paint on canvas. I hope to emulate his approach in the pages that follow.

Introduction

—

 S THE FIRST PART OF THIS BOOK WILL SHOW, I WAS DRAWN SLOWLY
to a life in science, after excursions in literature and clinical medicine.
But once committed to laboratory life at the relatively advanced age of
thirty, I had the good fortune to form a partnership with a like-minded
scientist, J. Michael Bishop, and to take part in work that uncovered a
central element in one of medicine's greatest challenges: the origins of
cancer.

In doing this work, as described in detail in the second part of the
book, we changed cancer research in a fundamental way. Before our work,
genetic damage was considered only one of several possible ways in which
cancer might arise. Especially after other scientists expanded on our findings, the cancer research community became generally united behind the
concept that mutations in certain cellular genes—largely, but not exclusively, the kinds of genes we discovered, the class now known as proto-
oncogenes—are the principal drivers of cancerous growth. These
advances and others are now revolutionizing the diagnosis and treatment
of cancers, diseases that remain leading causes of death throughout the
world.

Because our success brought prizes (especially the Nobel Prize in
Medicine in 1989) and prizes brought prominence, I became active in the

world of science policy. A few years later, in 1993, President Bill Clinton asked me to run the National Institutes of Health (NIH), the world's largest agency for biomedical research. The NIH directorship, discussed in part 3 of the text, proved to be much more than an administrative job. It was also a platform for engagement with some of the most interesting issues of our time, including three to which I have devoted chapters in the final section in this book: embryo and stem cell research, global health, and publication practices in science. In my position since 2000 as president of the Memorial Sloan-Kettering Cancer Center, I have been able to continue my involvement in these areas, while still directing a laboratory and overseeing a world-renowned cancer center.

As this book reveals, I have been dealt some very good cards—exemplary partners in life and science, talented trainees and co-workers, and strong institutions and propitious times in which to do scientific work That good fortune has allowed me to lead a charmed and exciting life in science. But I write at a time when science has strained relationships with the federal government, has been losing its financial support, and has become a less appealing career goal for many students on our campuses. In addition, some areas of science, including evolution and stem cell research, are under attack from the so-called religious right, which has a disturbing degree of influence in the White House at the moment.

By completing this book now, four years after giving the lectures on which it was originally based, I hope to transmit some of my own experiences in science and science policy to those who will guide the nation after the election of 2008. But I have been more persistently motivated by the idea of offering an enthusiastic view of a life in science to those who should be preparing to replace our generation of scientists. To be an effective advocate for a life in science, I have tried to explain why I chose a career in science over one in literature, why scientific work has captured my attention for so many years, and why science policy is both fascinating and important. To be convincing, I must also be specific. For that reason, I have tried to present the relevant parts of my education and some of the significant aspects of my own work, in the laboratory and in policy arenas, in some depth.

A central feature of this story is the scientific work that led to the discovery of proto-oncogenes. This discovery was, in more than one sense, pivotal to my life in science. By offering immense satisfaction to those of us involved in the discovery, it more than justified my choice of science as a career. By emerging from a collaborative effort—a long-term partnership with Mike Bishop, experiments involving many people in our own laboratories, and interactions among several West Coast research groups— it illustrated the strengths of cooperation in science and the importance of communities of scientists. And by making us notable as recipients of prizes, it made possible my excursions into the world of government and policy.

As I emphasize in discussions of our research, the discovery of proto-oncogenes and the mutations that activate them set the stage for a still-ongoing transformation of thought about cancer that affects all aspects of patient care. When Mike Bishop and I began working together in 1970, cancer research was often considered to be a field mired in largely unproductive technologies. People had been transplanting tumors in animals, observing animals with cancer, or growing cancer cells in petri dishes for decades, without much impact on the understanding of cancer or the improvement of its treatment. Most of the major new developments had come from epidemiology—linking smoking with lung cancer, for instance—or from empirical approaches to therapy, using surgery, x-rays, and highly toxic chemicals. Other branches of medicine seemed more highly informed by physiology or biochemistry—discoveries of hormones changed endocrinology and metabolic diseases, studies of salt balance affected the management of kidney diseases, analysis of electrical rhythms was fundamental to cardiology. But oncology seemed like a discipline of brute force and bad outcomes, without the guidance of operating principles and careful measurements.

As a recently trained physician and as a member of a family struggling with cancer, I was fully aware of cancer's human toll, and the need to make some progress against the disease. Then, as now, cancer ranked among the most prevalent—and the most feared—of the medical conditions that afflict human beings in this country and throughout the world. About half of all men and over a third of all women in the United States will receive a diagnosis of cancer at some point in their lives, and about half of the patients who develop a cancer, other than the common skin cancers, will die of it. While the disease can often be eliminated by surgery, the impact of a diagnosis is lifelong; everyone who receives it becomes a cancer survivor and is likely to live uneasily with the risk of recurrence. When efforts to eliminate a cancer do not succeed and the cancer spreads to other sites, patients are apt to battle the disease chronically. Such battles are rarely easy, often involving repeated surgeries, many sessions of radiation treatments, or drug therapies (chemotherapies) with unpleasant and even debilitating side effects. All of these features can inspire efforts to study cancer with some specific goals in mind: to prevent it; to detect it at earlier, more treatable phases; or to treat it and its symptoms more effectively, even to cure it.

Over the past thirty years our conception of cancer has been dramatically changed, even if mortality rates overall have declined only slightly.[1] What was once an unspeakable illness in which our cells mysteriously acquire the capacity to destroy us by incessant growth has become a comprehensible, if still dreaded, disease in which cells have experienced mutations of specific genes that can explain their wayward behavior. This means that we can think about cancers and the genes that cause them in very concrete ways, not unlike the ways we think about infectious diseases—the viral, bacterial, and parasitic agents that cause them and the specific vaccines and drugs that we now use to prevent and treat them. These changes are affecting how we think about cancer experimentally, how we diagnose and treat some cancers, and even how we talk about them when doctors must explain a diagnosis to patients and their families.[2]

The extent of these changes can be illustrated by two memorable telephone calls, separated by about fifty years. In about 1950, when I was ten years old, I recall watching my father, a physician working in Freeport, New York, receive a call that conveyed devastating news: one of my mother's favorite cousins, a robust man in the middle of his life, had just been diagnosed with leukemia. Of course, I did not know very much about leukemia, but I did know immediately from my parents' expressions—and, within a few days, from our cousin's death—that this disease was terrible, a veritable tidal wave.

About half a century later, early in 1999, when I was in my final year as director of the NIH, I received a call from Rick Klausner, then the director of the National Cancer Institute, telling me that a new drug had induced dramatic remissions in nearly all of more than fifty adults with a certain type of leukemia in an early-phase clinical trial. The drug, now known widely as Gleevec, was being tested as a treatment for that type of leukemia, chronic myeloid leukemia, because it had recently been shown to inhibit an enzyme that is made by a mutant gene considered responsible for the leukemia. That gene is a member of the class of cancer genes we had discovered nearly twenty-five years earlier. Twenty-five years before that, when my father heard about our cousin's leukemia, biologists were not even sure that genes were made of DNA, had no idea how genetic information could be encoded in genes, and, of course, had no way of knowing that cancers are driven by mutations.

The changes implied by this fifty-year transformation depend on an extraordinary range of new knowledge about biology and medicine. While it is not my intention to review these revolutionary developments in detail, I hope to provide a picture of one person's odyssey through unusual times in science, a sense of what it means to carry out scientific work with interesting colleagues, and an account of some of the social and political factors that affect how science is done and what we as a society can do to foster its potential.

Part One

BECOMING A SCIENTIST

CHAPTER 1

Origins and Beginnings

—

I GENERALLY THINK OF MY CHILDHOOD AS UNEXCEPTIONAL. CERTAINLY IT lacked the drama of familial unhappiness or divorce, the trials of poverty or discomfort, or the exhilaration of exotic travel or adventure. Still, my family represented an extraordinary and uniquely American phenomenon.

Less than fifty years before my birth, all of my grandparents were struggling to make a living in Europe—my father's parents in an unknown town in Poland, my mother's parents on farms near Linz in Austria. The computerized files at the Ellis Island Foundation have recently provided me with specific information about my grandfathers, although nothing to corroborate the little I know about the histories of my grandmothers. My mother's father, Hersch Barasch, later called Harry, arrived in New York on the Edam on August 5, 1898 at the age of seventeen, after sailing from Rotterdam; my father's father, Jakob Warmus, aged twenty-five, landed on October 26, 1904, on the Neckar, which had departed from Bremen. Although family legend claims that he had lived in a now exterminated suburb of Warsaw, the record shows that he called Lopuszna, a pretty farming village near Cracow, his most recent place of residence in Poland. Lopuszna is now a tour destination for cyclists and trout fishermen.

Like so many European Jews of their social class, my grandparents found their way to Ellis Island, then on to jobs in the environs of New York City. The change in class status between their generation and the next was electrifying. By 1932, at a time when the affluent country that had attracted my grandparents was in the depths of its Great Depression, my father, Frank, had attended Harvard College and graduated from Tufts Medical School, and my mother, Beatrice Barasch, had graduated from Wellesley College and was headed for the New York School of Social Work—achievements reasonable enough for people whose family had been in the country for a couple of centuries, but astonishing for the children of recent immigrants.

Still, I grew up thinking such accomplishments were ordinary and, of course, they were not uncommon. I knew there had been hard times in my father's past. His mother, Esther, had died in the influenza epidemic of 1918 when he was eleven, leaving him with a lifelong aversion to religion. Mostly, this aversion was expressed as a lack of interest in social events linked to the synagogue or good-humored mockery of rabbinical sermons. But as we followed my mother's hearse to the cemetery in 1971, he told me that he had never been able to believe in a God who would allow the mother of an eleven-year-old boy to die. His father, Jacob (an Americanization of Jakob), had never learned to speak much English and never earned more than what was possible for a small farmer near Newburgh or a hat factory worker in Newark. But, despite what must have been a relatively bleak home life, Frank was an academic star at Newark High (a culture that I have learned more about from the novels of Philip Roth than from my father's own accounts). Harvard offered a scholarship that was good enough to keep him at the college for two years, where he played lacrosse, mingled with aristocratic classmates (one, at least, was a Saltonstall), and must have felt very far from Newark. After that, he worked for a year as a waiter in Boston to stash away the funds necessary to pay for medical school.

My mother took an easier path—one that I can more readily picture, since I lived for most of my youth in the town, Freeport, New York, in which she, too, had grown up. Her parents, Harry and Regina, had come to America with access to relatives who had already established successful small businesses along the South Shore of Long Island. So my mother grew up, as did I, in a large house in a suburban community, in a family of some means and with conventional signs of respectability. Her father, Harry (for whom I was named), was among the founders of the first conservative synagogue in town, and the owner of Barasch's, a popular children's clothing store that held the Girls Scouts' franchise and provided employment for virtually everyone in the family, including my mother's two brothers and, much later, during school vacations, me. When the smart, popular Bea left for Wellesley in 1928 to study psychology and learn the traditions of a formidable New England college, she got no Horatio Alger send-offs. And when she returned home after graduation to train as a psychiatric social worker, her family seems to have greeted her choice as another sensible and quite ordinary step for a young woman of talent.

By this time, my father was a member of the house staff at Kings County Hospital in Brooklyn. A fellow trainee introduced him to my mother, initiating the sequence of events required for my own existence a few years later: a courtship, a honeymoon in the summer of 1936 at Lake George, and the settling down—living in a pleasant gray house, building a family practice of medicine, and having a first child (me, at the end of 1939)—in Freeport.

CHILDHOOD

The entry of the United States into a world war just two years later occasioned the most exotic segment of my childhood, life in a semitropical Florida suburb, Winter Park, not far from my father's post as a physician and officer at the Orlando Air Base, a situation that allowed evenings of fishing in a nearby lake with alligators. But by the start of 1946, we were back in Freeport, accompanied by a new family member, my younger sister, Ellen, in a larger, somewhat eccentric Victorian house, with a barn and an acre of land for vegetables and flowers, at short walking distances from three important influences: my maternal grandmother, my schools, and the public library.

How unremarkable all this history of comfortable living seemed to me during my childhood! It seemed entirely natural to belong to a family that in two generations had advanced from persecution and poverty in one part of the world to a contented existence in the professional class in another. Rarely did anyone in our family discuss the obligatory trials of this transformation or the alternative outcomes (the Holocaust being only the most obvious). Ellen and I took the benefits of our pleasant existence more or less for granted, growing up with a sense of entitlement and a confidence about the future that were probably unwarranted, however useful they proved to be.

In a small middle-class town like Freeport in the 1940s and 1950s, expectations about the future of its young were high, and closely tied to parental status. (Things seem to be different there now: Freeport's recent appearances in the *New York Times* have been triggered by a wave of drive-by shootings.) For me then, a bright and earnest Jewish son of a general practitioner whose friends were mostly physicians and dentists and businessmen, a career in medicine seemed preordained. Everything I can remember or document from browsing in my high school yearbook suggests that I did not resist that prescribed destiny.

Yet a number of signs implied that I might be an unlikely prospect for an education in science or for a professional alliance with my father. I did not have the kind of youthful romance with chemistry that Oliver Sacks describes in his recent book *Uncle Tungsten.*[1] If any of my relatives provided a similar sort of inspiration, it was Harvey Rattner, a second cousin in a nearby South Shore village, who introduced me in my teens to Kafka, other European writers, and existentialism. The sciences were never my favorite subjects in high school, and I did not aspire to enter, let alone win, any science fairs.

If I felt distinctive as a student in high school, it was because my family had packed me off, following my sophomore year, to summer work camp at the Putney School in Vermont, after many years of misadventures at a Boy Scout camp called Wauwepex, near Lake Ronkonkoma, on Long Island. I returned from Putney trying to write short stories and eager to spend weekends with my new and more sophisticated friends from Manhattan or the North Shore of Long Island. But I felt too insecure about my abilities and too loyal to my Freeport pals to transfer to Putney for the last two years of high school, as my parents thought I should. To try to imitate the high-mindedness of Putney in the more pedestrian two summers that followed, I managed to persuade William Hull, a young professor at nearby Hofstra University, to teach the novels of James Joyce to a group of my high school friends one evening a week. Hull proved to be a lively teacher and a serious scholar; I still treasure my copy of *Ulysses*, annotated with marginalia from his classes.

AMHERST COLLEGE

When I had to make a choice regarding college in my senior year, I did not think much about the scientific training I might receive at the schools under consideration, although I did pay attention to their success with medical school admissions. I sought a place where I would be certain to get a broad introduction to both arts and sciences, a school small enough to provide a reasonable chance of knowing members of the faculty. Largely on these grounds, I chose Amherst over Harvard. I perceived my father's enthusiasm for this choice as a measure of both his dissatisfaction with his own Harvard experiences, and his uncertainty about my abilities to thrive in what he portrayed as the more competitive and self-reliant atmosphere in Cambridge. I hope I was wrong about the latter perception, but I never asked.

In the 1950s, Amherst was distinctive among leading American colleges for its adherence to what was called the New Curriculum. Its 250 freshmen, all males, formed firm bonds from the common experience of taking the same set of courses, which included calculus, physics, European history, readings of the classics, and a justifiably famous course in expository writing called English 1-2, in which we all struggled with the same essay assignments. Memorably, the first assignments in the fall of 1957 asked us to describe our convictions, why we had them, and how they could be changed by our teachers, or "frisked," as Robert Frost had put it. Most of us found—and as I am still finding—that we didn't really know what we thought, what our principles were, until we tried to write them down. What we thought we believed was hard to put into ordinary sentences—so did we have any convictions at all? We discovered that we were more complicated than we knew, as we tried to define our opinions in words that others could comprehend.

Science classes also confronted us with the potential ambiguities of knowledge. I remember especially a cartoon shown by our first-year physics professor, Dudley Towne. A scientist sits on one side of a wall trying to make measurements of—and deductions about—the sounds produced by the antics of bizarre individuals on the other side of the wall. The implication was obvious. Science is limited by the tools we possess for measuring natural phenomena and by the imagination we exercise to interpret those measurements. Not so far from the lessons of English 1-2.

Exposure to many fields of inquiry, as then required by the Amherst curriculum, can be both invigorating and distracting to a curious student. In my first years at college, I toyed with the possibilities of majoring in philosophy (ultimately too abstract), physics (ultimately too hard), and English literature (ultimately selected). I remained loyal to my original intention of fulfilling premed requirements, but I never seriously considered majoring in biology. I couldn't understand how some of my close friends (among them, some now distinguished scientists) could spend long afternoons and evenings incarcerated in a laboratory, when they could be reading books in a soft library chair or reciting poetry on Amherst's green hills. I was once urged by a professor of organic chemistry, Robert Whitney, whose required premed course I was failing, to consider dropping the course and jettisoning my medical school aspirations, since I was so plainly headed for a career in literature. Because I doubted that Whitney knew much about me or what I should do, I moved out of my pleasantly boisterous fraternity house into a solitary dorm room and pulled myself up to a gentlemanly C. It later proved to be enough for at least one medical school.

My extracurricular obsession was the school newspaper, the *Amherst Student*. Serving as the chairman—the editor in chief—for a year was the headiest experience of my college career. The other members of the staff were among the most interesting students I knew at Amherst, and many later became academics, artists, journalists, and editors. We ran long reviews of books, lectures, readings, concerts, and movies; some issues had the appearance of a literary magazine. In addition, our editorials took on many controversial topics of the times, including student political activism (mostly to support racial equity in the South), college spending on athletics (our efforts to augment intramural at the expense of intercollegiate sports were very unpopular with some segments of the student body), the influence of philanthropic foundations on educational policy (equally unpopular with administration officials), and the presidential election of 1960 (favoring Kennedy over Nixon). These views were so often unpopular that a group of undergraduates attempted to recall some of us with a referendum, which we managed to survive. A few of the controversies made me uncomfortable, but I also found them exhilarating. A career in journalism seemed worth considering, too.

But English literature was the most powerful attraction. The Amherst English department had grown prominent, especially under the influence of Reuben Brower, who had departed Amherst for a Harvard professorship shortly before I arrived. Brower was a famously strong advocate for the literary movement known as the New Criticism, which argued that the interpretation of literature had become too heavily influenced by history and biography, and needed to return to the raw experience of directly confronting and analyzing the words on the page.

I remember particularly well my first exposure to the writings of I. A. Richards, one of the earliest prophets of the New Criticism.[2] Richards insisted on careful, close reading of primary texts and a clear exposition of what a writer is trying to say, before the reader seeks help from biographies of the author, scholarly or critical writings of others, or the historical context. I now see my enthusiasm for this approach to texts as not unlike the love I later developed for primary scientific data. Just as the data allow scientists to decipher natural systems, the texts allow literary critics to approach an author's state of mind. My devotion to the principles of the New Criticism probably delayed my appreciation of the ways texts and lives both shape and are shaped by cultures, aspects of the reading experience that I now find both instructive and enjoyable—and endorsed by new literary movements such as the New Historicism.*

I also fell under the spell of some extraordinary teachers at Amherst—Benjamin DeMott, a prolific essayist, with a national reputation, who lectured on Milton and eighteenth- and nineteenth-century novels; Theodore Baird, a rarely published, self-consciously eccentric teacher and an originator of the famous English 1-2 course, who taught Shakespeare; Roger Sale, an ebullient conversationalist and games player, who loved Spenser; Carter Revard, a young and imaginative scholar, who spoke on Chaucer.

Planning to write a senior thesis, I approached DeMott, who flattered

---

* My familiarity with these views of literature is among the happy by-products of my membership, many years later, in a group of academic bicyclists, including Stephen Greenblatt and Tom Laqueur, at the University of California at Berkeley.

me by saying that I should undertake the study of a major writer, such as Shaw or Dickens or Shakespeare, but then disappointed me by saying that he was already oversubscribed as a thesis adviser. Instead, I ended up working with William Pritchard, a recent Amherst graduate, newly arrived from Harvard, where he had studied for his Ph.D. with Reuben Brower. I didn't know much about Pritchard when we found ourselves assigned to each other. He then seemed very young and slightly insecure, but being the first thesis student of such a bright and lively man proved to be an enormous benefit. Certainly, by being his first, I received his attention and, I'd like to think, some special affection. We have enjoyed watching each other develop over the subsequent nearly five decades.*

I was intent on devoting the summer of 1960 to the choice of a thesis topic. In an act of pure nepotism, my father got me a featherbedded job at Jones Beach State Park, where he served part-time as the park physician for over thirty years. Jones Beach, an extraordinary expanse of sand, ocean, and recreation facilities, built by Robert Moses in the 1920s and 1930s, was only a few miles from Freeport. In the job-free summers of my boyhood, I would often spend the afternoon bobbing in the surf or reading on the beach, while my father removed fishhooks from the hands of careless fishermen or splinters from the feet of those who went shoe-less on the wooden boardwalks. But the job I was given was not much more onerous than no job at all, and gave me plenty of time to contemplate thesis topics. I was responsible for keeping barnacles from forming on the motors that propelled floats through the lagoon that separated the audience from the stage at Guy Lombardo's Jones Beach Marine Theater. This meant swimming briefly in Zach's Bay once a week to wipe off the propellers, and keeping out of the sight of supervisors or beachgoers the rest of the week.

I settled into a comfortable position in a shed protecting the motors at one end of a float and launched an attack on the major bodies of work that DeMott had advised me to read—especially plays by Shaw and Ibsen, any Shakespeare I hadn't read, and a few novels by Dickens. I had per-

---

* Pritchard has become one of America's best-known biographers and critics. A devoted and greatly admired teacher, he continues to carry a full course load in his mid-seventies without any loss of energy or enthusiasm.

suaded a small group of Freeport High School students to allow me to teach them a short literature course—featuring overly ambitious novels, like *The Wings of the Dove*, which I had only recently read in one of my courses at Amherst. So, lounging next to my motors, I also prepared those evening classes.

Back at Amherst in the fall, Bill Pritchard and I quickly settled on Dickens as the "major author" to tackle. This choice meant struggling to find something original to say about his lengthy, well-known novels. By reading several biographies of Dickens as well, I began to see a pattern. It seemed plausible to link Dickens's paternalistic attitude toward his family and friends with events in the novels that allow the pallid good characters, finally and mysteriously, to get the upper hand over the colorful and fully rendered evil ones. In the thesis that emerged, I argued that Dickens, as a narrator, was as protective of his weak, kind characters as he tried to be, in life, to his invalided sister-in-law and other relatives and friends. In his letters and his life, he seemed conscious of the enormous power of his personality and his anger at injustice; in his novels, he used that power and anger as a narrator to confront social ills and destroy wicked people. I called this narrative ploy "the murder of evil."

I knew that I wasn't starting a revolution in critical writings about Dickens. Still, I felt I had forged a coherent and creative statement about a major writer and his life. And, of course, I had moved away from the purity of the New Criticism, because my interpretation of the texts was strongly affected by my knowledge of the author's life and times. Weighing the evidence for my thesis, in the novels and the life of the writer, proved to be more consuming and satisfying than I had imagined. Encouraged by Pritchard and others in the English department, I began to think that I should consider literature as a career, not simply as an undergraduate adventure on the way to medical school.

But my mind was far from made up. My confusion was represented physically by a "career decision mobile" that I built in my dormitory room. From a ceiling fixture I had hung copies of my applications for admission to several graduate schools in English and to three medical schools; for a Fulbright Fellowship to study Ibsen and Shaw in Norway; for a visiting fellowship to a Japanese university; and for a couple of jobs in journalism.

My success rate with these options was not high, but there was good mail as well as bad. I was pleased to receive letters saying that I had been admitted to the Harvard graduate program in English and awarded a Woodrow Wilson Fellowship to pay my expenses in the program. On the other hand, a rejection letter from Harvard Medical School, which I now consider a small badge of honor, then seemed a stern judgment on my suitability for medicine. And my applications for various fellowships and jobs were rebuffed. So I readied myself for Harvard's Ph.D. program in English, to start a few months after college graduation, in the fall of 1961.

THE SUMMER OF 1961: A GLIMPSE OF THE NEW SCIENCE

My preparation for graduate school began that summer, immediately after the Amherst commencement, with my first adventure in Europe. I was eager to see places where the great English writers had lived, walked, and worked, and I was not intimidated by the distances or difficulties of travel. I was excited by the London street signs with names from Dickens's novels, but also by the haunts of Keats and Shelly in Rome and of Lord Byron on the Bosphorus.

One significant departure from my literary itinerary, a detour through the Soviet Union, starting in Stockholm and ending in Istanbul, provided an unexpected window on new developments in science. One of my classmates, Arthur Landy, now a well-known molecular biologist at Brown University, had won an Amherst biology prize that allowed him to attend that year's international biochemistry meeting, located in Moscow, and he invited me to join him.

I learned the enormous political significance of this meeting only years later. During Stalin's reign, the science of heredity and evolution, as conceived in the West by Charles Darwin, Gregor Mendel, Thomas Hunt Morgan, and others, was derided as bourgeois. Soviet scientific programs were dominated by T. D. Lysenko, a politically well-connected advocate of the theory of acquired characteristics. This now debunked theory is usually attributed to the late eighteenth-century biologist Jean-Baptiste Lamarck, who popularized the idea that traits imposed or learned during an organism's lifetime could be transmitted to offspring.

As later described by the enlightened Soviet historian Zhores Medvedev,[3] Lysenko was nearly single-handedly responsible for keeping Soviet science from applying modern genetics to agricultural and medical sciences until at least the early 1960s. The invitation to hold an international biochemistry meeting in Moscow was perhaps the first public sign that Lysenko's destructive domination of biological science in the Soviet Union was coming to an end, as the more moderate Nikita Khrushchev began to soften his government's stance toward the outside world in the wake of Stalin's death in 1953.

The biochemistry meeting in Moscow is also remembered for another and ultimately more significant event. Marshall Nirenberg, a young American scientist at the NIH, announced his success in deciphering the genetic code. That was a pivotal moment in the history of molecular biology. Even though I did not understand its meaning or its importance at the time, I was not oblivious to the excitement around me. Eventually, Nirenberg's discovery influenced everyone's thinking about biology and informed the work that all other biologists have done since then.[4]

What did it mean to decipher the genetic code? And why was its unveiling so significant? I could not have begun to answer these questions on my trip in 1961, but it will help with the story I aim to tell if I use the occasion of the Moscow meeting to introduce a few basic features of the revolution in molecular biology and genetics that was occurring at that time.

Eight years earlier, Jim Watson and Francis Crick had announced the structure of the DNA double helix—probably the pivotal discovery in twentieth-century biology.[5] Previous studies at the Rockefeller Institute and Cold Spring Harbor Laboratory strongly suggested that DNA, an enormous molecule discovered almost a century earlier, was the chemical form of genes.[6] If so, DNA had to contain the inherited instructions that were responsible for the contents, appearance, and functions of cells and organisms.

The notion that DNA was the repository of genetic information was accepted only reluctantly, since no one knew how an apparently simple molecule, composed of long chains of just four kinds of chemical building blocks, called nucleotides, could possibly encode so much information. Furthermore, it was not understood how DNA could transmit genetic information accurately to daughter cells during cell division or how it could direct a cell to make components, like proteins, that the information was supposed to specify. It was as though someone had claimed that a piece of paper contained information for making dining room tables, but could not explain three critical things: how the marks on the paper (letters) formed words with meaning, how the paper could be copied for others to use (e.g., by using a Xerox machine), or how the instructions would be carried out (with wood, nails, and tools) to build actual tables.

Within a period of about ten years, a golden age in molecular biology, all this uncertainty evaporated.* When Watson and Crick unveiled their aesthetically pleasing and now fabled double helix, some things were immediately apparent. First, the two strands of the DNA helix are held together in a highly provocative way. The double helix resembles a spiral staircase, with two very long interwound strands, each composed of thousands of the four types of nucleotides. Within the staircase, the "steps" holding the chains together are the parts of the nucleotides that differentiate the four types. These parts, called bases, hold the chains together by regular matches or pairings. Of the four types of bases—denoted by their abbreviated names, A, C, G, and T—A pairs only with T, and vice versa; likewise, C pairs only with G, and vice versa.

If it is assumed that the order of the bases somehow conveys information, then base-pairing provides the clue to perpetuating that information when DNA is duplicated to make two daughter cells. When the strands of DNA are copied, the order of the bases is transmitted, because each strand serves as a template to make a new and opposite strand. The components of the new strands are paired, base for base, with the template, thereby preserving the order. In other words, each new strand would be "complementary" to its template. In the concluding sentence of their paper in 1953, Watson and Crick famously recognized this possibility by saying, "It has not escaped our notice that the specific pairing we have postulated immediately suggests a possible copying mechanism for the genetic material."[8]

This may explain how the order of nucleotides is preserved when DNA is duplicated. But how does the order denote genetic information? And how does the cell use the information to build components like pro-

---

* This era is beautifully portrayed in Horace Freeland Judson's *Eighth Day of Creation*.[7]

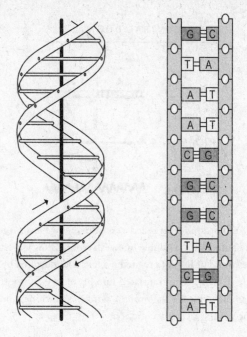

Odile Crick, the wife of Francis Crick, was the first to depict the beauty of the DNA double helix (left). A schematic cartoon on the right shows how base-pairing occurs, with As paired with Ts, and Cs paired with Gs.

teins? The first question poses the problem of deciphering the genetic code—of knowing what DNA says. The second question addresses the related problem of expressing genes to make proteins—of knowing how to use the information. To understand how these questions were tackled in that golden age, it is easiest to begin by saying a few things about the way in which cells convert information embedded in DNA to make proteins. (This is like finding out what tools are available for making a table before learning how to read the paper with lettered instructions.)

In its simplest form, anointed the Central Dogma of Molecular Biology by Francis Crick, gene expression consists of two steps, often summarized telegraphically: DNA makes RNA makes protein. More explicitly, cells are equipped with two sets of important tools. First, cells have enzymes that can copy the information in DNA to make chains of a closely related

CENTRAL DOGMA

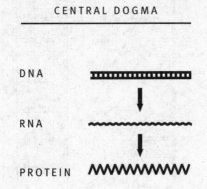

DNA, the stable double-stranded repository of genetic information (shown schematically by a double line with base-pairing), is transcribed into a single strand of RNA (a related nucleic acid indicated by the wavy line), and the RNA is then translated into proteins (saw-toothed line), a string of amino acids, by the protein-synthesis machine, under directions read according to the genetic code.

nucleic acid called RNA. This event, called transcription, resembles transcribing one text into another that is more easily read, like rewriting a cursive text into block letters. Because the chemical properties of RNA and DNA are so similar, this can be done, like the copying of DNA strands to make more DNA, by base-pairing—preserving the order of the bases and hence the information. In concrete terms, each G in DNA becomes a C in RNA, each T in DNA an A in RNA, and so forth. In this way, the information in DNA is accurately conveyed to the more readable RNA.

Second, a small intracellular machine, called a ribosome, can "translate" the RNA chain into a chain of protein, like turning a French text to an English one. This happens when the machine reads the information in the RNA and adds the appropriate amino acid, one out of the twenty possible ones, to a growing protein chain.*

---

* One of the important features of gene expression is its capacity to be regulated. That is, in different cells or under different conditions, each gene may be "read out" (expressed) at different rates or not at all, as determined, for example, by whether and how efficiently it is transcribed into RNA. Efforts to study gene regulation will resurface repeatedly in several subsequent chapters.

By 1961, the Central Dogma and the idea that information in DNA was inherent in the order of the bases had begun to gain wide acceptance. But the rules for reading DNA were far from obvious. Just as a language based on written letters would be impossible to understand if we didn't know the lengths of words and their meanings, it was equally hard to understand what DNA said or how a cell interpreted it, unless the analogous rules for genetic information were explained. For DNA to encode proteins—the long chains of amino acids that are among the most important and most various of the ingredients in cells—the order of the bases in DNA would presumably have to dictate the order of the twenty amino acids found in proteins. But how? Since four kinds of bases were available, sixty-four combinations of triplets were possible, more than enough to denote all of the amino acids. But which sequences of the four available bases signified which amino acids?

It was this question that Nirenberg (and also Severo Ochoa and his colleagues at NYU) had begun to answer in the experiments he described in Moscow, by means of a very clever approach.[9] By the early 1960s, it was possible to make RNA, the "readable" nucleic acid, in a test tube and then ask whether it can direct the protein-making machines to incorporate certain amino acids. In the simplest case, if RNA were made from a single type of nucleotide (e.g., only A's), it would contain only one kind of three-letter word (e.g., AAA). By identifying the amino acid added to proteins in response to RNA containing only that word, one of the sixty-four code words would be deciphered (in this case, as lysine). It was exactly that kind of experiment and discovery—AAA is the genetic word for the amino acid lysine—that excited the crowd of biochemists meeting in Moscow in 1961.*

Over the ensuing decade, the structure of DNA, the Central Dogma, and the genetic code were determined to be essentially universal—used in all plants, animals, and bacteria—with only minor deviations in a few species. These fundamental aspects are now so ingrained in our under-

---

* Nirenberg, with Gobind Khorana and Robert Holley (who helped to determine how cells read the genetic code to make proteins), received the Nobel Prize in Physiology or Medicine in 1968. Ochoa had earlier received a Nobel Prize with Arthur Kornberg for synthesis of nucleic acids.

standing of biology—and so strongly supportive of the idea that all life on earth evolved from a single constellation of fortuitous events—that it is hard to imagine the history of the last five decades of biology without them.

As an eighth-grader in 1953, I was understandably unaware of the discovery by Watson and Crick, and remained so for nearly a decade. When the first words of the genetic code were revealed at the biochemistry conference, I was a college graduate, but oblivious to science, riding Moscow's fabled ornate subways and roaming Russian art galleries, not sitting in the audience. In any case, it is unlikely I would have appreciated the force of Nirenberg's experiments. If I had been more knowledgeable, able to recognize that the challenge was learning to read and interpret genetic instructions, the questions might have been quite enticing to a student of language and literature! Still, listening to Art Landy's excited report at the end of the day in our rooms at Moscow State University, I began to understand that something of fundamental significance had occurred, and I felt that a seed of professional envy had been planted. Scientists seemed likely to discover new, deep, and useful things about the world, and other scientists would be excited about these discoveries and eager to build on them. Would this be true of literary critics and teachers?

CHAPTER 2

From Literature to Medicine to Science

—

[Mrs. Thrale] felt it was an odd misconception that scientists had no
taste for literature: "I have known many examples to the contrary."

—SHIRLEY HAZZARD,
THE TRANSIT OF VENUS (1980)

DESPITE OUTWARD SIGNS THAT I HAD CHOSEN A LIFE OF STUDYING
and teaching literature, soon after starting my graduate work at Harvard
I began to suffer some further internal doubts about abandoning medicine. The graduate curriculum in English literature was not especially
onerous, but it felt like a prolongation of college. Most of my courses
were heavily populated with Harvard and Radcliffe undergraduates.
First-year graduate students had little sense of identity as future scholars,
we were often taught by older graduate students, and Harvard's famous
professors, with the notable exception of the wonderful playwright and
poet William Alfred, paid little attention to us. Making a commitment to
literary scholarship under these circumstances was not easy.

I shared an apartment with an Amherst classmate and close friend,
Peter Berek, who was also in his first year of Harvard's English Ph.D. program. Now an Elizabethan scholar and professor at Mount Holyoke College, Peter was naturally suited to a literary life and didn't seem conflicted
about the long-term direction he was taking. But even he found it hard to
get out of bed in the morning and often missed classes. I attended classes
more dutifully, but felt less committed to the career.

A Reactivated Interest in Medicine

Occasionally, on Saturday mornings, I traveled across the Charles River to join some Amherst classmates at Harvard Medical School, while they sat in the Ether Dome at the Massachusetts General Hospital, entranced by diagnostic dilemmas discussed at the weekly clinical pathology conference. These stories struck me as far more interesting than those I was reading, and my medical school friends expressed genuine excitement about their work. They also seemed to have formed a community of scholars, with shared interests in the human body and its diseases and common expectations that they would soon be able to do something about those diseases.

These Saturday excursions probably account for an influential dream that I had one night about my continuing indecision. In that dream, my future literature students were relieved when I didn't turn up to teach a class, but my future patients were disappointed when I didn't appear. It seemed I wanted to be wanted.

As a distraction from some of the arcane texts I was being assigned at graduate school, I began reading Sigmund Freud, especially the case histories, dream theory, and efforts to explain history and literature in psychoanalytic terms. While not always persuaded by Freud's explanations, I was enchanted by his style and reach, his brilliant storytelling, his original efforts to understand the mind, and the connections he made to the larger world. Reading Freud made me feel as though some training in literary scholarship and criticism might prove useful if I went to medical school with aspirations in neurology or psychiatry.

A man named Bush may have had the most to do with reorienting me toward medical school. Douglas Bush, a well-known scholar in the Harvard English department, was cautious and pedantic in the classroom. I had no reason to doubt his love of literature, but I did not find evidence of passion in his fussy writings or in his flatly delivered lectures on Tennyson, Browning, and Arnold. He had reverence, but little apparent enthusiasm. His statements were muted and qualified—not what I was accustomed to at Amherst, and not what I found elsewhere at Harvard, especially in William Alfred's course on *Beowulf*, in Richard Poirier's on Henry James, or Harry Levin's on Shakespeare.

Nonetheless, Bush had a strong effect on me through a literary history he had published several years earlier, *English Literature in the Earlier Seventeenth Century.*[1] The book had no more verve or daring than his lectures, and the approach was soporifically inclusive, with, it seemed, at least a paragraph devoted to anyone who wrote anything that survived from the early seventeenth century. But something did capture my fancy: the biographical footnotes. Nearly every author Bush discussed appeared to have been involved in the practical, contemporary world—as lawyer, physician, courtier, clergyman, administrator, or businessman. This meant that they wrote on the side, as an avocation. Few writers *only* wrote, and those who could afford to do so were probably also managing inheritances and estates. The early seventeenth century, with the poetry of Milton, Donne, Herrick, Vaughn, and Marvell, was the period that most appealed to me, so Bush's book and its footnotes encouraged the idea that I could remain literary in some way, while taking on a profession that linked me more closely to the events and practical concerns of my time.

I decided to consult the augury again, by reapplying to medical school.* Harvard Med had the first deadline. I recall biking to the other side of the frozen Charles River to deliver my hastily assembled application at the very last minute. I was soon granted an interview with the notoriously confrontational dean of admissions, Perry Culver, who quickly made it clear, in a parental tone, that he found me too inconstant and immature in judgment to be admitted to his school. He then recommended something my parents would never have suggested: a maturing experience in the armed services. A spell in the military had much less appeal than anything I had contemplated when I built my "career decision mobile."

In contrast, the medical school at Columbia University (called the College of Physicians and Surgeons, or just P&S) greeted my reapplica-

---

* To my surprise, my parents found this vacillation quite perturbing. I had expected them to be relieved by my return to the course that everyone in Freeport seemed to have had in mind for me all along. But in our kitchen conversations during that year's Christmas holidays, I could see that they had liked my deviations from community expectations and had been defending my decision not to go to medical school to their more conventional friends. My apparent reversion to type seemed to distress them as much as did my apparently irresponsible flitting from field to field.

tion warmly. The Columbia interviewer, an esteemed physician and anthropologist named David Seegal, asked about the translation of the Anglo-Saxon phrase *Ich ne wat*. This was easy; it simply means "I don't know." Seegal used it to discuss why a physician might admit fallibility to a patient. I enjoyed this conversation a lot more than the one with Culver about the benefits of military service. By the fall of 1962, I was happily enrolled at P&S, helped for the first, but not the last, time by someone's exaggerated appreciation of my competence in two cultures.

MEDICAL SCHOOL AND MORE TRANSITIONS

At P&S, my plans for a medical future gradually evolved from being a practicing psychiatrist with literary hobbies to becoming an academic internist with scientific inclinations. In my first year, I had been sufficiently self-schooled by readings of Freud to win an essay prize in psychiatry, but my sense of a psychoanalytic destiny proved short-lived. Curiously, I found one of my exits from psychiatry through Freud's route of entry into it—the science of the brain. To my surprise, the subject that most powerfully captured my imagination during my first year of classes was perhaps the least literary: neuroanatomy. While many of my classmates viewed the subject as a tedious litany of nerve tracts and ganglia, to me it felt alive with potential for understanding motion, sensation, and thought. I was enchanted by the beautiful old drawings of the nervous system in Johannes Sobotta's three antique volumes and the clarifying illustrations in Frank Netter's more recent books, and I began reading the primary research literature for the first time. I found myself more interested in the physical brain than in the more elusive mind, more in the biochemistry and electrical impulses of nerve cells than in the thoughts and behaviors those cells presumably produced.

My disengagement from a psychiatric future was accelerated when my first hour alone in a room with a psychotic patient proved to be more difficult and less interesting than an hour reading Freud. The young woman, about my age and highly intelligent, was unwilling to answer any questions in a meaningful way, and was hostile to the idea of being interviewed by a medical student rather than her usual doctor. She made me feel incompetent (which I was) and humiliated. Of course, it should not have been my feelings that mattered. But the sense that I might not have the patience or the resolve to spend a lot of time alone with disturbed people made me dubious about my future in psychiatry. Furthermore, at the time, the prospects seemed remote for connecting what was understood about the brain, based on neuroanatomy and neurochemistry, with actual psychiatric disease.

But internal medicine held many charms. As in psychiatry, the case history was a biography. But the diagnostic process was a puzzle that could be solved with objective, quantitative data from x-rays, blood tests, and cardiograms and with systematic thought. Therapeutic options provided benefits and even some happy endings. Patients in kidney failure seemed more likely than psychotic ones to cooperate with the process of addressing their problems. And molecular biology promised to reveal the origins of some common diseases in the near term.

This promise seemed most apparent in the fields of blood diseases (hematology), infectious diseases (microbiology), and disorders of the immune system (immunology), and all three were especially well represented at P&S at that time. Paul Marks—many years later my immediate predecessor as president of Memorial Sloan-Kettering Cancer Center— made a special impression on me in his lectures about the anemias (conditions in which patients have too few red blood cells). This was especially true of his lectures describing what was already known about a few genetically determined anemias, such as sickle-cell disease and the thalassemias. In these disorders, the patient is born with genes unable to direct synthesis of the right amount or the normal form of hemoglobin, the protein in red cells responsible for carrying oxygen from the lungs to other tissues.

The nature of the genetic code, as revealed by Nirenberg, Ochoa, and their colleagues in the early 1960s, explained how simple changes in the nucleotide sequence of DNA could affect the composition and hence the function of proteins, including hemoglobin. A change in a single base would change a three-letter word in DNA and could change a critical amino acid in an important protein. As Marks's lectures made clear, such changes (mutations) could cause diseases when they affected physiologically important proteins. Given a knowledge of such things, the classification, diagnosis, and treatment of diseases could become rational, based upon the fundament properties of genes and proteins. More subtle, but powerful, genetic changes might also cause disease, such as changes in DNA sequence that did not alter the amino acid sequence of a protein, but did affect protein abundance. For instance, mutations of this type might corrupt the signals in DNA that normally govern the time, place, and efficiency of gene expression, the making of RNA and protein. So the fundamental rules of biology could tell clinicians how, finally, to understand some of the most perplexing and ancient of diseases— sickle-cell anemia, in which red blood cells fold into sickle-like shapes, or thalassemias, in which blood is as watery as the sea (*thalassa*, as I had learned in my brief exposure to Greek as a graduate student). DNA, protein chemistry, medical genetics, gene expression, and hematology were not unrelated subjects. Taken together, they offered comprehensive views of organisms and cells and stimulated new ideas about how to diagnose and control diseases.

A more distant prospect was even more exciting: that what was true for the diseases of hemoglobin—a very abundant protein, and thus among the first to be studied thoroughly for its biochemical properties, physiological functions, and three-dimensional structure—might also be true for diseases that were more difficult to understand. Any protein that serves an important function—to interpret a hormone's signal, to contract a muscle, to promote cell division—could be altered by changes in DNA sequence and thereby contribute to an endocrine disorder, muscle disease, or cancer. By learning such things, medicine could become molecular and genetic, and diseases could be better understood and better controlled. Those medical school lectures planted some important seeds.

Still, during the next four years, two as a medical student at P&S, then two as a house officer in medicine, I devoted my mental energies to the medical rather than the molecular side of this equation. I seemed to be heading for a career as an internist at an academic health center, a position in which I might be knowledgeable about the science behind medicine, but primarily as a practitioner and teacher, with an interest in clinical investigation, but not as a laboratory scientist.

I also entertained a temporary interest in tropical medicine, the result of an exciting course in parasitology and participation in Columbia's

International Fellows Program.* To test my curiosity about tropical diseases more rigorously, I spent most of my final months as a medical student at a mission hospital in Bareilly, a provincial town in northern India. As recounted in more detail in chapter 14, this experience turned me away from the idea of practicing medicine under the difficult circumstances prevailing in developing countries. Because of this trip, I learned about my acceptance into the medical staff training program at Columbia-Presbyterian Medical Center while opening my mail in a rat-infested hotel bathroom in Calcutta.** A couple of months later, while climbing toward the Kolahoi glacier with a horse and a Kashmiri guide, I celebrated my graduation from medical school.

FINDING AN ALTERNATIVE TO SERVICE IN VIETNAM

In thinking about career options at medical school, however, I had not fully considered the potential implications of the Vietnam War. Fervently opposed to the war, I was determined not to serve in it. Medical graduates were subject to the draft; however, we did have the more palatable option of two years of training at one of the agencies of the Public Health Service: the CDC (then the Communicable Disease Center, now the Centers for Disease Control), the Indian Health Service (IHS), or the National Institutes of Health (NIH). The CDC was famed for training epidemiologists, medical scientists who study disease trends in populations and trace sources of novel or epidemic infectious diseases. The IHS sent its physicians to practice medicine at reservations throughout the country, an assignment likely to be culturally interesting but unlikely to foster my interests in academic medicine. For most of my classmates with academic

---

* This program, organized by the School of International and Public Affairs, brought together students from all of Columbia's components, exposed us to the theory and practice of foreign policy, and provided a weeklong opportunity to view Washington, D.C., in action, an excellent preview of a world I would get to know much better as director of the NIH. We were granted moments of self-importance when leading politicians, such as Hubert Humphrey, Robert Kennedy, and Claiborne Pell, seemed eager to meet with us. I also watched with amusement as one of the fellows, Franklin D. Roosevelt III, FDR's grandson, pocketed a couple of notepads during our tour of the White House.

** Once again, I had been rejected by the Harvard medical establishment; I didn't do well during my interviews at the Massachusetts General Hospital, which had been my first choice.

ambitions similar to my own, the NIH was the favored choice. As the largest biomedical research campus in the world, it offered unequaled opportunities to learn virtually any form of biomedical science, from biophysics to clinical trials. Afterwards, many NIH trainees became faculty members in departments at distinguished medical schools.

So, despite a woeful lack of laboratory credentials, I entered the competition for these highly desirable slots at the NIH. Those applicants selected for interviews were asked to come on a single day, just after graduation from medical school, but two years in advance of joining the Public Health Service. (Virtually every candidate was anticipating two years as an intern and resident at some major academic hospital before actually starting work at the NIH.)

I hoped to secure an NIH research position with a focus in one of the clinical disciplines I considered most likely to be affected by advances in molecular biology and genetics—immunology, infectious disease, hematology, and endocrinology. I did not think much about cancer (oncology) at that point, perhaps because cancers seemed to be such intractable diseases, perhaps because I was not sufficiently familiar with the recent progress toward studying cancer in animals with viruses that contain only a few genes. But more about that later.

During my long interview day, I met with several well-known laboratory chiefs, most of whom were not especially encouraging. But one sympathetic senior scientist, the endocrinologist Jack Robbins, saw that my limited experience would probably keep me from being selected, and he suggested that I speak with Ira Pastan, a young NIH investigator who had recently established his own laboratory to study the production of hormones by the thyroid gland.

This recommendation proved to be wise and fateful. My schooling in literature turned out to be more important than my interest in endocrinology, Ira's field, because Ira's wife Linda, a poet, had often complained that Ira's colleagues seldom talked about books. Ira, himself an enthusiastic reader, thought it might be helpful to have someone with my background in his lab. When the matches were announced, I was told I would become Ira's first clinical associate, having been passed over by the more famous senior investigators I had ranked higher on my list. This outcome could not have been more fortunate.

GETTING READY FOR THE PASTAN LAB

Before heading for Bethesda and the NIH, I was committed to completing my two-year clinical training program in internal medicine. One day in 1967, midway through my traineeship, while caring for patients on the medicine ward of Presbyterian Hospital, I received a shocking phone call from Ira. He told me that he was curtailing his work on the thyroid gland—the endocrinology that I sought—because he and a colleague, Robert Perlman, had made a startling discovery about gene regulation in bacteria.[2] What he said was something like this: "We've found that cyclic AMP reverses catabolite repression of the lac operon of E. coli." I had no idea what that meant. I didn't know whether it was important or even interesting. And I certainly didn't want to undertake a project in what seemed to be an esoteric domain. But I was too busy tending my patients to continue the conversation with him.

That night I went to the small library maintained for hospital trainees to try to read for the first time about the Nobel Prize—winning work by Jacques Monod and François Jacob at the Pasteur Institute in Paris.[3] Monod and Jacob were among the first to venture productively into one of the great areas of modern molecular biology: regulation of gene expression. The central question can be envisioned in simple terms. Cells have hundreds or thousands of different genes, each with instructions for making different proteins. But to make cells with different behaviors, not all the genes are "read out" (or expressed) at the same levels or all the time. If genes are being regulated in some way, as seems sensible for the economy of the cell, what signals and conditions control expression? And how is expression controlled? Do cells do this by governing the synthesis of RNA, the messenger of genetic information in Crick's Central Dogma? (See the figure on page 22.) By governing the destruction ("turnover") of the RNA? Or by changing the rates of synthesis or destruction of the encoded protein?

Monod and Jacob and their colleagues had approached the issue of gene regulation by concentrating on a small set of genes in a simple and extensively studied cell type, the common intestinal bacterium, *Escherichia coli* (*E. coli*), the traditional workhorse of microbiology. These three genes were discovered because they help *E. coli* to eat—namely, they allow one of the organism's food sources, the sugar called lactose, to enter the cell and get metabolized. For that reason, the genes were said (charmingly!) to compose "the lac operon." Changes in the growth conditions, by the addition or subtraction of lactose or other sugars, are followed by changes in the levels of the proteins, such as those encoded by the genes in the lac operon, that allow the bacterium to feed on those sugars. For instance, the addition of lactose (or something closely resembling lactose) to the growth medium increased the amounts of the three lac operon proteins, and the amounts fell when lactose was withdrawn.

In a series of experiments whose beauty I came, eventually, to appreciate, Monod and Jacob developed evidence that supported a simple but powerful idea.[4] They proposed that the bacterial cell possesses a mechanism that shuts down—represses—the expression of the lac operon unless lactose (or its equivalent) is present. So if lactose is added to the growth medium, the lac operon is "turned on"; lactose induces—or derepresses—the operon. In the now accepted view, when expression of the operon is shut down, a protein (called a repressor) is bound to a part of the operon, thereby preventing the synthesis of the RNA "message" for making lac operon proteins. But lactose can reverse this, by binding and inactivating the repressor protein, thus allowing the lac operon to be expressed. In other words, the bacterium's food itself (lactose) can induce the tools (the lac operon proteins) needed to eat it.

Not only was this scheme pretty; it also marked a giant stride toward understanding how many kinds of genes, both in bacteria and in the more complex cells of plants and animals, are regulated—that is, turned on and off in response to various kinds of signals. But another early observation by Monod was less well understood: glucose, a sugar different from lactose, blocks—rather than induces—expression of the lac operon.[5] How did this happen?

Ira started thinking about this problem—one well outside his own area of investigation, hormone release from the mammalian thyroid gland—after hearing a visiting lecturer, Earl Sutherland from Vanderbilt University, mention a curious finding during a seminar at the NIH. Sutherland had received a Nobel Prize several years earlier for the discovery of a small molecule, called cyclic AMP, that is made in animal cells after the cells have been stimulated by certain hormones.[6] Because cyclic AMP increases the activity of an enzyme that can profoundly alter cell behavior, cyclic AMP came to be known as a second messenger, relaying to an animal cell's interior a signal triggered by hormones outside the cell.

No one had given much thought to the possibility that cyclic AMP might play a role in simple organisms like bacteria, let alone one similar to its well-established role in animal cells. But Sutherland had found cyclic AMP in bacterial cultures. So Ira and his colleague, Bob Perlman, began to think about what cyclic AMP might be doing in bacteria. One of their early stabs at a solution paid off: addition of cyclic AMP (actually a close relative of cyclic AMP) to *E. coli* growing in glucose induced the expression of the lac operon.[7] In other words, cyclic AMP reversed glucose repression of the lac operon. This suggested that addition of lactose was not the only way to turn on the lac operon. While lactose blocked a repressor, cyclic AMP might act in a completely different way. To pursue these ideas, much more needed to be known about how cyclic AMP affected the regulation of expression of genes in the lac operon, and the next questions would fall, in part, to me.

CHAPTER 3

The First Taste of Scientific Success

—

THE EXCITING RESULTS FROM PERLMAN AND PASTAN ABOUT CYCLIC AMP and the lac operon raised many unresolved issues, but they also made some highly instructive points to a newcomer like me. First, they encouraged a boldness of approach: medically trained scientists, like Perlman and Pastan, could step beyond the boundaries of their studies of the thyroid gland and make a startling finding that helped solve a long-standing mystery in a very different field. Moreover, this discovery showed how ideas and findings from multiple sources—from Jacob and Monod's work on E. coli, from Sutherland's study of cyclic AMP in animal cells, from Perlman and Pastan's interests in hormonal action—could suddenly converge, producing a new vista, from which further interesting questions arose. Of equal importance, by showing that cyclic AMP transmitted a key signal in bacterial as well as in animal cells, the new findings reasserted the theme of universality in biology, a theme also apparent in the genetic code, the Central Dogma, and the mechanism of protein synthesis, as well as the mediators of gene regulation. At an early stage in my experience as a scientist, this shaped my conviction that simple, experimentally accessible organisms, like bacteria, can reveal parallel features of more complex organisms, like mammals. What is true for E. coli is true for the elephant, Jacques Monod had prophesied. Everything that has happened in biology in the past four decades has confirmed the wisdom of his prophecy. We have learned as much about human biology from yeast, worms, flies, and mice as from human cells.

LEARNING TO DO SCIENCE AT THE NIH

When I arrived at the NIH in July of 1968, my growing ability *to understand* science proved to be very different from my ability *to do* science. My early days in the laboratory were disastrous. The very first day, I spilled radioactive filters into the sink, contaminating the sink and ruining the experiment. Soon thereafter, I asked Ira to tell me the meaning of "Tris" —the name of a common reagent that virtually all biochemists use to prevent solutions from becoming too acidic or basic. He looked up with an anguished expression and said, only half joking, "Now remind me why I took you into the lab."

But things got better. One day, a few months later, with a machine rattling off the results of a test I was trying to devise, I first felt the joy of being a scientist. Although I had not yet discovered anything, I realized that I had developed a reliable way to measure what I wanted to measure. Science consists largely of measurement. When the metaphorical ruler— what we call an assay—is in hand, results and happiness generally follow.

The assignment I had accepted began with a straightforward question: Does cyclic AMP augment expression of the lac operon by increasing the amount of RNA made from the lac operon's DNA? Conceptually, that would be the simplest way to begin to explain why the proteins for metabolizing lactose were more abundant after cyclic AMP was added to bacteria growing in that other sugar, glucose. Although the question was straightforward, the answer was not. The measurement of RNA from a single gene (or a single small set of genes) is complicated by the presence of many other genes and RNA molecules in any cell. Was it possible to make a tool for measurement, an assay, that would specifically determine the concentration of lac operon RNA? And, if so, how?

The strategy I used for doing this turned out to be important, for reasons that extended well beyond the immediate experiments I was performing in the Pastan lab in 1968. The strategy required learning about two topics, virology and molecular hybridization, both of which proved to be crucial in the studies of cancer genes that I will describe in the following chapters.

Virology—the study of viruses—introduced me to the importance of genetic simplicity. Like most of my generation, I grew up with a fear of viral contagion. I knew the devastating history of smallpox, my grandmother had died in the influenza epidemic of 1918, and as a boy I was told to avoid summer activities, like swimming in public pools, that were thought to promote transmission of polio.* As a medical student, I had also learned about the common viral diseases and which can be prevented with vaccines.

But viruses are not just worthy of scientific attention as agents of disease; they are also important tools in biological research on a wide variety of topics. This was brought home to me in my first days in the Pastan lab, when I learned about the usefulness of bacteriophages, viruses that infect bacterial cells. Because some bacteriophages can destroy the bacteria they infect, scientists and novelists alike have considered them as potential means for treating bacterial diseases, like the plague or pneumonias. Other bacteriophages can lift single bacterial genes from the cells they infect and carry those genes along for the ride when the viruses infect subsequent cells. In this way, a virus can provide what an experimentalist is often seeking: a source of a single gene uncontaminated by other cellular genes.**

Viruses are small and simple. In essence, they are small bags of proteins enclosing a single copy of a few viral genes (which may be in the form of DNA or RNA). When a virus picks up a gene from an infected cell, that gene is separated from the many other genes in the cell. Its other genes, the viral genes, are essential for multiplication of the virus and are generally unrelated to any cellular genes. For the experiments Ira and I hoped to do, we needed a source of isolated lac operon DNA. Fortuitously, parts of the lac operon had been found incorporated into some bacteriophages growing in *E. coli.* Therefore, once we obtained those

* In an address at the Harvard commencement in 1996,[1] I talked about those early fears of polio and my admiration for those scientists, especially the Nobel laureate John Franklin Enders, who used the basic methods of virology to grow polio virus, thereby making the fundamental advances that allowed two now more famous scientists, Salk and Sabin, to formulate their vaccines.
** Recombinant DNA technology, introduced in the 1970s, markedly reduced the dependence of molecular biologists on serendipitous phenomena like those described for bacteriophages, by allowing specific pieces of DNA to be grown as engineered DNA clones. Bacteriophages remain important vehicles (vectors) for growing those engineered clones of DNA.

viruses and learned to grow them, we could prepare bacteriophage DNA that had genes from the lac operon, but no other *E. coli* genes.

With this source of lac operon DNA, we hoped to be able to measure the levels of lac operon RNA in bacterial cells growing under various conditions—with or without cyclic AMP or in the presence of different sugars. Procedures for measuring amounts of nucleic acids, RNA or DNA, had been under development since the early 1960s and were called "molecular hybridization" (or "nucleic acid hybridization"). These methods took advantage of a critical property of nucleic acids that I have already emphasized: base-pairing. If a double helix of DNA is separated into its single-stranded components—for example, by heating the DNA—the single strands can reform double helices under certain conditions, such as cooling, when a strand with several bases in the correct order can form pairs (As with Ts, Cs with Gs) with a complementary sequence in another strand, as in the top panel of the figure on the following page.

We were focused on measuring the RNA that had been copied from lac operon DNA. Recall that the order of bases in RNA is the same as that of the bases in the DNA from which it was made. So if messenger RNA is added to separated strands of that DNA, base-pairing will allow the RNA to form an RNA-DNA hybrid, composed of the RNA bound to one of the two DNA strands. But how could the hybrids we cared about be detected and measured? We used a method developed some years earlier by Sol Spiegelman, a feisty molecular biologist I had briefly encountered at the famous meeting in Moscow because my traveling companion, Art Landy, wished to study with him when he entered graduate school at the University of Illinois. For the essential feature of their method, Spiegelman and his colleagues had learned to stick the separated strands of DNA onto a piece of filter paper.[2] When stuck to the paper, the strands cannot re-form DNA-DNA duplexes, but they can form base pairs with any well-matched RNA in a fluid bathing the DNA-containing filter paper—for example, with an RNA that was copied from the gene whose DNA is fixed to the filters, as shown in the lower right panel of the figure on the following page.

But if we wanted to use this method to measure RNA from the lac operon, how would we *know* that lac operon RNA had, in fact, formed

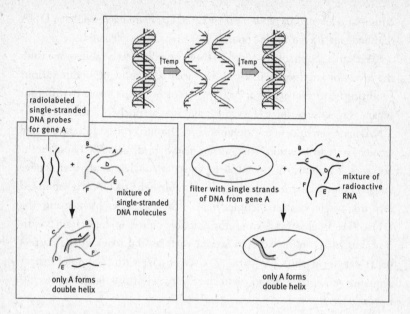

radiolabeled single-stranded DNA probes for gene A

mixture of single-stranded DNA molecules

only A forms double helix

filter with single strands of DNA from gene A

mixture of radioactive RNA

only A forms double helix

The drawings show three types of molecular hybridization. In the top panel, the strands of a double helix of DNA that have dissociated (for example, when heated) then reassociate or "hybridize" (after cooling), with the bases reforming their original pairings. The principle of base-pairing can be used to look for more informative hybrids, as shown in the bottom panels. On the left, radioactive (dark) strands of DNA from one gene (A) can find their "complementary" partner strands among many non-labeled strands from other genes. On the right, strands from gene A are fixed to a filter; when a complex mixture of radioactive RNA strands are exposed to the filter, only RNA that forms base-pairs with gene A-type DNA will be retained on the filter. Because of the specificity of base-pairing, molecular hybridization can be used to measure the amount of a specific gene sequence in DNA or RNA.

base pairs with the lac operon DNA on the filter? We added radioactive RNA building blocks to growing cultures of *E. coli*, so that the RNA in the bacterial cells would become radioactively labeled. Then any lac operon RNA that hybridized to (formed base pairs with) the lac operon DNA on the filter could be detected as radioactivity remaining on the filter after washing, by means of a machine resembling a Geiger counter. In this fashion, Ira and I could learn how much lac operon RNA was being made in bacteria grown under different conditions. If the filters containing lac operon DNA bound more radioactive RNA from the cells treated with cyclic AMP than from untreated cells, then we could conclude that cyclic AMP enhances the synthesis of lac operon RNA. That is exactly the result that I observed.[3]

To develop our molecular hybridization assay, Ira and I worked closely together—he, too, needed to learn molecular biology and bacterial genetics, despite his extensive experience with enzymes and hormones. We shopped around for the best strains of bacteriophages with lac operon DNA, learned by trial and many errors how to grow them and optimally prepare the DNA, and then played with conditions to find the best way to measure lac operon RNA specifically in a sea of irrelevant molecules. We also took advantage of *E. coli* mutants from which lac operon DNA had been deleted; these deletion mutants provided additional "controls" that further strengthened our results.

These experiments with the lac operon proved to be analogous in several ways to experiments that revealed the first proto-oncogene a few years later. As I will describe in subsequent chapters, viruses that carry cellular genes, molecular hybridization, and deletion mutants all figured in important ways in that discovery, just as they did in our studies of the lac operon.

The hybridization assays that Ira and I developed allowed me to enjoy my first eureka moments. I could accurately measure the amount of lac operon RNA in a bacterial cell. This method of measurement enabled me to show that when cyclic AMP was added to *E. coli* grown in glucose, the rate of synthesis and the concentration of lac operon RNA increased. This meant that the relief of glucose repression of the lac operon by cyclic AMP is the result of changes in "transcription"—more efficient copying of lac operon DNA into RNA. Other possibilities, such as slowed degradation of lac operon RNA, were eventually ruled out. Of course, it was not obvious how the regulation of transcription from the lac operon occurred. But others in Ira's lab were beginning to probe the mechanism of regulation; these studies later led to the discovery of proteins that, in conjunction with cyclic AMP, augment the synthesis of lac operon RNA.[4]

Having made some unambiguous observations about how cyclic AMP regulates genes in bacteria, I was now ready to write and talk about my results—another important moment in the process of becoming a scientist. The eminent biologist Gunther Stent claimed that he would not do science alone on a desert island, because so much of the joy comes from telling others about the results.[5] Once I learned the established rituals for organizing a scientific paper—title, abstract, introduction, methods, results, discussion—the writing itself was a pleasure. Clear exposition. Grammatical rectitude. Some nice turns of phrase to give the manuscript some class. I did not have to be taught this part of the process. And then came the stimulating exchanges with anonymous, but penetrating, reviewers of our articles. The closely argued several pages of single-spaced comments and criticisms that were sent to us by the editors at the *Journal of Biological Chemistry* set a standard for constructive peer review that I am grateful to have learned early in my career. Happily, the editors were also persuaded by our responses and revisions, so that I could learn the joys of having a paper accepted, seeing my work on glossy pages of a respected journal, and knowing it has been sent forth to potential readers.

My first public presentation of our findings from a lectern, rather than on the page, occurred at a remarkable meeting—a large gathering devoted to the lac operon at the Cold Spring Harbor Laboratory on Long Island. Cold Spring Harbor, one of the birthplaces of modern biology, is renowned as the site of some of the most important meetings in biology. I found many aspects of this meeting beguiling: the diversity of scientists from around the world, my first glimpses of Jim Watson and other pioneers from the golden age of molecular biology, the political and social dynamic, the setting at the famous laboratory in Gatsby country, even the title—the Lac Operon Symposium—sounding like something out of *A Midsummer Night's Dream.*

Under these circumstances, I was both grateful and anxious when Ira generously proposed to carve up his assigned speaking slot to allow others in his lab to talk. Since the audience included the suave Jacques Monod, seated in the second row, wearing a cravat, and always ready with a thoughtful question or two, this moment was especially important for a young scientist. Having Monod pay attention and ask questions mattered for Ira, too, since the Pastan group had emerged unheralded from a background of medical endocrinology to crack open a large unsolved problem about the lac operon, territory that bacterial geneticists, especially those working or trained at the Pasteur Institute, seemed to believe they owned.

REASSESSING RESEARCH DIRECTIONS: MOVING TOWARD CANCER VIRUSES

My pleasures and successes in Ira's lab were leading me away from clinical medicine and toward basic biological research. But I realized after the first year that I was going to need a closer connection to the problems of disease to find complete satisfaction in the laboratory. I also felt that I would always be disadvantaged by the lack of a formative, early experience with bacterial genetics—it is like a language, best learned when young. And I wanted to use my medical knowledge to do work that promised to be socially beneficial.

Two events that occurred earlier in my days at the NIH, in the summer of 1968, profoundly affected my life and my career. First, I fell in love—with Connie Casey, who soon became (and is still) my wife.* Less than a month after I was smitten with Connie, I learned that my mother had discovered a mass in her breast. Connie and I drove to Freeport on the day of her biopsy and immediate mastectomy. Over dinner at a seafood restaurant, my father told us that tumor cells had spread to many lymph nodes. The outcome was inevitable, though it took three years, two of them good ones, to play out.**

I am unwilling to draw a straight line between my mother's breast cancer and my career in cancer research, but the connection is unarguable. The experience did not pull me back to clinical medicine, drive me to training in oncology, or set me on a quixotic quest to "cure cancer." Instead, I have felt determined to understand what happens when normal cells become cancerous, by means of the instruments of modern biological science, hoping that benefits for patients would follow.

* Connie is also the mother of our two children, Jacob and Christopher, a deft journalist, a sensitive reader, a tireless professional gardener, my foremost editor and critic, and nice to look at, too!

** My mother's death took its toll on my father as well. In less than a year, he died of coronary artery disease, at the age of sixty-five.

In 1968, when my mother's cancer was discovered, I knew very little about cancer research. Fortunately, in the Vietnam era, the NIH was host to many young people like me (nearly all of them men, as is evident from the photographs of our group), who had been excellent medical students, but knew relatively little science. Courses taught by senior NIH scientists were offered on virtually every aspect of modern biology and medicine, without any intention to award degrees, simply to prepare our group (called, unfairly but good-naturedly, the Yellow Berets) for an academic life that was at least partly based in a laboratory. These courses exposed and repaired my deficiencies in many areas of basic research, and they also introduced me to two topics I found especially exciting: animal viruses and cancer.

I was particularly intrigued by the provocative link between these two topics that was provided by cancer-causing viruses in animals ("tumor viruses"). Already there were several reasons, described in a later chapter, for thinking that cancer might have its origins in mutations (changes in DNA). But the idea that genetic changes were the underlying explanations for cancers was far from established, especially since direct, simple, specific evidence, such as an example of a mutant gene in a human cancer, was not available. It was also apparent that such evidence would not be easy to obtain: animal cells were exceedingly complex, like machines with numerous functions and hundreds of thousands of parts—genes, RNA molecules, and proteins.

Work with bacterial cells, based on my own experience and that of many others, indicated that genes were essential targets in efforts to understand how cells work. But, just as it would be hard to sift through many thousands of machine parts to discover why a machine was malfunctioning, there was no obvious way to carry out a search for cancer-causing genes, especially in animal or human cells, which were then much more difficult to study than bacterial cells. If, however, a virus, with its relatively small repertoire of genes—as few as four or five, no more than a hundred—could convert a normal animal cell into a cancer cell, surely that would be a good place to start, certainly better than starting with the entire machine, the cell itself.

Viruses capable of causing cancers in chickens and rodents had been discovered and studied intermittently since early in the twentieth century,[6] but efforts to understand how they worked had been stymied by limited experimental tools. Initially, there seemed little more to do with tumor viruses than to observe the growth of tumors in infected animals. But that began to change when methods were developed to characterize the effects of these viruses in cells growing in culture dishes in the laboratory—advances I will discuss in more detail in succeeding chapters. Amounts of infectious, cell-altering viruses could now be accurately measured, the effects of viruses on cells could be examined closely, experiments could be done in weeks instead of months or years, and viruses could be grown to large amounts to determine their chemical composition. By the time I was taking courses at the NIH, tumor viruses had been assigned to two categories, according to the chemical material, DNA or RNA, that constitutes their genes. The DNA tumor viruses carry their genes, as do bacteria, plants, and animals, in the form of double-stranded DNA. The RNA tumor viruses carry their genes as single strands of RNA.

Of these two types, I was more strongly drawn to the RNA tumor viruses. John Bader's course in virology had introduced me to these viruses (later known as retroviruses), which have formed the basis for much of my subsequent scientific work. Even by the 1960s, RNA tumor viruses had been encountered in fish, birds, and many kinds of mammals, and they were known to cause a diversity of cancer types, including leukemias, lymphomas, sarcomas of bone and connective tissues, and a few carcinomas.[7] Furthermore, the RNA tumor viruses posed a special problem. If they could persistently affect the behavior of infected cells, making cells permanently cancerous, it seemed likely that they had some way of perpetuating their genes in animal cells. But it was hard to see how this could happen, since the genes of these viruses were composed of single strands of RNA, not double-stranded DNA. Because the viral RNA, the genetic material of the virus, differed substantially from the genetic material of animal cell chromosomes (DNA), a long-term attachment of viral genes to a cell's chromosomes seemed implausible. Something novel seemed likely to happen.

Bader, a long-standing member of the NIH intramural scientific staff, was among a still relatively small number of virologists drawn to these perplexities of RNA tumor viruses. Howard Temin, a young virologist at the University of Wisconsin (about whom I will say much more in subsequent chapters), had attracted a good deal of attention and criticism for proposing that the situation might be explained if the genetic information in the viral RNA were converted into a DNA form (which he called a provirus) and then associated stably with a chromosome in an infected animal cell.[8] Bader himself had published some work in support of this idea,[9] but his experiments, like most of Temin's early results, were indirect and open to multiple interpretations.

Two things about this work were exciting to me. First, the idea that an RNA cancer virus might give rise to a DNA form of its genes was novel, an apparent violation of Crick's Central Dogma, in which biological information was known to flow from DNA to RNA to protein, not from RNA to DNA.* Second, the most obvious prediction of the model—the presence of at least one copy of the proposed viral DNA (the provirus) in every infected cell—seemed experimentally testable with the molecular hybridization methods I had adapted to study expression of the lac operon in bacterial cells. Here was a problem—important and also cancer related—that I might be able to solve.

Another NIH course, one taught by the eminent tumor biologist Mike Potter, surveyed the many proposed causes of human cancer and the model systems for studying them. Virtually every result from these experimental systems, whether based on viruses or chemicals, on animals or cultured cells, implied that genetic changes were important in cancer. But what genes were changed when cancers developed? It seemed nearly impossible to answer that question by putting mutagenic chemicals on animal skin or into cell culture fluids. Or by doing what Potter was famous for—producing myelomas, cancers of antibody-producing cells, by irritating the abdominal cavity of mice with mineral oil and other chemicals. But if cancer genes were present in tumor virus particles, the small protein-covered packets of viral nucleic acid, then cancer genes might not be so difficult to isolate, identify, and study—even then, before recombinant DNA technology made molecular biology such a powerful

---

* As Crick later explained after the provirus hypothesis received resounding support,[10] RNA to DNA was an acceptable variation from the previously observed flow of information, not a violation of his rules; this is more fully explained in the next chapter.

form of science. Like Bader's course, Potter's classes made me appreciate the advantages of using viruses—in combination with the molecular methods that I was then mastering in Ira's lab—to pursue the genetic basis of cancer.

FINDING MIKE BISHOP AND UCSF

In response to these interesting possibilities, I began to look for places and people that offered further research training with cancer viruses. After recent vacations to visit friends in the San Francisco Bay area and to learn fly-fishing in the Sierra Nevada, I was strongly inclined toward a California experience. (Connie had never been west of Iowa, but welcomed the prospect of adventure.) However, when I wrote to ask the already famous virologist Renato Dulbecco, at the Salk Institute in La Jolla, just north of San Diego, for a postdoctoral position, I was rebuffed by not one but two letters from his secretary.*

I had more welcoming responses from investigators in the Bay Area, so I paid a visit to them in the summer of 1969. During a conversation with Harry Rubin, a veterinarian and famed expert on Rous sarcoma virus at the University of California at Berkeley, I learned about a new group at the then burgeoning UC medical school in San Francisco (UCSF). He told me that the group included Warren Levinson, one of his former students; Leon Levintow, previously a senior virologist at the NIH; and Mike Bishop, a smart young virologist and physician who had trained with Leon as a Yellow Beret, working on polio virus, and had joined the UCSF faculty a year or two before. Rubin himself was one of the founders of the field of RNA tumor virology and had groomed its new star, Howard Temin. But he was outspoken about his disdain for Temin's new ideas, and these were the ideas I wanted to pursue. I needed to visit UCSF.

I went there in an almost insultingly casual way, without any forewarning. I walked through the halls of UCSF until I found the right labs, then asked whether Levintow, Levinson, or Bishop was around. I learned they were having lunch in the Golden Gate Room; this sounded roman-

---

* Now that Renato and I are friends, I am glad that I saved these rejection letters.

tic, but it was just the UCSF hospital cafeteria. When they returned, we had a round of impromptu conversations. Happily, they did not stand on ceremony and were unabashedly interested in finding new research fellows. Since all four of us were medically trained (only Warren also had a Ph.D.), since three of the four had worked at the NIH, and since we all spoke about the power of viruses to reveal biological truths, the warm welcome may have also come from a recognition that we were already part of the same professional club, with a shared point of view. And the camaraderie itself implied that I would find the intellectual pleasures and rewards of group efforts in California, just as I had at the NIH.

Although Mike and I were born to very different circumstances—his father was a Lutheran minister in rural Pennsylvania—we recognized from the first moments that we seemed to have been destined to work together. We had similar undergraduate experiences (his in history at Gettysburg College), similar medical training (his at Harvard Medical School and the Massachusetts General Hospital), and similar laboratory experiences at the NIH (his using molecular hybridization, among other things, to study the multiplication of polio virus). More importantly, we had similar ideas about using modern biology and animal viruses to study cancer, exploiting new methods (like molecular hybridization) and the genetic simplicity of tumor viruses to try to understand how normal cells could be converted into cancer cells. And I suspect that we recognized, from rapidity of speech, intensity of purpose, and moments of good humor, common characteristics that would work well in partnership. In short order, I agreed to begin work in San Francisco in the summer of 1970, as soon as I fulfilled my Public Health Service requirements at the NIH.

My decision to join Mike Bishop in San Francisco to study cancer-causing viruses has proven to be a pivotal point in my career. To arrive at such a point in any life, circumstances, connections, and coincidences are likely to have played their parts. But, at least in retrospect, an internal logic seems also to have influenced the events in mine. After many years of ambivalence and indecision—the prolonged adolescence that this country permits and that has served me well—I appeared to be headed in a clear direction, even if not toward medicine or literature.

Part Two

DOING SCIENCE

CHAPTER 4

Retroviruses and Their Replication Cycle

—

THE SUMMER OF 1970 WAS, FOR ME, A TIME OF REORIENTATION, IF NOT rebirth. I was thirty years old, taking a transcontinental journey with my new wife, to a new job, in a new and romantic place, San Francisco, California. The preceding two years at the NIH had begun to prepare me for the new problems I'd be working on. My studies of the lac operon in the Pastan lab had introduced me to some of the important methods in the expanding field of molecular biology, and NIH courses had stimulated my interest in—and repaired my deficient knowledge about—tumor viruses. Still, our monthlong trip across America was a symbolic as well as a physical transition. Up to that time, I had wandered in literature, medicine, and science. Afterwards, for at least twenty years, I would focus on two large questions presented by the class of viruses, the RNA tumor viruses, that I had chosen to study: How do these viruses multiply? And how do they cause cancer?

THE TWO QUESTIONS

I was drawn to the first question when I learned at the NIH about Howard Temin's unorthodox proposal that these tumor viruses convert their genes, carried in virus particles as RNA, into a piece of DNA that is then joined to host chromosomes.[1] Did this apparent deviation from the Central Dogma of molecular biology actually occur? If so, how was the viral DNA made and joined to chromosomes? And how were viral genes, once embedded in chromosomes, then used to make the RNA and protein needed to assemble thousands of new virus particles in each infected cell?

The second question—how do RNA tumor viruses cause cancer?—was a refined version of the more general issue that had initially attracted me to tumor viruses. At that time, despite several kinds of evidence that abnormal or mutant genes might be determining elements in the generation of human cancers, most of the scientific community remained skeptical about this idea, in the absence of the most direct support: the demonstration that mutant genes were present in and specifically responsible for cancers. But how could this objective be pursued, when so many genes, tens of thousands, were present in human and animal cells? Whether they carried their genes as RNA or DNA, tumor viruses promised to simplify this intractable problem. Most tumor viruses were thought to carry no more than a few genes, fewer than five or ten, so it seemed plausible to figure out whether and how any of them were, in fact, cancer causing. That kind of strategy might even lead to the identification of similar genes in cells, and those cellular genes might subsequently be directly implicated in human cancers.

Virtually everything I accomplished as a scientist over the next twenty-three years at UCSF can be linked to my curiosity about these two central questions. The RNA tumor viruses—and one in particular, Rous sarcoma virus—proved to be fertile starting points for asking the two broad questions, and many narrower ones as well. These questions led us—me, my faculty colleagues, and our trainees—to explore some of the most exciting areas of modern biology: DNA synthesis and recombination; gene expression (the synthesis and processing of both RNA and proteins); genetic change during evolution; biochemical pathways that allow an external signal to change a cell's behavior; and the genetic basis of cancer, influencing the diagnosis and treatment of the disease.

The outcomes of these many forays into tumor virology can be measured by different indicators: productivity, insight, significance, even aesthetic quality. It is certainly not my intention here to follow every line of work. Instead, I have given the most weight to significance, focusing on the story line that led to our Nobel Prize—the discovery of genes with cancerous (oncogenic) potential. But even that story is not strictly linear. To understand it in any depth, it is necessary to know something about molecular biology and its methods, a little bit about how RNA tumor viruses multiply, and quite a lot about work that followed our own major discovery and ultimately established its significance.

So what was our discovery? In simple outline, it was this. Rous sarcoma virus has one gene, called v-src (for viral src), that is fully responsible for the cancer-causing capacity of the virus. We found a very similar gene, called c-src (for cellular src), in the chromosomes of normal chickens and many other animals. This normal gene had been pilfered by some benign precursor of Rous sarcoma virus and turned into a viral cancer gene (an viral oncogene), at least in part because of concordant changes (mutations) in its nucleotide sequence that altered the properties of the protein it encodes. c-src is now called a proto-oncogene because it has the potential to become an oncogene, either by viral capture or by mutations, including mutations that may affect the gene without the involvement of a virus. The Nobel committee summarized this work by citing our "discovery of the cellular origin" of RNA tumor virus oncogenes.[2]

But why did the discovery of c-src prove to be prize worthy? For at least two reasons. First, because c-src was just the first of many cellular proto-oncogenes. More than thirty have been discovered in more or less the same way—by finding in cellular DNA a gene closely related to a retroviral oncogene—and still more have been discovered later in other ways. And, second, because many proto-oncogenes are medically important: they help turn normal cells into cancers, including human cancers, when they undergo mutations.

That may have been enough to convince a Nobel committee in 1989, but the story did not end there. In recent years, after our prize was awarded, mutant proto-oncogenes and the proteins they encode have become critical tools for the classification of cancers and promising targets for drugs and antibodies—treatments that have, in some cases, proven to be effective for a significant and growing number of cancers, including leukemias and lymphomas; lung, gastrointestinal, and kidney cancers; and cancers of the breast. In this part of the book, I will explain some of these developments.

PEYTON ROUS AND THE ORIGINS OF RNA TUMOR VIROLOGY

During my two years as a trainee at the NIH, I had learned a bit of the history of the field of science I was driving to California to enter in 1970.

But I did not yet know about the founding event, which had occurred sixty years earlier, in the brand-new laboratory of a young physician named Peyton Rous. Rous had just joined the Rockefeller Institute (now Rockefeller University) in New York City, where he was to work until his death, which happened to occur in the year of my transcontinental migration. In an amazingly short time after his arrival in New York in 1909, Rous discovered the virus that would immortalize his name—Rous sarcoma virus, or RSV—a virus that would play a dominant role in studies of RNA tumor viruses and take center stage in my own laboratory work and the work of my closest colleagues.

At the time of Rous's great discovery, very little was known about viruses. One defining attribute was (and is) their size; they are small enough to pass through filters that prevent the passage of bacteria, the larger microbes that were then the best-studied infectious agents of disease. In addition, they were already recognized to be parasites, unable to grow on their own, thus requiring cells —animal, plant, or bacterial, depending on the virus— to allow them to multiply. To look for viruses that can cause cancers, as a means of asking whether cancers might have infectious origins, Rous worked with tumors from animals. He presumed that if the tumor cells were making a virus that caused the cancer, he could demonstrate its presence by grinding up the tumor, passing the extract through a filter to block any animal cells or bacteria, and then injecting the filtered material into another animal to see whether it induced another cancer.

Amazingly, this worked—very early in his career, Rous had made an astonishing discovery.[3] In his report to his institute's supervisors, written in April of 1910, the thirty-one-year-old Rous noted (as a fourth item on his list of several projects), "I have propagated a spindle-celled sarcoma* of the common fowl into its fourth generation [by transplanting it from one chicken to another]. . . . The neoplasm grows rapidly, infiltrates, metastasizes, and remains throughout true to type. Experimental work has not been begun with it."[4] By January 1911, however, this work had pushed all other items out of consideration. He had shown that "the chicken tumor has been several times transmitted by means of a filtrate

* This is a cancer arising in so-called connective tissue cells, such as fibroblasts or muscle cell precursors.

free of its cells. The 'virus' [he explained] will pass through a Berkefield filter which holds back *Bacillus prodigiosis* [a bacterium much smaller than an animal cell]. . . . Work is now being pushed on the natural mode of transmission of the chicken tumor, and the character of the 'virus.' "[5]

Thus Rous sarcoma virus (RSV) was discovered, even though not directly observed; it could not have been seen before the invention of the electron microscope a few decades later. Unfortunately, because the methods of modern biology were not yet in hand, the work that Rous was ready to "push" on his virus never went much beyond the discovery of the virus itself. Rous may have known about the rediscovery of Mendel's laws of heredity a decade earlier and about the concept of the gene as a still mysterious entity that was responsible for many traits of an organism. But, at the time he was trying to work with his virus, no information was available about the composition of a gene or about the processes by which genes, viral or cellular, were duplicated or expressed to make proteins. It was simply not possible at that time to think productively about how viruses reproduced or about how they might cause a cancer such as his "spindle-celled sarcoma." So he went on to explore other aspects of cancer research, including work on another kind of tumor virus, wart-causing viruses of rabbits that belong to the DNA tumor virus class.[6] Ironically, he eventually became an opponent, rather than a proponent, of the genetic origins of cancer that his virus ultimately helped to reveal.[7]

The discovery of RSV paved the way for many later discoveries, including viral cancer genes, proto-oncogenes, and many of the cardinal features of the multiplication strategy for retroviruses, the large class of viruses that includes HIV, as well as RSV and many others. But even before these later discoveries, RSV and Peyton Rous were not forgotten. RSV finally brought him a Nobel Prize—in 1966, fifty-five years after his crucial experiments, when he was eighty-seven years old.

PERPETUATING THE GENES OF RNA TUMOR VIRUSES IN INFECTED CELLS: REVERSE TRANSCRIPTASE

In 1969, I had learned from John Bader, one of the scientists who lectured in my virology course at the NIH, about the fierce debate that had been raging for several years among virologists about Howard Temin's radical idea, called the provirus hypothesis, an idea that could, in principle, solve a persistent mystery: How can viral genes be perpetuated in cells infected with RNA tumor viruses?

Temin was then a young faculty member at the University of Wisconsin, having emerged as a new bright light in tumor virology when he was a postdoctoral fellow at Caltech with Harry Rubin in the late 1950s. Although I did not get to know Howard until the early 1970s, I can readily imagine what he was like in his brashest and most inventive period, because he retained a youthful, appealing, if argumentative intensity about all of his experiments and their possible interpretations until his premature death, in 1994. The older and more melancholic Rubin, whom I met during my search for a postdoctoral position in 1969, had trained as a veterinarian and recognized the importance of viruses that caused diseases affecting poultry stocks; he was among the few who had kept alive an interest in RSV that even Peyton Rous had lost. Many of those who were active in tumor virology during the years when RSV became so influential had been trained in Rubin's laboratories at Caltech or UC Berkeley. Still, as I had learned from my own visit to his lab, he was no fan of Howard's provirus hypothesis and had, in general, a surly attitude toward molecular explanations of cell behavior.

Together, several years earlier, Temin and Rubin had turned the study of the cancer-causing potential of RSV into a quantitative science. In 1957, they published a method for scoring the number of infectious, biologically active RSV particles in a virus preparation.[8] This measurement (or assay) depended on the fact that infection of a single chicken embryo cell, growing amid a layer of other similar cells on a glass plate, with a single infectious virus particle caused a dramatic change, a "transformation," in the appearance and growth properties of the cell. Unlike the existing assays for other kinds of animal viruses that destroy the cells they infect, these new tests for tumor viruses recorded enhanced growth of cells—producing a mound or "focus" of overgrown cells, rather than an empty space left behind by dead cells.

Within a few days after infection, a normally extended, flat cell would round up, divide repeatedly, and become a pile of rapidly growing cells with features of malignant tumor cells, including the ability to form cancers in animals. By testing progressively diluted virus preparations and counting the number of so-called transformed foci, one could determine the number of transformation-competent particles in the original preparation. Moreover, cells transformed by RSV produce infectious virus particles persistently; the newly made virus can infect immediately adjacent cells and thereby accelerate the formation of foci, even if the cells are covered by a viscous layer of agar to prevent the spread of virus to cells throughout the culture dish. The number of infectious, cancer-causing particles of RSV in the inoculating fluid taken from any source can then be measured by counting the foci of transformed cells.

In this way, using chicken embryo cells in a petri dish, Temin and Rubin showed that it is possible within just a week or so to perform quantitative assays for two cardinal properties of RSV: the ability of the virus to multiply (replicate) and its ability to induce cancerous change in cells (transform). These two properties, replication and transformation, are central to any serious consideration of RNA tumor viruses and to the questions that attracted me and many others to study these viruses.

In the early 1960s, Temin had proposed—on the basis of slim evidence, crafty intuition, and strong conviction—that the single-stranded RNA of RNA tumor viruses (in effect, its "genome," the collection of all the genetic information in the virus particle) was converted into double-stranded DNA after a virus particle entered a cell. Temin argued that later in the infectious process the resulting DNA was inserted into one of the cell's chromosomes, forming a "provirus," an integrated segment of viral DNA, that could then be perpetuated along with the rest of the cell's DNA when cells divided.[9] Furthermore, proviral DNA, ensconced in a cell chromosome, could be used, like any cellular gene, to direct synthesis of the RNA and proteins required to produce new virus particles and to transform the cell into a cancerous state. The provirus hypothesis could thus explain some of the unusual features of RSV, especially its ability to change cell behavior permanently, even though it contained only the labile type of nucleic acid, RNA, not the stable form, DNA, in its particle.

The provirus hypothesis was, at that stage, both heretical and, at best, weakly supported by evidence. It was widely considered heretical because, in proposing that viral genes were converted from RNA to DNA, it ran counter, as I've noted before, to the usual flow of genetic information in biological systems—from DNA to RNA to protein—as described by

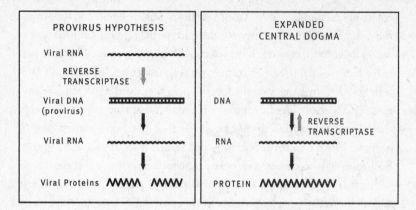

The provirus hypothesis requires that viral RNA be copied to form double-stranded DNA, the provirus, expanding the ways in which genetic information can be used in cells and thus complicating the Central Dogma (right panel). Once reverse transcriptase, an enzyme able to make DNA from RNA, was found in RNA tumor virus particles, a coherent view of the virus multiplication cycle began to emerge (left panel). Viral RNA in the infecting particle is copied early during infection to form DNA, which then joins to a cell chromosome; afterwards many copies of viral RNA are made. The viral RNA can be either translated to make abundant viral proteins or packaged into new, infectious virus particles assembled from the newly synthesized proteins. Hence one particle can make thousands of new ones each day, as long as the cell remains viable.

Francis Crick as part of his Central Dogma of molecular biology. Even more importantly, the provirus hypothesis lacked two crucial elements of support: no enzyme was then known to copy RNA into DNA, and the proposed proviral DNA had not been convincingly detected in, or isolated from, infected cells. I hoped that molecular hybridization—which I had been using in my studies of the bacterial lac operon with Ira Pastan at the NIH—could be used to measure proviral DNA directly and unequivocally, thus helping to resolve this important controversy.* But

---

* As was described and illustrated in chapter 3, molecular hybridization takes advantage of the ability of single strands of nucleic acid, RNA or DNA, to form double strands by pairing their nucleotides, A with T, C with G, when the order of the nucleotides is perfectly, or nearly perfectly, complementary.

that would not have resolved the question of how the viral DNA was synthesized.

The tipping point in the debate over Temin's provirus hypothesis occurred in the spring of 1970, just as Connie and I were getting ready to move to California and UCSF. David Baltimore, working at MIT, and Howard and one of his postdoctoral fellows, Satoshi Mizutani, announced, first at important meetings and soon thereafter in adjacent papers in *Nature* magazine, that they had found—not in cells, but in the virus itself!—an enzyme that could copy the RNA genome of an RNA tumor virus into DNA.[10] For these experiments, Temin used the classic virus, RSV; Baltimore used another virus of the same type that causes leukemia in mice (murine leukemia virus, or MLV).

Baltimore's experiments were inspired, in large part, not just by Temin's hypothesis but also by his experience as a molecular virologist studying several other kinds of RNA viruses that do not cause cancer. During infection, some of these viruses use schemes for multiplication that depend on enzymes that the viruses both encode and carry with them into cells. In other words, those enzymes (which copied viral RNA to make more viral RNA) are in the infectious virus particles themselves, not just made in the cell after infection. This work—much of which Baltimore had performed with his wife, Alice Huang, working on a virus related to the rabies virus[11]—encouraged him to think that the enzyme needed to support the provirus hypothesis might also be found in isolated particles of RNA tumor viruses.

The enzyme that these two laboratories found in RNA tumor virus particles transcribed viral RNA to make DNA. Thus it reversed the commonly observed flow of information (in which DNA is transcribed to form RNA) and quickly became known as reverse transcriptase. Packaged in purified virus particles, it accompanies the invading virus when the virus enters a cell, and it initiates the process of viral multiplication by synthesizing viral DNA from the RNA "template." The viral DNA could ultimately become embedded in a host chromosome, forming the provirus that Temin had prophesied, and its genes could be expressed to make new viral RNA and proteins, to be assembled later into many infectious viral particles. Because the enzyme was found in viral particles and not then known to exist in normal cells, it seemed likely that it was encoded by the viral RNA; that was soon shown to be true.

The discovery of reverse transcriptase was stunning, among the most dramatic events in the history of modern biology. In 1975, a mere five years after its discovery, reverse transcriptase brought the Nobel Prize in Physiology or Medicine to Temin and Baltimore.* Why was the discovery of reverse transcriptase so dramatic? First, it clarified the meaning of the Central Dogma of molecular biology. The conventional flow of information transfer "from DNA to RNA to protein" was the essence of the Central Dogma, so to some the discovery that information could flow from RNA to DNA appeared to violate of the rules. But soon after the discovery of reverse transcriptase, Francis Crick, the dogma's high priest, pointed out that he had never excluded the possibility that RNA could be used as a source of information to make DNA.[13] He had excluded only the possibility that protein could be used as a source of information to make nucleic acid (RNA or DNA). With the discovery of reverse transcriptase, the "reversed" flow of genetic information, from RNA to DNA, was now clearly possible and seemed likely to happen when RNA tumor viruses infected cells. The "reverse" feature, of course, accounts for the colloquial name of the enzyme.** The notion that information flowed "backward," in the unaccustomed direction, from RNA to DNA, also inspired the new and now universally used name for RNA tumor viruses: retroviruses.

The discovery of reverse transcriptase by Temin and Baltimore in 1970 had profound effects on molecular biology in general and on cancer research in particular. For example, reverse transcriptase proved essential to the growth of the biotechnology industry. Importantly, it allowed messenger RNA, the RNA that directs synthesis of proteins, to be directly copied into DNA. The newly synthesized DNA could, in turn, be used in various ways: to be amplified to very large amounts in bacteria or other types of cells; to direct synthesis of large amounts of proteins, including such medically important ones as insulin or growth hormones; and to

---

* Temin and Baltimore shared their prize with Renato Dulbecco, at the Salk Institute, who had shown that the small genomes of certain DNA tumor viruses also persisted in cells by lodging within cell chromosomes.[12]

** The official name is too cumbersome to use here and is rarely used by scientists either.

make radioactive DNA that can serve as gene-specific probes in many kinds of experiments, especially molecular hybridization tests.*

FINDING RETROVIRAL DNA IN INFECTED CELLS

Reverse transcriptase persuaded most of the skeptics to accept Temin's provirus hypothesis, even before anyone had convincingly measured viral DNA directly in infected cells by molecular hybridization. Even though the discovery of reverse transcriptase took some wind out of the sails of my ambitions to test the provirus hypothesis in this way, the new enzyme also proved to be a crucial element in my scientific future. It provided a way to make DNA copies of RNA tumor virus genomes. If radioactive DNA building blocks (nucleotides) were used in the enzymatic reactions, the DNA copies were also radioactive and thus readily measured. These DNA copies were essential probes in the molecular hybridization experiments that allowed us to find the first proto-oncogene just a few years later. The radioactive probes made by reverse transcriptase were also crucial for measuring newly synthesized viral DNA and integrated proviruses in infected cells, the experiments I had first set out for California to do. Because viral DNA could be measured and characterized during infection of cells by RSV and other retroviruses, it was possible to determine how viral DNA was made in infected cells and to learn how it was integrated into host cell chromosomes to form a provirus. These methods and others also made it possible to follow the expression of viral genes through the conventional phases of the Central Dogma—proviral DNA to viral RNA to viral protein.

As I soon learned, though, the task of detecting new molecules of viral DNA, synthesized by reverse transcriptase after animal cells are infected by a single retrovirus, was not trivial. One viral RNA molecule has some eight thousand nucleotides, and it is copied to make one DNA molecule

---

* Reverse transcription later also turned out to be an essential feature of the multiplication strategy for other viruses (such as the hepatitis B viruses); it is central to the mechanism by which the ends of chromosomes (telomers) are kept intact; and it is the driving force in the expansion of copies of certain recognizable segments of DNA that are found in up to thousands of copies in human and other genomes, in animals, plants, and even simpler organisms like yeast.[14]

of about the same length. However, the cells in which the viral DNA is made have (in the case of chicken cells) about two *billion* nucleotides of DNA—nearly a millionfold more. So detecting the relatively minute fraction of viral DNA is like searching for the proverbial needle in a haystack. Success would require both a strong signal—provided by highly radioactive DNA probes, copied from viral RNA with reverse transcriptase—and high specificity. The specificity is achieved by means of molecular hybridization, which demands accurate base-pairing between the radioactive probe and the DNA from an infected cell to form the double-stranded molecules that are measured.

But this kind of experiment, to detect newly made viral DNA in RSV-infected chicken cells, plausible though it seemed, turned out to be difficult for a reason that I hadn't fully anticipated: the DNA of a normal chicken cell is already endowed with DNA closely related to the infecting virus, RSV. This means that the radioactive RSV probe would hybridize to DNA prepared even from uninfected cells, creating a "background" signal against which a small increment, the newly synthesized RSV DNA, would be (and in fact was) hard to detect in DNA from RSV-infected cells.

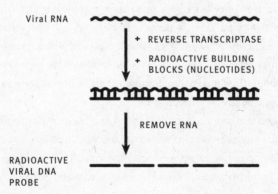

Reverse transcriptase and isotopically labeled nucleotides are used to synthesize short radioactive DNA copies of viral RNA. After removal of the RNA from the base-paired RNA-DNA hybrids, the readily detected DNA can be used as a probe to measure complementary RNA or DNA from cells, as discussed in this and subsequent chapters.

ENDOGENOUS PROVIRUSES

Beyond the technical challenge of detecting new RSV DNA in infected chicken cells, deeper questions were lurking. What was implied by the presence of RSV-related DNA in the normal cells? And how did the viruslike DNA get there? During the 1960s, as methods improved for detecting RNA tumor viruses and their proteins—for example, by making antibodies that reacted with proteins in chicken or mouse viruses— several investigators noted that cells from normal embryos made, or could be induced to make, such viral proteins or even infectious particles containing those proteins.[15] Such findings were too common to be dismissed, and a consensus developed that animals must have RNA tumor virus genes that were "endogenous" —that is, viral genetic material that was intrinsic to normal chromosomes and transmitted through the germ line to progeny. At that time, it was hard to know how those genes were organized in animal chromosomes or how they had come to exist in the germ lines of animals. But, regardless of their origins, they appeared to be transmitted through successive generations of animals and hence had to be part of cell chromosomes.

Many years later, we know that these endogenous viral genes in cell chromosomes are organized just like a provirus created during an infection of cells in a laboratory dish. For this and other reasons, we now believe that most "endogenous proviruses" were synthesized many generations ago by reverse transcriptase when certain retroviruses managed to infect an animal's germ cells (egg or sperm precursors). In fact, thanks to modern methods for examining DNA from various kinds of organisms, it has become evident that the chromosomes of virtually all nucleated cells, from yeast to man, are littered with hundreds or thousands of "endogenous proviruses" and with shards of other pieces of DNA that show signs of having been synthesized by a reverse transcriptase.[16] Although the purpose and significance of such virus-related DNA remain a mystery,* its presence can—and, in the early 1970s, did—

---

* The situation was nicely summarized in the *New Yorker* magazine of December 7, 2007, in an article by Michael Specter entitled "Darwin's Surprise."

confound efforts to monitor the synthesis of viral DNA in newly infected cells. (Endogenous proviruses also influenced the design of experiments that revealed proto-oncogenes, as I will describe in the next chapter.)

To eliminate the confounding effects of endogenous viral DNA on measurements of newly made DNA during viral infection, we took what seems now to be an obvious step: we looked for normal cells that were susceptible to infection by RSV but did not have any detectable RSV-related DNA in their chromosomes. Duck embryo cells, for example, proved to be a convenient host cell.[17] Ducks doubtless carry endogenous proviruses, but they are not sufficiently closely related to RSV to confound molecular hybridization tests that use radioactive RSV DNA probes. Fortunately, fertilized duck eggs were readily available from farmers in Petaluma who served the Bay Area's large Chinese population. The embryos were conveniently large, and the cells derived from them were easily infected by RSV. By measuring viral DNA after infection, we were able to show (during several years of work) that the DNA was made in the cytoplasm rather than in the nucleus of the infected cells; that it was then transported to the nucleus, where both circular and linear forms of viral DNA were observed; and that the linear form of viral DNA was ultimately joined to (integrated within) host chromosomal DNA, allowing its perpetuation in progeny cells, just as Temin had predicted.[18]

PROVIRAL INTEGRATION

But exactly where in the chromosomes did the joining occur? How was the viral DNA arranged at each joining site? And how were the joints between viral and cellular DNA made? To answer these questions, other approaches were required. For some experiments, it was helpful to use yet another kind of host cell—cells that were derived from rodents (mice or rats). Although also devoid of RSV-related endogenous DNA, these cells had one other useful property: after infection, cells became transformed (that is, they acquired the growth properties and appearance of tumor cells), but they didn't produce RSV. That meant that it was quite easy— or, at least, our collaborator in this work, Peter Vogt, made it seem so—to isolate the progeny of single infected cells (clones). Using many such clones made it possible to analyze the proviral DNA to determine its position in chromosomes and its internal organization.[19]

Two important messages emerged from these studies. First, viral DNA could enter many different sites in chromosomes. Imagine a piece of newly synthesized viral DNA to resemble a missile descending to earth. If the missile can set down anywhere, random chance and the size of each target determine whether it will land in a city or on a farm or in the wilderness or in the ocean. In each instance, the missile gets to earth but the effects on the surroundings will vary dramatically. If, however, the missile is specifically targeted to cities or to one particular city, then the consequences of the landing will be the same or nearly the same in all cases. Now we know that the integration of retroviral DNA can occur almost randomly, probably at any of millions of potential sites. This promiscuity has important implications with respect to the consequences of retroviral infection, as will become evident later, when we consider how the positioning of new proviruses can affect nearby proto-oncogenes.

Second, proviral DNA has a uniform and symmetrical appearance.[20] The genes of the virus are always arranged in the integrated DNA in the same order in which they are found both in viral RNA and in the linear form of viral DNA before it is integrated. This suggests that the linear DNA form, rather than the circularized forms, is the one that integrates, and we now know that to be true. More important for our story, proviruses have an unexpected and striking physical property: the same long sequence of nucleotides—called a long terminal repeat, or LTR—is present at both ends of the provirus (see the figure on the following page). This sequence at the termini of viral DNA is made up of sequences present at both ends of viral RNA. This may sound complicated (and it is), but it also suggested unexpected and fascinating aspects of the process of reverse transcription. In due course, detailed studies that we need not review here established that reverse transcriptase uses a number of tricks to synthesize the LTRs from the ends of viral RNA.

While this is especially interesting to experts who study how DNA is made, it has a more general message, too: retroviral proviruses, the products of DNA synthesis by reverse transcriptase, have a structural "signature" that is hard to miss: the LTRs at both ends. When a region of chromosomal DNA has the LTR signature, it has very likely originated

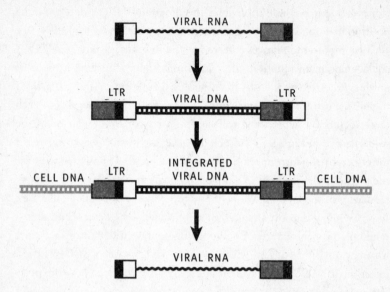

Retroviral proviruses (integrated viral DNA; third line from top) have a distinctive organization, with long terminally repeated sequences (LTRs) at each end. These are also found at the ends of the linear DNA precursor to the integrated provirus, are composed of sequences present at the ends of viral RNA, and contain signals that determine where viral RNA begins and ends, as suggested by the boxes in the cartoon.

from a retroviral infection. Conversely, when the signature is missing, the DNA has probably arrived in the chromosome in some other way.[*]

Given its importance in the virus growth cycle, one final point about the integration of viral DNA should be made. Cells have many enzymes that can cut DNA and paste it together, so it was conceivable that such enzymes would be corralled by retroviruses to mediate the joining of viral DNA to chromosomes. But the integration of viral DNA is an efficient

---

[*] Our laboratory's early work on synthesis and integration of viral DNA, the organization of a provirus with its LTRs, endogenous proviruses, and other related topics was performed over several years by a remarkably congenial team of postdoctoral fellows and graduate students, including Ramareddy Guntaka, Stephen Hughes, Peter Shank, Hsien-Jien Kung, Barbara Baker, John Majors, Ron Swanstrom, Craig Cohen, Larry Donehower, and others. Although the emphasis of my story will soon shift to proto-oncogenes, the communal pleasures and successes of our experimental efforts in this domain can hardly be exaggerated.

and highly specialized process, and it was not surprising to find that retroviruses have developed their own refined tools for performing it. By the mid-1980s, a small group of us—including Mike Bishop; a graduate student, Bruce Bowerman; and a postdoctoral fellow, Pat Brown (who will resurface in chapter 15 as a leader in the movement to provide greater access to the scientific literature)—demonstrated that stripped-down retroviral particles could carry out the integration reaction in a test tube.[21] Later, on the basis of work in several laboratories, most of the necessary cutting and joining steps were attributed to a single enzyme, called the viral integrase.[22]

ANTI-RETROVIRAL THERAPIES

One benefit of learning how retroviruses multiply—the identification of potential targets for antiviral therapies—was not often discussed in the 1970s, when much of the work was done and the known retroviral diseases were confined to a few animal species. But the discovery of the lethal human retrovirus HIV, in the early 1980s, changed all that. Everyone studying the multiplication of animal retroviruses quickly realized that studies of the retroviral replication cycle could identify targets for drugs that might be useful in treating human beings infected with HIV and suffering from AIDS. Most of the anti-HIV drugs now in wide use inhibit reverse transcriptase, and several block another retroviral enzyme I haven't discussed, the viral protease (which cuts viral proteins to make the final components of virus particles).[23] Recently, an inhibitor of the viral integrase has also been approved for treatment of HIV infection,[24] yet another vindication of efforts to pursue the sometimes esoteric strategies for virus replication.

The discovery of reverse transcriptase in 1970, like so many important advances in science, marked not just the crossing of a finishing line. It was also the starting point for examining other aspects of the multiplication cycle of retroviruses, the integration of viral DNA, the nature and distribution of endogenous proviruses, and the potential targets for treating people infected with HIV. Moreover, as we shall soon see, it played a critical role in the search for the origins of viral oncogenes and the discovery of proto-oncogenes.

CHAPTER 5

The RSV Oncogene and Its Progenitor

—

*Usually the beginning of a piece of research is when something strikes
a spark on one's imagination: something one does not know seems a
particularly fascinating thing to try and find out. Partly the thing
itself seems important and fascinating in its own right, partly one has
intimations that one can find it out. That is where the spark comes
in—the intimation that one actually can find it out gives one a
particular thrill that is irresistible. There is a flash, and as with love
one knows that one is in it.*

—WILLIAM COOPER,
THE STRUGGLES OF
ALBERT WOODS (1952)

IN 1970, WHEN I WAS LEAVING THE NIH AND WASHINGTON WITH CONNIE FOR
a new life in cancer research at UCSF, very little was known about how
cancer arises, and it was not easy to think about cancer in molecular terms.

As a physician and the son of both a family physician and a woman
struggling with breast cancer, I knew well the toll cancer takes on families and on populations around the world. But my commitment to cancer
research required more than public health statistics or a personal, emotional stimulus. I needed to sense that there were new possibilities for
discovery: in the phrase that William Cooper assigns to his fictional
chemist, Albert Woods, something needed to "strike a spark on [my]
imagination."[1] For me, this came from seeing the experimental potential
inherent in viruses that cause cancer in animals. Of course, I was not
alone in seeing that potential. But now that cancer has become such an

exciting area of research, it is much easier to understand why it increasingly commands the attention of scientists interested in a broad array of problems in cell biology, development, and medicine.

THE ATTRACTIONS OF CANCER RESEARCH

Cancer is one of nature's great mysteries, a disease that directly alters the behavior of cells, the basic unit of biology—not by destroying cells, but by conferring on them greater than normal powers to do many of the things that cells must normally do. Most cells can grow and divide when appropriate to do so; cancer cells do this, even when it is not appropriate. Most cells are programmed to die at some point after providing useful service; cancer cells often persist because they have lost the potential to die. Most cells do not exercise their capacity to recruit new blood vessels; but many cancer cells emit signals to build new vessels, ensuring that sufficient oxygen and nutrients are provided to growing tumors. Many types of cells can move in an orderly response to signals; cancer cells move locally beyond their normal boundaries without obvious purpose, and they can sometimes spread to invade distant tissues, producing lethal metastasis. These acquired characteristics mean that cancers grow in size and fail to follow the rules that normally keep our tissues and organs in check.[2]

Because cancers can occur in virtually any type of cell in the body and display a wide variety of characteristics, they have an obvious, important, and sometimes bewildering diversity. But cancers are also unified by the capacities acquired by cells to grow, to move, and to survive beyond normal limits. We now know that these common properties presage an overriding, recurrent theme: despite the heterogeneity of cancers, they have common properties and arise by common pathways, involving measurable changes (mutations) in the DNA that constitutes genes. These fundamental aspects of cells—how they function normally, how they become dysfunctional in cancers, and how they are governed by genes—are powerful attractants to biologists of all kinds and have drawn many to the study of cancer over the past few decades. This is especially so now that we know many of the genes that experience the mutations that lead to cancer. How we have come to know some of those genes is central to the story I will tell here.

By 1970, the time of my transcontinental relocation, several clues pointed to the importance of mutations in cancer. For example, some families were known to have very strong tendencies to certain kinds of cancer (such as early-onset colon cancer or the rare childhood tumor of the eye, retinoblastoma).[3] The existence of these families implied that abnormal genes, the consequence of mutations in the germ line of an ancestor, could be transmitted from generation to generation and spur the development of tumors. But, at that time, without modern methods for isolating and analyzing human DNA, there was no obvious way to look for the mutant genes or to know exactly how they predisposed someone to cancer.

Other observations suggested a connection between cancer and genetic damage occurring after birth. In fact, it appeared that damage to genes during childhood or adult life, in individual cells in various tissues or organs, might be more frequent and important for the generation of human cancers than were inherited mutations. (Such damage is called somatic because it affects cells of the body, the "soma," not cells of the germ line, the sperm and eggs, as is the case for inherited mutations.) For example, abnormal chromosomes were often observed in cancer cells,* but not in normal cells from the same patient; such chromosomal damage must have occurred in a somatic cell, not a germ cell. High rates of cancers had been reported in people occupationally exposed to known DNA-damaging agents, such as radiologists exposed to x-rays.[5] And, in the 1960s, Bruce Ames at UC Berkeley startled the cancer research world when he found that chemical compounds that induced cancers in animals also caused mutations in simple bacterial systems: mutagens and carcinogens appeared to be nearly synonymous.[6]

APPROACHING THE GENETIC ORIGINS OF CANCER

In 1970, anyone interested in trying to study the genetic origins of cancer— in somatic cells or germ cells—was plagued by a simple perplexing question:

---

* This is most dramatically and informatively illustrated by the peculiar "Philadelphia chromosome," which was first reported in a form of adult leukemia in 1960[4] and is discussed extensively in later chapters.

How could anyone possibly find and characterize the mutated genes with the methods then available? Hypotheses supported only by associations, such as those between exposure to DNA-damaging agents and a higher incidence of cancer, are unlikely to be fully embraced until they are more directly verified—for instance, by characterization of mutant genes in cancers. Without new techniques for isolating single genes from the cells of complex organisms, however, it seemed inconceivable to be able to say which genes, out of the roughly one hundred thousand genes then thought to be in human cells, were affected by the mutations proposed to drive the cancer-forming process. In the absence of such evidence, most scientists were reluctant to accept a gene-based explanation of cancer's origins. The identification of some cancer-causing genes, even one, would greatly strengthen the idea that cancer had a genetic basis and would foster studies of some important issues: What kinds of proteins did such genes encode? How could alterations in those genes cause cancer? Did they eliminate a protein's function? Or did they strengthen that function? What kinds of mutations—simple changes in the protein-coding sequence of DNA, such as changes in a single base, or more drastic deletions or rearrangements of DNA—could make genes cancer causing?

Without the answers to such questions, many of us thought, it would be impossible to understand cancer at the most fundamental level and to control it in a rational fashion. And if we didn't come to understand these things, the treatment of cancers that had spread beyond the reach of a surgeon's knife would likely continue to be toxic and limited in efficacy, confined to the drugs and radiation that kill any growing cell in their path, normal or cancerous.

It is difficult today to appreciate how inaccessible answers to those questions seemed to be in 1970, less than forty years ago. In the current era, we know how to isolate, copy, analyze, and manipulate any of the individual genes from the genomes of animal cells.* We know how to determine the complete sequence of the building blocks (nucleotides) of a gene, or even an entire genome, with ease and with a speed that continues to accelerate. And we can return normal or altered forms of a gene to animal cells in petri dishes, or to somatic or germ cells in experimental

---

* A genome comprises the complete set of genetic instructions in any organism.

animals, to discern the gene's functions. These technical advances have allowed us to learn the sequence of the DNA comprising nearly all human genes (approximately twenty-two thousand of them, a much lower number than earlier predicted); to assess the kinds of proteins encoded by those genes; and to seek changes in the genes that might account for diseases, for variability among individuals, or for differences between species. We are now even on our way to determining the nucleotide sequences of many or most of the genes in many different kinds of human cancer.*

TUMOR VIRUSES AND CANCER GENES: AN INFORMATIVE MUTANT OF RSV

Although strategies for gene discovery were quite limited in 1970, investigators interested in the possible genetic origins of cancer were becoming increasingly optimistic that fundamental features of cancer could be gleaned by a deeper study of the several kinds of viruses—RSV and other retroviruses, and the DNA-containing tumor viruses—that had been shown over the preceding several decades to induce cancers in experimental animals and change the behavior of cells grown in culture dishes. Because most of these viruses contain only a few genes, usually fewer than five or ten, in contrast to the tens of thousands of genes in animal cells, they were self-evidently attractive to anyone wanting to learn what a cancer gene might be and how a gene might cause a normal cell to become cancerous. But to make even these relatively simple viral genomes useful for studying cancer, it was crucial to seek direct evidence implicating specific viral genes, perhaps just one among the few genes in a viral genome, in the process of transforming cells and inducing tumors. At that time, before the advent of powerful methods to isolate genes, even viral genes, and characterize them biochemically, the best way to identify a cancer-causing gene in a tumor virus was to harness the traditional tools of viral genetics.

I first saw how effectively this approach could be applied to tumor

---

* The National Cancer Institute and the National Human Genome Research Institute at the NIH have recently committed substantial funds to an effort, now becoming international, to describe the genetic changes in about fifty types of human cancer in great detail; the project is called The Cancer Genome Atlas (TCGA) and can be followed via the Internet.[7]

viruses when Connie and I took a several-day detour to attend the annual Gordon Conference on Animal Cells and Viruses in Tilton, New Hampshire, on our way to California in 1970. This venerable meeting was held, as always, at a derelict boarding school, with bad food and hollowed-out beds. For several years to come, I would make a regular pilgrimage to this meeting, absorbing new results in the ramshackle auditorium for four hours in the morning and the evening, but avoiding the school's amenities by renting cabins with Mike Bishop, David Baltimore, other colleagues, and our families at a nearby lake. In 1970, though, Connie and I were strangers among the attendees and endured the accommodations and the meals.

The general mood was buoyant. Reverse transcriptase had been announced only weeks earlier, and several other research groups, including Mike Bishop's, were already confirming and extending the findings. At one evening session, I learned about another startling discovery that, like reverse transcriptase, would profoundly influence everyone's thinking about retroviruses. Steve Martin, then a graduate student with Harry Rubin (and now a professor) at UC Berkeley, described his isolation of a mutant version of Rous sarcoma virus.[8] As a student, Steve did not appear much different from how he looks now, in his sixties—bookish, but boyish, with dark curls, a cherubic face, and an enthusiastic manner. His intent was not to create a cancer gene by mutating a normal one, but instead to mutate and thus inactivate any of the genes in RSV that might be responsible for its cancer-causing ability. This would allow him to say that the virus had a gene (or genes) required for transformation and might help to define the position of that gene (or genes) along the viral RNA genome.

In his talk at the meeting, Steve recounted how he had used a traditional approach to generate and look for mutants. First, he used a chemical to damage viral nucleic acid and thus make mutants of RSV. He then screened through large numbers of surviving viruses, using the transformation assays developed by Temin and Rubin, to seek rare interesting mutants deficient in the ability to transform cells.

Steve had succeeded beyond expectation. Not only was his best mutant defective when tested for its ability to transform chicken cells in the focus-forming assay developed by Temin and Rubin; it was defective only when cells were grown at an elevated temperature, not at a lower temperature. Furthermore, the mutant virus was able to multiply well at either temperature, despite its temperature-sensitive defect in transformation. These findings implied that the mutant virus had an altered gene that was specifically required for RSV's transforming activity and that altered gene made a faulty protein that was less stable at high temperature than the protein made by the starting version of RSV.

The mutated viral gene was soon thereafter called the viral src oncogene, or v-src. The name, pronounced "sark," was chosen to indicate the ability of RSV, and its transforming gene, to induce *sarcomas* in animals, as first shown by Peyton Rous in chickens. In a formal sense, the mutation that Steve Martin had characterized *defined* the gene by disturbing the

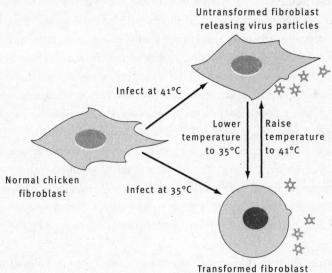

The illustration shows how the v-src mutant strain of RSV isolated by Steve Martin affected the behavior of infected cells at high and low temperatures. When a normal chicken cell is infected by the virus (left) and kept at the lower temperature (lower right), the cell changes shape (transforms); if inflated and kept at the higher temperature, it retains its normal spread-out appearance. At either temperature, the cell makes new virus. If the growth temperature is later changed, the transformed cell will return to normal or vice versa.

gene's cancer-causing function, just as variants of Mendel's pea colors allowed him to define color-determining genes.

Steve's experiments did even more; they also indicated that the function of the src gene was required to *keep* cells in a transformed state, not just to *initiate* cancerous change. By changing the incubation temperature at any time after infection, he could alter the behavior of infected cells, even long after infection. That is, if the temperature of cells transformed by the mutant virus was later raised, the cells returned to a normal shape and pattern of growth, even though viral genes, in the provirus, were still present. Conversely, if the higher temperature of infected, normal-appearing cells was lowered, the cells displayed the properties of transformed cells.*

Because the mutant virus multiplied normally at *both* temperatures, making many new infectious particles, an additional principle could be deduced: the v-src oncogene is not required for virus multiplication. This implied that the other genes in the RSV genome are sufficient to make all of the components that assemble to make new, infectious virus. Although this separation of functions—of replication from transformation—seems logical in design, it was hardly a foregone conclusion. For instance, most oncogenes of DNA tumor viruses turn out to be also important for virus growth, a feature that has historically complicated studies of those viruses. The distinct separation of RSV's cancer-causing and multiplication functions also raised some profound questions: Why does the virus bother to carry the v-src gene if it is dispensable for virus replication? What kind of gene is it? Where did it come from originally? Why is it in the virus? Do other cancer-causing retroviruses carry that gene or something like it?

Many of these provocative questions about cancer genes seem more obvious in retrospect than they did at the time. At the Gordon Conference in 1970, the several follow-up studies on reverse transcriptase attracted the limelight. Steve Martin's v-src mutant was warmly received, but the findings weren't viewed with the fervor accorded to reverse tran-

---

* Because temperature-sensitive mutants usually make proteins with a heightened vulnerability to heat, it was assumed that the src protein encoded by Steve's mutant was inactivated when the cells were shifted to the higher temperature, preventing it from maintaining the cell's transformed state, and then reactivated or resynthesized in a normal form when the temperature was lowered.

scriptase, which was so obviously a revolutionary development. There were, after all, other laboratories isolating other mutants of RSV, studying other retroviruses, and pursuing DNA tumor viruses, and some of their findings were interesting, too. Clearly, time would be required to understand the full significance of what Martin had to say.

After the meeting, I did not race to San Francisco to exploit what I had learned. Instead, Connie and I drifted happily across the country in our recently acquired Volvo, stopping to camp in the Boundary Waters, Glacier National Park, and a few other places. When we arrived in San Francisco, we spent time exploring the city, looking for an apartment, and visiting the places (Stinson Beach, the Sierras) that had attracted me to California. I was settling into my new laboratory, too, but my focus was on attempts to measure RSV DNA in infected cells. Viral oncogenes and their progenitors would have to wait.

DISCOVERING THE SRC PROGENITOR: A CELLULAR PROTO-ONCOGENE

Methods and materials drive discovery as much as do new ideas. This certainly proved to be the case when we found the src proto-oncogene.

The notion that genes related to retroviral oncogenes might be found in normal cells had been in the air, even in the 1960s, when viral oncogenes, like v-src, had not yet been defined experimentally. The best-known exposition of the idea was the so-called virogene-oncogene hypothesis described in 1968 by Robert Huebner and George Todaro, two senior scientists at the NIH.[9] Their hypothesis was built on the increasing evidence for genes in normal cells that could direct the production of retroviral proteins and even infectious retroviruses. Expression of these viral genes (genes we would now call parts of endogenous proviruses, and they called virogenes) sometimes occurred in response to specific "inducers," such as chemicals applied to normal mouse embryo cells growing in a dish. If genes for retroviral proteins were present in normal cells and could be turned on and off, perhaps genes for retroviral oncogenes were also present in normal cells and susceptible to signals that turned virogenes on and off. This led Huebner and Todaro to propose the widely discussed idea that human cancers might arise when chemical or physical factors, like x-rays, switched on a viral oncogene that had been lying dormant in the chromosomes of normal cells as part of a virogene.

A rigorously defined retroviral oncogene, most obviously the v-src gene of RSV, seemed to offer a way to test the Huebner-Todaro hypothesis. Was a viral oncogene, like v-src, in fact present in the DNA of normal cells from chickens or any other animal? But there were also problems with this approach. If DNA related to v-src was found in normal cells, there could be explanations other than the virogene-oncogene proposal. For instance, any DNA related to v-src might not be a true oncogene, as envisioned by the NIH scientists; instead, it might be a normal gene that could be converted into a cancer-causing gene (for instance, if captured by a retrovirus or if changed by mutations).

Regardless of the motivations for doing it—or of the uncertain interpretations of a positive result—it seemed that efforts to seek v-src-related DNA in normal cells might be rewarding. But the proposed experiment also presented major technical hurdles. The era of recombinant DNA methods that now allow any gene to be isolated, amplified, dissected, and used for further experiments was still several years in the future. In the early 1970s, it remained difficult to make radioactive nucleic acid, DNA or RNA, that would represent only a single gene, like v-src, in molecular hybridization tests for related DNA in normal animal cells. Without a means to prepare such a highly specific probe for v-src, the best that could be done was to use the entire RNA genome of RSV, or DNA copied from it, in molecular hybridization experiments. Radioactive probes representing the entire RSV genome would be derived largely from RSV genes devoted to virus multiplication, with the v-src gene constituting at best about 15–20 percent of the probe. Under these conditions, misleading results were possible. In fact, an effort by others to use radioactive RSV RNA in a search for v-src sequences in normal chicken cell DNA had yielded a negative (and, we now know, incorrect) result.[10]

The solution to this dilemma depended on some fortuitously helpful mutants of RSV. These mutants allowed us to prepare a radioactive probe that represented only the v-src gene, not any of the replication genes of RSV. The path that led us to these mutants was also notable—the consequence of an unusual, long-term collaboration with the remarkable RNA tumor virologist Peter Vogt. A brilliant, unflappable, and artistic man who had escaped from the Sudetenland as a high school student during the Soviet occupation, Peter was another acolyte of Harry Rubin and RSV. Shortly after I arrived at UCSF, two of his postdoctoral fellows, Robin Weiss and Robert Friis, had written to us from their lab at the University of Washington in Seattle, asking whether we'd like to use our molecular hybridization methods to look for endogenous proviruses in various species of birds. This request led to collaborative projects, published papers, and increasingly frequent meetings in San Francisco or in Los Angeles (after the Vogt laboratory moved to the University of Southern California in 1972)—meetings at which Peter's knowledge of virus biology and genetics nicely complemented our skills in molecular biology.

Among the interesting RSV mutants that Peter discussed at these gatherings was a class of deletion mutants, viruses that appeared to be devoid of the v-src gene, having lost about two thousand nucleotides of the original nine or ten thousand in the genome of RSV.[11] This loss spared the genetic information required for multiplication of the mutants; indeed, they multiplied even more vigorously than the parental strain of RSV. While the behavior of these mutants resembled Steve Martin's v-src mutants in one way, by retaining their full potential for multiplication, they differed by lacking the ability to transform cells at any temperature, consistent with the complete loss (rather than a subtle alteration) of the transforming gene, v-src.

In our discussions with Peter, it was generally assumed (and later proven by experiments)[12] that the deleted region of the RSV RNA represented the v-src gene and nothing else of significance. This region had been mapped to one end of RSV RNA by another of Peter's collaborators, the UC Berkeley chemist Peter Duesberg.* Duesberg and his colleagues also became regular attendees at our meetings with the Vogt laboratory; as the group grew, to include scientists from other institutions

---

* Duesberg's early reputation as an insightful and exacting analyst of retroviral genomes has regrettably been overshadowed in the past two decades by his damaging demagoguery as an advocate for the unsupportable position that HIV is not the cause of AIDS.

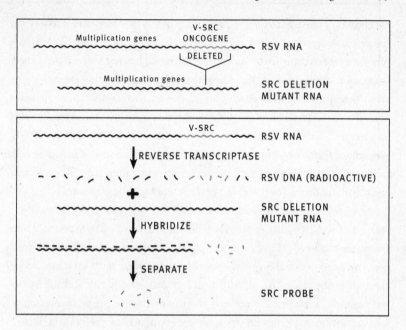

The preparation of a radioactive probe specific for the src gene depended on the isolation of RSV deletion mutants lacking the src gene (top). When short pieces of radioactive DNA were made by copying normal RSV RNA with reverse transcriptase, the src-specific pieces of DNA were isolated by hybridizing the rest to RNA from the src deletion mutants and separating the RNA-DNA hybrids from the src probe.

in California and Washington State, it evolved into what we eventually called the West Coast Tumor Virus Cooperative.

The RSV deletion mutants inspired some thoughts about ways to make a radioactive probe for the v-src gene, so that we could test whether src-like DNA was present in normal cells. The situation reminded me of experiments I had undertaken on the lac operon in Ira Pastan's lab. To develop a sensitive and specific molecular hybridization test for lac operon RNA, we had taken advantage of genetic differences between bacterial viruses, using strains that did and those that did not carry the operon. Similarly, our contemplated strategy for making a probe specific for the v-src gene of RSV took advantage of genetic differences between the normal (wild-type) strain of RSV and Peter Vogt's deletion mutants, as shown in the figure on the previous page. First, we would make small pieces of radioactive DNA representing the entire, wild-type RSV RNA genome. RNA from Peter's deletion mutants, lacking v-src, would then be used to capture all of the radioactive DNA representing everything in RSV except v-src. The remainder of the labeled DNA would then be specific for v-src. It was possible to do this because molecular hybrids between the RNA lacking v-src and radioactive DNA could be physically separated from the unhybridized v-src DNA, with a simple procedure. If all worked according to plan, the unhybridized, radioactive DNA would be a specific probe for v-src, the gene deleted in Vogt's mutants.

Exploratory work by one postdoctoral fellow in our group, Ram Guntaka, showed that this strategy would indeed serve our purposes. Then more extensive work by another fellow, Dominique Stehelin, delivered on the promise of the initial experiments, producing what came to be known as the src probe* in sufficient amounts and purity and validating its essential features. Dominique then used the src probe in molecular hybridization experiments to look for evidence of src-related DNA, revealed by base pairing, in normal DNA from a variety of birds. The results were unambiguous and stunning: DNA closely related to the viral src gene was present in normal DNA—first from chickens and then from other birds, such as duck, turkey, quail, and even, most memorably, an emu we obtained from the Sacramento Zoo.[14] Later, src-like DNA was detected in mammals, including man, by another postdoctoral fellow, Deborah Spector.[15] Still later, src-like DNA was described, mostly by others, in essentially all multicellular animals, including flies and worms.[16] These findings immediately suggested that src DNA was conserved during evolution; the genetic information we were measuring in DNA was presumably a gene that conferred some benefits on organisms. In this way, src became one the first genes of uncertain function—unlike, say, the globin genes that were known to encode proteins that carry oxygen in the blood—shown to have been conserved over hundreds of millions of years of animal evolution.

* Notably, the successful preparation of the src probe warranted publication in a prominent journal;[13] today, with recombinant DNA methods and information from genome projects, such probes are trivial to make and would deserve only passing comment in the methods section of a research paper.

But these experiments were not confined to the simple question of whether any src-like genes were present in normal DNA from birds. It was also possible to judge just how closely a cell's src DNA resembles the RSV src gene, how well it had been conserved in evolution, and whether the cellular gene was likely to do the same thing that the viral src gene did. We were able to explore these questions, at a time well before direct sequencing of the bases in DNA became routine, by measuring the fidelity of base-pairing between the radioactive src probe and the various cellular DNAs. Highly faithful base-pairing would imply that the v-src probe was identical or nearly identical to the src DNA in normal cells, whereas less perfect base-pairing would imply differences between v-src and the cellular DNA.

Dominique's measurements showed that the src-like DNA in normal chicken cells was not identical to the v-src gene—as one might have expected, for example, if the oncogene-virogene hypothesis had been correct. Moreover, as we surveyed DNA from birds that were more and more distant from chickens on the evolutionary tree, the base-pairing became less and less accurate, implying that the cellular DNA detected by the src probe had evolved in accord with the evolutionary distances between the birds estimated by more traditional methods, like anatomical differences. These findings had the markings of results that would be expected if the probe detected a normal and highly valued cellular gene related to v-src, rather than a viral oncogene that had been inserted in cell chromosomes by infection, as part of an endogenous provirus.

These conclusions were reinforced by parallel experiments with a radioactive probe for the parts of the RSV genome that were present in Vogt's v-src deletion mutants—a probe that detects the sequences that are required for virus multiplication and are expected to be in endogenous proviruses (or "virogenes"). This kind of probe formed molecular hybrids with normal chicken DNA, because chickens harbor endogenous proviruses closely related to RSV (although lacking an oncogene like v-src). But no hybrids were formed with the DNA of other birds. These results also had evolutionary implications. The infections of the chicken germ line that established endogenous, RSV-like proviruses most probably occurred within the past few million years, possibly even quite recently, but after divergence of avian species. In this model, any endogenous proviruses in the other avian species must have little or no similarity to RSV. Alternatively, the infections that established endogenous proviruses in chickens might have occurred before species diverged; but, in that case, the proviral sequences were not conserved during evolution.

Regardless of evolutionary interpretation, it was evident that probes for the multiplication genes and for the transforming gene of RSV produced very different results, consistent with a profound biological distinction. We now have much more evidence to say that the sequences in normal cells related to v-src are part of a normal cellular gene that has slowly evolved along with other valuable genes and has features characteristic of cellular genes in animal cells.* In contrast, the sequences in normal chicken DNA related to the RSV replication genes are part of endogenous proviruses that inserted into chicken chromosomes during relatively recent infection of the germ line of chickens.[18] The endogenous proviruses have the terminally repeated sequences and other peculiarities first noted in proviruses produced during infection of cells in culture dishes, as described in the preceding chapter.

In the paper that described the initial findings of src-related DNA in normal birds,[19] published in *Nature* early in 1976, we drew conclusions and made inferences that, while still speculative, were revolutionary. Happily, they also later proved to be correct. We proposed that a normal cellular gene, closely related to the viral oncogene src, was present in the genomes of normal animal cells. We also argued that this normal cellular gene, called c-src, is the presumptive precursor to the viral oncogene and that the small differences we were able to detect between the viral and cellular genes might be responsible for making the viral gene oncogenic—that is, capable of contributing to the development of a cancer. (For these reasons, we later categorized c-src and other genes with the potential to become oncogenes as "proto-oncogenes.") Having observed src-like DNA in multiple avian species, we proposed that c-src had been conserved during evolution and that such conservation implied essential functions for c-src, most likely during cell growth or development.

---

* The protein-coding portions of cellular genes are, for example, normally found as segments separated by noncoding regions, and are not associated with the LTRs present in proviruses. Both features of cellular genes have been shown to be true for src.[17]

Finally, we suggested that changes in cellular genes like c-src might be cancer causing, even without the involvement of a retrovirus. It is this last prediction that is most likely to be viewed with time as the greatest legacy of the search for cellular precursors of retroviral oncogenes. As subsequent sections will show, c-src was merely the first of many proto-oncogenes, and many of them have been directly implicated in human cancers.

BEYOND THE DISCOVERY OF C-SRC

Like all startling developments, our discovery of src sequences in normal cells and our proposal that such sequences constituted a c-src proto-oncogene provoked more questions than they seemed to answer.

We had already tried to answer an obvious one—is c-src involved in cancer formation independently of RSV and viral src?—and we came close to publishing a significant error. During the studies that revealed src sequences in normal avian cells, we had also begun to ask whether the putative proto-oncogene was "read-out" (expressed) in the form of RNA that could, in turn, be translated to make src protein. Our initial findings, which were included in the manuscript describing the c-src proto-oncogene when it was submitted to *Nature*, were provocative. Although we could not find src RNA in normal bird fibroblasts, we did detect it in a line of tumor cells that one of our favorite colleagues, Carlo Moscovici, had derived from a chemically induced sarcoma in quail.

This was potentially exciting because it implied that the sarcoma-causing chemical might have acted by turning on an otherwise silent proto-oncogene, thereby conferring oncogenic activity on it. But the experiment was criticized by a skeptical reviewer, who thought publication of it was premature, and we ultimately (and, in retrospect, happily) removed it from the paper. Not long thereafter, other members of our laboratory group, Deborah Spector and Daisy Roulland-Dussoix, were able to detect src RNA in normal cells, undercutting the argument that chemical carcinogens could cause sarcomas by turning on a normally silent c-src gene.[20] We now know that many proto-oncogenes can be turned into active oncogenes by several routes, including mechanisms that augment gene expression. But, as we shall soon see, showing that proto-oncogenes can participate in oncogenesis without first being abducted from cells by retroviruses required the discovery of proto-oncogenes other than c-src.

One of the most pressing questions that followed the discovery of c-src concerned other retroviruses. It was becoming clear that many of them caused cancers, mainly sarcomas and leukemias, because they carried in their RNA genomes genetic information unrelated (or, at best, distantly related) to src or to the multiplication genes of retroviruses. Was this information, like v-src, derived from normal cells? If so, what kinds of genes were involved? What kinds of proteins did they encode? What was their relationship to src? Questions of this sort attracted enormous interest among retrovirologists—indeed, several had been working on these questions even before our findings about c-src were obtained, talked about, and published.

Some of the ferment in this new field of oncogene research has been memorialized in a cartoon drawn by Jamie Simon at the Salk Institute in 1983 to decorate the cover of abstracts at an annual Cold Spring Harbor RNA tumor virus meeting. This now totemic image faithfully and amusingly depicts some of the better-known, senior scientists who pursued a variety of retroviral oncogenes to their origins as proto-oncogenes in several different species, including chickens, mice, rats, cats, and monkeys. In one case that will be discussed later, an oncogene found in a human tumor cell, not in a retrovirus, also turned out to be a mutated form of a previously discovered proto-oncogene—one of the ras proto-oncogenes, precursors to oncogenes found in mouse and rat sarcoma viruses.

By the time Jamie drew his cartoon, at least twenty retroviral oncogenes were known from studies of a wide variety of highly oncogenic retroviruses that had been isolated by virologists, working in the tradition of Peyton Rous by looking for viruses in cancers arising in many kinds of animals. In the late 1970s and early 1980s, most of these viral oncogenes had been traced to a normal gene, a proto-oncogene, that was almost certainly the precursor of the viral gene. (By now, about forty cellular genes have been discovered in this way; yet more proto-oncogenes, perhaps five- to tenfold more, have been found in recent years by other experimental routes, discussed in subsequent chapters.)

The upper half of Jamie Simon's drawing shows a simplified, symbolic version of the events that allow a common form of a retrovirus, one lacking any specific viral oncogene, to become an efficient cancer-causing agent by capturing genetic information from a cell, converting a cellular proto-oncogene into a viral oncogene. Arrayed along the lower half are some of the leading figures in the study of retroviral oncogenes and their cellular progenitors, in a fashion that suggests the animal species they worked with and some of the genes that they found. Among these are the author and Mike Bishop with birds and the src gene (Mike also found avian genes called myc, erbA, erbB, and myb); Charles Sherr with the feline gene fes; David Baltimore with the mouse abl gene that became important in the deciphering of the Philadelphia chromosome; Ed Skolnick with the mouse ras genes that proved to be so frequently mutated in human cancers; Bob Weinberg with one of the early human oncogenes that turned out to be a mutant form of ras; Stuart Aaronson with the sis gene of monkeys, a gene later shown to encode an important growth factor; Inder Verma with a mouse gene called fos, first implicated in bone cancers in animals; and George Vande Woude with yet another mouse gene, called mos.

Of those proto-oncogenes found first as the predecessors of retroviral oncogenes, a few are closely related (e.g., two ras genes), and others make proteins with similar biochemical properties (e.g., src, erbB, and abl). But the major theme is diversity. Most of these proto-oncogenes are different in fundamental ways, encoding proteins that differ chemically, functionally, and positionally within cells, with many different roles in the normal business of animal cells. Some are secreted hormones, growth factors, that affect cell behavior. Others are receptors for growth factors, protruding from a cell's outer membrane and able to recognize and bind growth factors. Still others relay signals through the cell cytoplasm or instruct the cell nucleus to turn certain sets of genes on or off.

That the protein products of proto-oncogenes play such a wide range of roles in cell physiology underscores the idea that cancer occurs when some fundamental cell process, like growth, differentiation, or cell death, goes awry, the consequences of mutations altering the genes that govern those processes.[21] When proto-oncogenes become cancer genes (for instance, when incorporated into retroviral genomes[22]), they display mutations that make their protein products more active—dangerously active, because they disrupt normal patterns of cell growth, cell differentiation, or cell death, promoting the development of cancers. Furthermore, significant numbers of proto-oncogenes have repeatedly been found in a mutant, oncogenic form in a variety of human cancers, as we shall soon discuss.

Although the diversity of proto-oncogenes can be bewildering and mostly beyond the territory we need to cover here, it will be important later in this chapter to know that some of the proteins made from proto-oncogenes are enzymes. The most important type of enzyme is one first encountered, once again, by the study of RSV. During the late 1970s, in the few years following the discovery of c-src, src genes were shown to encode a medium-sized protein, first detectable with antibodies present in the blood of animals that had developed tumors caused by RSV.[23] With these specific antibodies, one could partly purify the src protein and ask whether it might exhibit an enzymatic activity. That would provide a glimpse of how a normal cell is transformed into a cancer cell and, at the same time, offer a simple test for a cancer-causing biochemical event and even a possible target for cancer therapies.

These efforts have paid rich dividends. With the src antibodies in hand, two groups, Ray Erikson's and ours, found that v-src protein is an enzyme called a protein kinase, an enzyme that moves phosphate from ATP (a cell's energy source) to amino acids in proteins.[24] Several other proteins made by viral oncogenes and proto-oncogenes were also shown to be protein kinases.[25] Even more surprisingly, many of these protein kinases, including those encoded by v-src, v-abl, and other viral oncogenes and their progenitor proto-oncogenes proved to place phosphate specifically on a single type of amino acid, tyrosine.[26]

The significance of the tyrosine target cannot be overemphasized. We now know that just over 500 of the 20,000-odd genes in human chromosomes make protein kinases, enzymes that transfer phosphate to proteins and thereby regulate the functions of proteins that gain the phosphate. Nearly all of that phosphate is added to amino acids other than tyrosine (serine and threonine) in the protein chains. But the remaining 1 or 2 percent, added to tyrosine, is critical. The importance of tyrosine as a target is underscored by the fact that as many as 90 of the roughly 500 human genes that encode protein kinases make kinases that are specific for tyrosine (hereafter called tyrosine kinases). Moreover, among those 90 genes, several, like c-src, c-abl, and c-erbB, are proto-oncogenes.

When the proto-oncogenes are converted into oncogenes by mutation, the enzymes they encode become stronger. For example, when the c-src gene was captured by a retrovirus to become the v-src gene of RSV, the gene was altered in a way that removed a brake on the enzymatic activity of the resulting v-src protein. In other words, the v-src protein adds phosphate to tyrosine residues much more efficiently than does the c-src protein.

These findings represent a remarkable advance in our understanding of cancer—an advance that exceeds what might have been predicted to emerge from the study of animal tumor viruses and their cancer genes. For instance, work with the v-src gene and its encoded protein immediately suggested that excessive phosphorylation of tyrosine might mediate cancerous change and that inhibitors of protein kinases, if they could be made to work with sufficient specificity, might be useful in treatment of cancers caused by genes of the src type. Indeed, as we shall soon see, several kinds of human cancer are caused by such genes and can be treated with appropriate inhibitors.

In the course of about a dozen years, from the early 1970s to the mid-1980s, scientists working with cancer-causing retroviruses had moved from a state of virtual ignorance about viral oncogenes to knowing that there were several kinds of retroviral oncogenes, encoding several kinds of proteins; to knowing that the viral oncogenes all had cellular progenitors (proto-oncogenes); and to knowing that some of the properties of oncogenic proteins were potentially useful for the treatment of cancers.

Unfortunately, we still do not know the full repertoire of proteins that are phosphorylated by enzymes like src and other tyrosine kinases. But we do know something about how the kinases affect cell behavior. More importantly, small molecules that inhibit those enzymes efficiently and specifically have recently been found, and some of them have become drugs approved for use in cancer patients. In chapter 7, I will discuss some of the ways in which these tyrosine kinase inhibitors have improved the treatment of cancers in which proto-oncogenes related to src, like abl and erbB, are mutated.

CHAPTER 6

How Proto-oncogenes Participate in Cancer

—

WITHIN FOUR OR FIVE YEARS AFTER PUBLICATION OF OUR PAPER ON THE discovery of the c-src gene in 1976, a large community of investigators around the world was at work on many retroviral oncogenes, their cellular progenitors, and the proteins they encode. But essential questions remained unanswered. Proto-oncogenes may be numerous and varied, but can they play a role in cancer without being captured by a retrovirus and converted to a viral oncogene, like v-src? And, if so, are these genes involved in the generation of human cancers?

An extensive search over many years for retroviruses in human cancers had come up mostly empty-handed, after producing a number of false alarms.[1] But there were notable exceptions. In the late 1970s, Robert Gallo and his colleagues at the NIH, as well as groups working in Japan, had found the human T cell leukemia/lymphoma viruses (HTLVs), retroviruses that cause relatively uncommon human diseases, especially a cutaneous lymphoma.[2] But the HTLVs do not carry a cell-derived viral oncogene, and it remains unclear, even today, how they cause cancer in a few of many people infected with the HTLVs. Without any evidence for human retroviruses that carry oncogenes, the importance of proto-oncogenes in human cancer hinged on the question of whether proto-oncogenes could become cancer causing even if they were not first captured by a retrovirus.

PROVIRAL INSERTIONS CAN TURN ON
PROTO-ONCOGENES

One of the first demonstrations that proto-oncogenes don't need to be captured by a retrovirus to cause cancers came from an unexpected direction, but one that again illustrated the revelatory power of retroviruses. In the late 1970s, a couple of years after the discovery of the src proto-oncogene, some of us began to consider a long-standing and vexing problem in the study of retroviruses. Unlike RSV and many other powerfully oncogenic viruses, some retroviruses cause tumors in animals and yet do *not* carry a cancer gene derived from a cellular proto-oncogene! In fact, they don't have any specific gene to which their cancer-causing ability can be ascribed. It was acknowledged that such viruses differ from the highly oncogenic retroviruses, like RSV, because they are not able to transform the growth and shape of cultured cells and because they require a relatively long time to induce tumors. But, indisputably, many kinds of genuine cancers—especially leukemias, lymphomas, and breast cancers—do occur after infection of animals with these oncogene-deficient retroviruses. How does this happen?

My own interest in this question became more focused in 1978, when I decided to take a yearlong sabbatical at the Imperial Cancer Research Fund laboratories in Lincoln's Inn Fields, in central London.* My sabbatical was itself an oddity; most scientists I know do not take long leaves from their labs, especially when work is going well. We are not solitary scholars, so we hesitate to be separated from the technicians, students, and fellows who compose our laboratory groups. But I was curious about doing science in different company and a different cultural environment after eight years in San Francisco. I would also be protected from laboratory disasters at home and from the irresponsibility of leaving trainees in the lurch by my partnership with Mike Bishop and by the vigilant oversight of my research associate Suzanne Ortiz.**

---

* A few years ago, the ICRF fused with another charity-based cancer research organization to form Cancer Research UK, or CRUK; the Lincoln's Inn Fields laboratories are still in operation as part of CRUK.

** Suzanne began working with me in 1972 and has for many years since then been the

My reliance on Mike and Suzanne would be supplemented by telephone calls, letters, and an occasional visit to San Francisco in that age before electronic mail and videoconferencing made daily contact all too easy. Connie and I were further motivated by our eagerness for a sustained dose of London theater, and by the prospect that, in a foreign setting, we could at least temporarily readjust the pace of my work against the growth of our family.

Christopher, our second son, was about four months old when we arrived in London in July of 1978. (Jacob, our first, had been born late in 1973.) We devoted quite a bit of time to wheeling Christopher through Islington's St. Mary's Churchyard and other London parks in an over-sized English carriage, with the nearly five-year-old Jacob in tow. Part of our group at UCSF was then focused on the organization of proviral DNA and on the locations of proviral integration sites in cell chromosomes. One evening, while pushing Christopher's pram in front of some royal palace, I began to think about the possible consequences of an increasingly likely conclusion from our studies. Proviruses seemed able to insert into virtually any position in the chromosomes of an infected cell, like missiles landing anywhere on earth (to return to an earlier analogy). This quasi-randomness meant that virtually any cellular gene could be affected by proviral integration. For example, a provirus might interrupt a gene and inactivate it, or a provirus landing near a gene might disturb the gene's regulatory signals, causing inappropriate levels of expression, as indicated in the figure on the following page.

In mammalian chromosomes, there is generally a lot of poorly understood DNA between the sequences that are recognizable as genes encoding proteins. So most proviruses might have little or no disruptive effects on known genes when they enter a chromosome more or less randomly. The odds would favor insertion outside of the coding regions of genes, like missiles landing in the desert or plunging into the sea. Insertion within a genome's most recognizable regions, the roughly 2 percent of sequences that encode proteins, would inactivate a gene, like a missile

managerial force that has kept my laboratory and trainees functional, despite my two sabbaticals, the lab's two geographical transitions, and the distractions of my recent administrative positions.

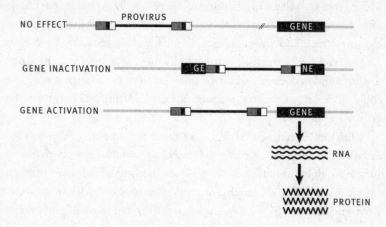

When retroviral DNA inserts into a chromosome, it may have little or no effect on cellular genes (top), it can disrupt and inactivate a gene (middle), or it may perturb the expression of a gene, for example, by turning it on inappropriately to make RNA and protein (bottom). If the perturbed gene is a proto-oncogene, the integration event may initiate cancerous growth.

destroying a major building.* On the other hand, if the insertion occurred close to a gene, leaving the protein-coding regions intact, production of the gene's RNA and protein might be increased or decreased, thanks to regulatory signals at the ends of the provirus—not unlike the increased human activity that would follow a missile's landing next to a major building. If the gene were a proto-oncogene and the proviral insertion increased production of the gene's RNA and protein, a potentially oncogenic protein might rise to abnormal levels and trigger cancerous growth. The single cell in which the growth-promoting insertion had occurred could then form a tumor composed of the cell's descendants. As a result, all of the tumor cells would contain the inciting provirus at its landing site next to a proto-oncogene.

---

* During my London sabbatical, I performed a successful test of this idea. When cells transformed by a single RSV provirus were infected by another retrovirus (murine leukemia virus, MLV), rare cells reverted to a normal shape and behavior if an MLV provirus happened to integrate within the RSV provirus, thereby disrupting expression of the v-src gene.[3]

A proviral integration event of this type could, in theory, explain the cancer-causing properties of those retroviruses without viral oncogenes. Among the best characterized of these oncogene-deficient viruses are the avian leukosis viruses (ALVs). The ALVs are a serious nuisance to poultry farmers because they frequently cause lymphomas in a type of blood cells in chickens. The ALVs are closely related to RSV, the progenitor of which is assumed to have been an ALV; but the ALVs lack a src gene or any other cell-derived oncogene. These features made me wonder, as I wheeled Christopher up and down the English lanes, whether the ALVs cause tumors by this kind of insertional mechanism, with an ALV provirus randomly inserting near a proto-oncogene and switching it on to initiate abnormal cell growth. How could this idea be tested? Could we identify the gene that might be switched on?

I considered two kinds of approaches: trial-and-error tests with probes for the very few proto-oncogenes then known, or a systematic study of ALV proviruses in several virus-induced lymphomas. Trial and error would be quick but limited. Probes for the src proto-oncogene or any other known proto-oncogene could be used to ask whether ALV proviruses were inserted near those genes in DNA from lymphomas. At that time, though, we knew about no more than a few proto-oncogenes, and many—certainly tens, perhaps hundreds—might exist. So why bother testing the few in hand?

The systematic approach would be more laborious, but more likely to succeed in the long run. It would require characterizing proviral insertion sites from multiple tumors and determining whether the insertion sites were near regions of DNA containing a likely proto-oncogene. A clue might come from finding that proviruses in different lymphomas were in the same region of the chicken genome, despite the apparent randomness of proviral integration. There was an important idea behind this: a cell with a provirus inserted in certain regions, near a proto-oncogene, would acquire a growth advantage and thus be "selected"—a version of Darwinian evolution, occurring among cells in a single animal. Random mutations (proviral insertions) would activate a proto-oncogene in one among millions of infected cells, providing a growth advantage. Then the affected cell, growing vigorously, would appear to be selected when its progeny formed a tumor.

I persuaded a graduate student in San Francisco, Greg Payne, to set off on the second, more challenging, but perhaps more secure, path. In surprisingly short order, Greg had evidence that the same region of the chicken genome was disrupted by insertions of ALV proviruses in different tumors.[4] But before we could figure out what genes lay nearby, we were shocked to learn from Bill Hayward, a friendly competitor at Rockefeller University, that the answer was not only simple; it had been within our grasp. Hayward and his colleagues had discovered that the sites at which most lymphoma-inducing, ALV proviruses were located were next to the c-myc gene[5]—a proto-oncogene that Mike Bishop himself had found a few years earlier by tracing an avian retroviral oncogene, v-myc, to its origins in cellular DNA.[6]

I had made a common and embarrassing error: Thinking Too Much. Instead of doing the quick-and-simple experiments on the trial-and-error path, I sent Greg on the more rational, but also slower and more extensive, route. Gallingly, molecular probes for the myc genes had been available in our own lab freezers. When we used them, we too could see what Bill Hayward had seen: c-myc was next to the ALV proviruses. And, as predicted, the ALV proviruses dramatically augmented expression of the proto-oncogene—by overproduction of myc RNA—in the lymphomas.

This was more than momentarily disappointing for us—when we get together more than twenty-five years later, Greg, now a professor at UCLA, and I still sometimes bemoan my choice of strategy—but it was also exhilarating. After all, the basic premise was correct. Proto-oncogenes could cause cancers when their normal control is reversed by a randomly invading provirus. Proto-oncogenes did not need to be captured by retroviruses to have cancer-causing effects. In the years ahead, there would be many other kinds of evidence for the latter point, in human patients as well as animal models.

It was still possible, moreover, to extend the story beyond the account by Hayward and his colleagues. In very short order, Greg showed that, in the chicken lymphomas he had been studying, ALV proviruses could be found on either side of the myc gene and in either orientation, not just on one side and in one orientation, as in the report from Hayward's group.[7] This was surprising and had important implications for how proviruses affect expression of adjacent proto-oncogenes.

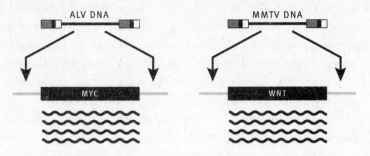

The two drawings show how retroviruses without a viral oncogene can initiate tumor growth by inserting near a proto-oncogene and activating its expression. On the left, an ALV provirus inserts on either side of the c-myc gene (a gene initially found as the precursor to a retroviral oncogene, v-myc) to cause a B cell lymphoma in infected birds. On the right, an MMTV provirus inserts on either side of the wnt-1 gene (a gene found by studying integration sites in tumors) to cause a breast cancer in infected mice.

By the time this story came to fruition in 1981, I was long back from our London sabbatical. Learning how ALV causes lymphomas in chickens spurred my interest in undertaking a similar search for proto-oncogenes that might be switched on by proviral insertions in another and especially provocative setting—in breast cancers that occur in mice infected with another retrovirus, the mouse mammary tumor virus (MMTV). I had been working with MMTV for several years because, as an infectious agent of breast cancers, it was among the few animal tumor viruses that regularly cause a cancer similar to the common cancers of adult human beings.*

In 1980, a Dutch postdoctoral fellow, Roel Nusse, already well trained in the biology of MMTV, agreed to join me in this search. Since no retrovirus carrying a cell-derived oncogene was known to induce breast cancers, I felt justified in advising Roel to take a systematic, rather than a trial-and-error, approach. But this time my predilection for *not* presuming that the target gene would be a known proto-oncogene paid off. (For-

---

* About 90 percent of the daunting human cancers are carcinomas, arising in epithelial cells of the breast, lung, colon, pancreas, prostate, and other organs.

tunately, Thinking Too Much sometimes has advantages.) Within less than two years, Roel and I were able to report the isolation of an apparently novel gene that was turned on when an MMTV provirus happens to integrate nearby, initiating the growth of breast cancers.[8] This gene, now called wnt-1, was not among the known proto-oncogenes, having never been found as a viral oncogene, like v-src, in a retrovirus.

Now, over twenty-five years later, we know that the wnt-1 gene has many close relatives, and that these members of "the wnt gene family" have crucial roles in normal development of all animal species.[9] The discovery of wnt-1 also helped others show that genes functionally associated with wnt genes are nearly always mutated in human colon cancer, as will be discussed briefly near the end of this chapter. While the details about wnt genes and their actions lie beyond the scope of my purpose here, the strategy that later revealed their importance in embryonic development is a useful illustration of the importance of model organisms, like fruit flies (*Drosophila melanogaster*), for making connections that lead to broad conclusions about biology. In this instance, Roel, working in his own laboratory in Amsterdam, figured out that a version of the wnt-1 gene, its evolutionary equivalent, in *Drosophila* was a gene that had been identified several years earlier in a Nobel Prize–winning search for genes that determine the first steps in development of the fly embryo.[10] *

PROTO-ONCOGENES ARE MUTATED IN HUMAN CANCERS

While it was extraordinary to find proto-oncogenes, like c-myc and wnt-1, activated by proviral insertions in chicken lymphomas and mouse breast cancers—and reassuring to those of us who had speculated about the importance of proto-oncogenes—the proviral insertion mutations had produced cancers in animals, not in human beings. So, in the early 1980s, the jury was still out on a crucial question: Do proto-oncogenes

---

* In the fly, the gene is called Wingless, reflecting the absence of wings in one of the developmental mutants of that wnt gene. Elimination of a functional wnt-1 gene in the mouse produces animals that lack part of the midbrain and cerebellum and run in circles.[11] More recent work, again involving Roel, in his current laboratory at Stanford, indicates that wnt genes have crucial roles in maintaining the behavior of stem cells,[12] including embryonic stem cells.

undergo mutations to cause human cancers? Within a few years, a wide array of evidence was saying that, yes, they do.

Some of the first evidence came from efforts to understand the abnormal chromosomes that had been observed for many years in certain types of tumors, especially leukemias and lymphomas. One path led again to myc genes, the proto-oncogenes that are targets for cancer-causing ALV proviral insertions in chicken lymphomas. In the human childhood tumor called Burkitt's lymphoma, for example, a myc gene on chromosome eight is joined to other chromosomes in a fashion that places strong signals for gene expression next to the myc gene, enhancing the production of myc RNA and protein.[13] In another childhood tumor, called neuroblastoma, a different member of the myc gene family was often reduplicated ("amplified"), so that many copies of the gene and dangerously large amounts of myc protein were made in the cancer cells.[14]

But other kinds of proto-oncogenes were also affected by these cancer-causing rearrangements of chromosomes, and some of them have come to provide targets for new cancer therapies. Perhaps the most instructive of these rearrangements involves the proto-oncogene, c-abl, one of those encoding a protein kinase specific for tyrosine and thus a relative of c-src. In 1960, David Hungerford and Peter Nowell, who happened to work together in Philadelphia, spotted a small, peculiar-looking chromosome in the leukemic cells of most patients with chronic myeloid leukemia (CML), one of the most frequent leukemias of adults.[15] In a moment of civic pride, they gave this chromosome a parochial name, the Philadelphia chromosome.

Initially, the abnormal chromosome was considered to be simply a truncated form of human chromosome 22. But thirteen years later, Janet Rowley, a medical geneticist at the University of Chicago, used improved methods for staining chromosomes to show that the Philadelphia chromosome was actually a pastiche, with most of chromosome 22 attached to a small piece of chromosome 9.[16] Although the analysis could not go deeper at that time to ask which specific genes might be affected by the joining of these two chromosomes, about a decade later several groups converged on a remarkable discovery. A proto-oncogene on chromosome 9, c-abl, the precursor to the viral oncogene in a mouse leukemia virus, was always found at the junction point in the Philadelphia chromosome, joined to another gene from chromosome 22.[17] Furthermore, the abl protein made from the translocated gene in the Philadelphia chromosome was a fusion protein, encoded mostly by c-abl and partly by the adjacent gene brought in from chromosome 22. This fusion protein was much more active enzymatically than the normal c-abl protein, just as the v-src protein kinase is more active than the c-src kinase.[18] All of these observations are consistent with the idea that the abnormal abl protein in CML cells might be responsible for the leukemia. Perhaps the leukemia could then be controlled with a tyrosine kinase inhibitor, if it was effective against the kinase activity in the fusion protein. As we shall soon see, all of this is true.

SIMPLE MUTATIONS OF PROTO-ONCOGENES IN HUMAN CANCERS

Another line of investigation provided evidence for even more dramatic mutations of proto-oncogenes in human cancers. These mutations were dramatic because of their frequency and their biological effects, but were usually subtle at the DNA level, requiring as little as a single nucleotide change in a proto-oncogene, without insertion mutations or large-scale chromosomal disturbances, to turn a normal gene into a powerful oncogene.

Finding such mutations in proto-oncogenes initially depended on one of the oldest and now standard methods in molecular biology: the introduction of naked DNA into cells in order to test for gene function.* Oswald Avery, Colin MacLeod, and Maclyn McCarty at the Rockefeller Institute used this approach in the 1940s to show that DNA is the material that embodies genetic information in cells.[20] When they put DNA from one bacterial strain into another strain, the second acquired the shape and surface characteristics of the first. In other words, apparently pure DNA could transfer a genetic trait from one cell to another.

---

* When these discoveries were made, DNA sequencing and other methods were still in their infancy, and the Human Genome Project had not yet even been formulated. Now, of course, mutations affecting human proto-oncogenes are being found at a much greater rate with those new and powerful, if less aesthetically satisfying, methods. The Cancer Genome Atlas, TCGA, is the most visible manifestation of that enterprise, and the COSMIC database provides a readily digested listing of the genes involved thus far.[19]

More than three decades later, in the late 1970s, Bob Weinberg at MIT's Cancer Center scored a very similar achievement, by transferring a genetic trait (transformation) from one cell to another by means of naked DNA. He and his colleagues prepared DNA from various kinds of rodent and human cancer cells, added it to normal-appearing mouse cells in petri dishes, and watched "foci" of transformed cells arise,[21] just as Temin and Rubin had done many years earlier in their focus assay for RSV. Weinberg and his students, and other investigators as well, hunted down the responsible genes in the transferred DNA, expecting and perhaps hoping that they would be novel genes. But the first transforming genes in cancer cells also turned out to be mutant versions of known proto-oncogenes, precursors to retroviral oncogenes, members of the ras gene family.[22]* (Bob's surprise, and perhaps displeasure, at the revelation of ras is recorded in Jamie Simon's cartoon on page 85.)

The mutations that Weinberg and others found in ras genes had an especially remarkable feature: a single nucleotide change was sufficient to convert a normal gene into a potent oncogene. Moreover, the single nucleotide changes that turned a ras proto-oncogene into an oncogene were essentially identical to changes also observed when retroviral ras oncogenes were compared with the proto-oncogenes. Furthermore, one of the ras proto-oncogenes, the K-ras gene, is now known to be mutated in a vast number of human cancers, including a quarter of lung cancers, half of colon cancers, and nearly all pancreatic cancers.[23] Again, in virtually all cases, the responsible mutations consist of no more than a single change affecting one nucleotide in the DNA sequence, and almost always at a few characteristic sites in the gene, altering a specific portion of a ras protein. The consequences of such a small change are nevertheless devastating: one altered nucleotide changes one amino acid in a protein, irreversibly producing hyperactive behavior by that protein, driving the cell into a cancerous state. Unfortunately, no one has yet come up with drugs,

---

* These proto-oncogenes, called Harvey-Ras (H-ras) and Kirsten-Ras (K-ras), are the progenitors of viral oncogenes found in mouse and rat sarcoma viruses, highly oncogenic viruses named for two American virologists, Jennifer Harvey and Werner Kirsten, who discovered them many years ago. The Ras genes make small proteins that reside in the cell's cytoplasm and have strong influences on many aspects of cell behavior by binding to many other proteins.

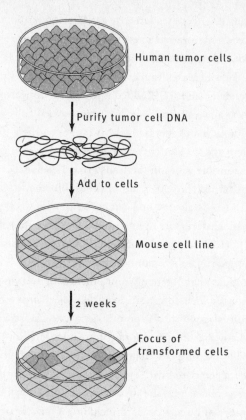

Human tumor cells

Purify tumor cell DNA

Add to cells

Mouse cell line

2 weeks

Focus of
transformed cells

To detect mutant proto-oncogenes in human cancer cells, DNA was
purified from the cells, then introduced into normal-appearing mouse
cells to watch for the rare cells that acquired properties of transformed
cells. By further study of the foci of transformed cells, the introduced
gene—one among many—that was responsible for transformation can
be identified, as described in the text.

like those that block activated tyrosine kinases, to inhibit the effects of
the supercharged ras proteins. If we had such a weapon, a large fraction
of the most lethal human cancers would suddenly become much more
amenable to treatment, for reasons that will be apparent in the next
chapter.

One final example of the now numerous instances of proto-oncogenes
participating in human cancer warrants mention. Wnt genes, one of

which Roel Nusse and I found because it is often turned on by MMTV proviruses in mouse breast cancers, encode proteins that are secreted from cells. Genetic studies of the wnt-1 gene in *Drosophila* revealed that several other genes are required for the actions of secreted wnt proteins. These other genes encode proteins that make up a communications chain, called a signaling pathway, that tells a cell how to respond to a wnt protein when it is present in a cell's environment. Knowledge about this pathway has proven to be vital information for understanding human colon cancer. Amazingly, some of the genes involved in the wnt signaling pathway in mammalian cells, genes often identified as the homologs of the fly genes that allow wnt proteins to act, are mutated in nearly all human cancers of the colon and in some other human cancers as well.[24] So the basic science of insect development has been influential in deciphering common human cancers. Again, unfortunately, the means for blocking these lethal pathways in patients with cancers driven by wnt signals have yet to be found.

CHAPTER 7

Targeted Therapies for Human Cancers

—

As the preceding chapters reveal, the scientific community learned a great deal about proto-oncogenes in the decade following the discovery of the c-src gene. There are many proto-oncogenes, not just c-src; many, but not all, of them were discovered because they were once captured and converted to viral oncogenes by retroviruses; proto-oncogenes can be activated to induce cancers in several ways, including adjacent insertion of proviruses and mutations of several types (chromosomal rearrangements and subtle changes in the DNA sequence); and mutant proto-oncogenes are often found in human cancers. The next questions were obvious, but more difficult to answer. Is this information useful to patients, as well as exciting to scientists? Can doctors use this knowledge to diagnose, classify, monitor, or, most importantly, treat or prevent human cancers?

ANOTHER PROBLEM OF TWO CULTURES

One potential barrier to answering these questions is a cultural divide between laboratory and clinical investigators that can impede the application of new science to old diseases. Although the barriers are surmountable, they are real. For twenty-three years at UCSF, most of my scientific career, I thought of myself as a basic scientist, one with medical training but lapsed clinical skills, trying to answer questions that were often relevant to diseases, mainly cancer and later AIDS. But I was rarely engaged in direct efforts to put what I was learning into the service of controlling those diseases.

There were several reasons for this, some strong and some weak. In my occasional attempts to work with clinical colleagues, I encountered a kind of "two cultures" problem, one both similar to and different from the more famous one that C. P. Snow described. Most clinicians, even academic ones, and basic scientists, even those trained originally as physicians, do not necessarily converse easily. They know different things, seem to speak different dialects, have somewhat different goals and standards, and even organize their days differently—clinicians arriving early, scientists arriving late—hampering opportunities to meet. Clinicians often lack the laboratory support that would be required to store and keep track of patient materials for research, they are extremely busy, and their primary responsibilities lie outside of the laboratory. Furthermore, the time from biological discovery to clinical advance can be extraordinarily long, and the process may be encumbered with administrative and regulatory hurdles. These things can try the patience of those accustomed to frequent gratification in the laboratory.

In earlier phases of my career, I enjoyed the opportunities to work on scientific frontiers where the implications for the mechanisms of disease were abundant, while leaving to others—to people with clinical skills, or to those in the biotechnology and pharmaceutical industries—the responsibilities to apply in the setting of health care whatever my colleagues and I might discover. However, during the years immediately after I left UCSF in 1993 to become the NIH director, the gulf between lab science and clinical application appeared to narrow. The Human Genome Project was developing tools that greatly simplified tests of the role of human genes in disease and promised further rapid advances in every domain of the NIH's work. In my new job at the NIH, I was exposed nearly every day to patients or their families, who hoped that new knowledge would open avenues to control disease, and to legislators who asked how the billions of dollars appropriated to NIH-funded research might soon improve public health.

Although the practice of oncology, the clinical specialty most likely to be affected by our own work, had yet to change dramatically, numerous signs indicated that information about cancer genes in individual tumors would soon be guiding diagnosis, classification, prediction of outcome, and choice of therapy. During the 1980s and 1990s, antibodies had been developed against some proteins encoded by proto-oncogenes, and at least one showed some promise in the treatment of certain breast cancers.[1] In addition, a few molecular tests for mutant genes, like the translocated c-abl gene in CML[2] or mutated K-ras in colon cancer,[3] appeared to offer new ways to detect cancers or monitor their responses to therapy.

SUCCESSFUL TARGETING OF ONCOGENIC PROTEINS

Then, in 1999, suddenly there was Gleevec—a molecular oncologist's dream come true, and the best evidence to date that the most fundamental aspects of cancer research had dramatic benefits for patients with cancer.* Unlike most chemotherapies, Gleevec is easy to take (as a daily pill), causes only mild side effects, usually remains effective for many years, and is remarkably potent, reversing virtually all of the findings associated with chronic myeloid leukemia (CML) within a couple of weeks in virtually all patients, especially those in the early phases of the disease. More to the point here, it confers these benefits by inhibiting the action of a mutant proto-oncogene, specifically the c-abl fusion protein made from the Philadelphia chromosome that is found in every leukemic cell.

The development of this drug was serendipitous and not straightforward.[4] In the early 1990s, the pharmaceutical company Ciba-Geigy (now part of Novartis) was working with scientists at the Dana Farber Cancer Institute to find drugs that would block the action of another tyrosine kinase, not c-abl, one that contributes to a very common disorder, atherosclerosis in blood vessels. One drug, called STI-571 (now known officially as imatinib and commercially as Gleevec), had specific inhibitory effects on that target protein in blood vessels (although apparently no clinical effect). But it also strongly inhibited the abl tyrosine kinase and at least one other tyrosine kinase. This raised the question of whether the drug might be useful in patients with CML.

The company was initially concerned about the costs of developing and testing the drug to treat a disease as uncommon as CML.** Brian

---

* This was the drug that occasioned Rick Klausner's call, described in the introduction.
** There are about six thousand new cases of CML in the United States each year, many fewer than the millions at risk of atherosclerosis.

Druker, an oncologist who had moved from the Farber Institute to the University of Oregon, persuaded the firm to sponsor a early-phase clinical trial. The results were near-miraculous and virtually unprecedented for what was, in principle, a preliminary (so-called phase one) test of drug safety. In just a few days or weeks and in virtually every patient, amounts of the drug adequate to inhibit the tyrosine kinase activity of the abl fusion protein reversed the symptoms and most of the evidence of disease in the blood and bone marrow, without causing major side effects.[5]

The FDA approved Gleevec for treatment of CML in near-record time for an anticancer drug.[6] Seven years later, its use has been widely adopted around the world. Most patients who continue taking the drug remain in remission, Novartis is making money and enhancing its stature, and Gleevec has been used effectively in at least five other cancers (one of them a sarcoma of the intestinal tract,[7] the others mostly rare blood disorders). Each of these cancers is driven by a mutation affecting one of the three tyrosine kinases known to be targeted by the drug. This is rational, targeted therapy at its best.

Among CML patients who respond initially to Gleevec, the disease recurs in a few percent each year, despite continued use of the drug. Why? It turns out that, in virtually all of these leukemias that have acquired drug resistance, another mutation has occurred in the c-abl gene on the Philadelphia chromosome.[8] These new mutations change the amino acid sequence of the abl fusion protein and prevent Gleevec from inhibiting its tyrosine kinase activity. Other inhibitors have been tested against the Gleevec-resistant mutants, and, in surprisingly short order, two compounds active against most of the Gleevec-resistant abl fusion proteins have been found, shown to be effective in patients, and approved for use.[9] It seems increasingly likely that CML, whose diagnosis was once a death sentence, will soon be a disease that is regularly controlled for decades, until patients develop some other mortal condition. Short of complete cures or prevention, this is about as good an outcome as anyone studying the molecular basis of cancer could have hoped for.

Gleevec's success is an obvious boon to patients. It is also a vindication for those of us who had hoped that drugs that interfere with the actions of oncogenes would be effective weapons against cancers. That wasn't necessarily the case. Most, if not all, cancers have multiple kinds of genetic damage, and it was certainly conceivable, even probable, that all of the damage would have to be reversed—a daunting task—to produce benefits. Moreover, it was not anticipated that a drug like Gleevec would dramatically reduce the number of cancer cells, rather than simply arrest the growth of cells already formed. (I will say more about this in a moment.)

When Gleevec appeared, some said that it might be singular, even an anomaly, or that CML was an atypical cancer. The effectiveness of Gleevec against some other blood cancers and a gastrointestinal sarcoma shows that CML is not uniquely responsive to this kind of targeted therapy.[10] But are there other Gleevecs, other targeted treatments that work by inhibiting proteins made by mutant proto-oncogenes? Gleevec certainly is not alone. Among the new generation of treatments for cancers are several drugs that inhibit other wayward tyrosine kinases, some that block other proteins implicated in cancer, and antibodies that bind to proteins on the surface of cancer cells or proteins that move between cells.[11] Most of the proteins targeted by these treatments are encoded by mutant proto-oncogenes or by proto-oncogenes that are too abundantly expressed. None of the other therapies has the extraordinary impact that Gleevec shows in CML, but several have been approved by the FDA and are widely used. Perhaps the best known is Herceptin, an antibody that recognizes a cell surface protein found on about one-third of breast cancers, produces remissions in patients with disease that has spread, and can substantially reduce the incidence of metastasis when used at the time of initial surgery.[12*]

New Treatments of Lung Cancer Based on Mutant Oncogenes

Recently, through our own work at the Memorial Sloan-Kettering Cancer Center (MSKCC) on lung cancer, I have been able to observe and participate directly in efforts to improve cancer therapies by harnessing

---

* This protein, incidentally, is encoded by a proto-oncogene that Bob Weinberg discovered by introducing DNA from rat brain tumors into cultured fibroblasts to look for transforming activity.[13]

new knowledge about cancer genes. In this role, I have seen the promise of such targeted therapies, as well as their limitations.

The virtual disappearance of cancer cells in CML patients treated with Gleevec implied that cancer cells might die, not simply stop growing, when the drug deprived cancer cells of the enhanced tyrosine kinase activity of the abl fusion protein. That notion has been reinforced by many other observations, in patients, cultured tumor cells, and experimental animals over the past several years. This phenomenon is now called "oncogene dependence" or (more colorfully) "oncogene addiction."[14] The underlying idea is that a cancer cell is so drastically altered by the mutations that converted it from a normal to a malignant state that it can't survive without the signals emitted by the mutant oncogenes; in other words, the cancer cell will direct itself to die, to commit cell suicide, if one of the oncogenes driving abnormal cell behavior is suddenly suppressed.

Genetically engineered mice offer a dramatic and experimentally attractive means to demonstrate and study the phenomenon of oncogene dependence. In the late 1990s, Mike Bishop and Dean Felsher, one of his trainees at UCSF, were among the first to show this, using a clever trick to turn an oncogene, myc, on and off under the control of the antibiotic tetracycline.[15]* When they turned the myc oncogene on in blood cells, large tumors appeared; when it was turned off, the tumors rapidly disappeared. Similarly dramatic findings were reported with experimental melanomas caused by a mutant H-ras gene[16] and leukemias caused by an abl fusion gene.[17] Subsequently, by means of this general strategy for regulating oncogenes, several oncogenes have proven to be essential for maintaining the viability of a broad array of mouse cancers.[18] In a sense, turning off an oncogene in this setting is analogous to using a very effective drug in a patient, so the dramatic regressions have been spurs to efforts to find ways to block the actions of relevant oncogenes.

CML, the adult leukemia that taught us how potent a targeted drug like Gleevec can be, is a highly instructive, but relatively uncommon, can-

---

* Tetracycline itself has no direct role in the cancers that resulted; it is used only to regulate expression of the oncogene.

cer. Lung cancer, on the other hand, is the leading cause of cancer mortality in the United States and the world. Near the end of my time as director of the NIH, a postdoctoral fellow in my group, Galen Fisher, constructed a laboratory mouse in which a mutant K-ras gene—a gene known to be involved in about a quarter of human lung cancers—could be turned on and off at will in lung cells.[19] When mutant K-ras is turned on, lung cells grow, some becoming small tumors and later large invasive carcinomas, resembling adenocarcinomas, now the most common form of human lung cancer. But when the K-ras gene is turned off, the tumors rapidly disappear, another example of oncogene dependence. The lung cancer cells require the mutant K-ras gene to survive—reemphasizing the great need to have what we do not have: an effective way to neutralize the effects of mutant ras proteins.

When my laboratory moved these mice from the NIH to MSKCC, the challenge of studying them was transferred to William Pao, then an oncology fellow with a primary interest in lung cancer. An accomplished lab scientist as well as an excellent clinician, Will was trying to understand why mouse lung cancer cells die when K-ras is turned off. To follow this process in living animals, we use magnetic resonance imaging, so Will looked at many pictures of mouse lungs in which cancers had rapidly disappeared after the K-ras gene was turned off. One day in the winter of 2002, while looking at x-ray images of a middle-aged woman with advanced lung cancer, he was stunned to see the same kind of dramatic clearing of disseminated lung cancer—just five days after the patient had received a new experimental drug called Iressa.

This drug, like Gleevec, is an inhibitor of tyrosine kinases. It was being tested in advanced cases of lung cancer that had failed to respond to other therapies, without any certainty about the specific tyrosine kinase that might be a target for the drug. About 10 percent of such patients showed good initial responses to Iressa, albeit responses rarely as dramatic as in Will's patient.[20] On the basis of work with mouse models and the experience with Gleevec, we thought that the cancer cells in the responsive tumors must be addicted to a mutant proto-oncogene, one that makes a tyrosine kinase inhibited by Iressa.

But which gene and which kinase? No tyrosine kinases had yet been clearly implicated in the genesis of lung cancers, drug responsive or not.

Iressa's manufacturer, AstraZeneca, had developed the drug for its inhibitory activity against a particular tyrosine kinase, a cell-surface receptor for a hormone called epidermal growth factor (EGF). The gene that encodes the receptor itself, abbreviated as EGFR, has been recognized as a proto-oncogene for two decades.* There was, however, no reason to presume that EGFR was the target for Iressa in the responsive lung cancers. The receptor was sometimes abundant in the cancer cells, but that, by itself, did not mean much. Abundance of EGFR did not correlate with the remissions, and no mutations in EGFR had been reported in lung cancers. The question was an open one.

The Human Genome Project had revealed about ninety genes encoding tyrosine kinases in the human genome; in principle, any of them could have been the relevant target of action for Iressa. But testing them all—for mutations, or for a response to Iressa—would be a large job, and the drug company did not have much motivation to do this. It had more to gain by giving Iressa to all patients, rather than to the pre-identified few—expected to be about 10 percent in this country—who would be likely to respond.

Will and I were excited about the prospect of looking for the mutations in lung cancers that conferred sensitivity to tyrosine kinase inhibitors like Iressa. We had some significant advantages. Both Iressa and a closely related drug, called Tarceva (produced by Genentech), had been tested in patients by our lung cancer specialists at MSKCC, so we had access to tumor samples from patients who either had or had not responded to these drugs. The idea was straightforward: to look for proto-oncogenes that were mutant in those tumors that responded, but normal in the tumors that did not. A correlation between mutations in a specific gene and responses to Iressa or Tarceva would imply that the drugs blocked the tyrosine kinase encoded by the mutant gene.

To undertake this search, we first pulled together a multidisciplinary team at MSKCC, a coalition of oncologists, surgeons, radiologists, pathologists, molecular biologists, and others, that came to be called the

---

* At first called erbB, the EGFR gene was discovered by, among others, Mike Bishop, as indicated in Jamie Simon's cartoon, through studies of an avian retrovirus that causes erythroleukemia.[21]

Lung Cancer Oncogenome Group (LCOG).* To look for mutant genes that might encode the targets for Iressa, we then sought help from Rick Wilson, the head of the famed DNA sequencing center at Washington University.

Of course, the human genome is large, so we had to narrow our focus. Even concentrating on the ninety genes that encode tyrosine kinases, the likely drug targets, would be a challenge, because most of the tumor samples had been embedded in paraffin to make slides for microscopic observation and diagnosis; this made extraction of DNA from the samples difficult. As a result, we could prepare enough DNA to examine only a few of the many possible genetic targets. Under these circumstances, with the amount of DNA limited, should we take our cue from AstraZenaca's intent to inhibit the EGFR tyrosine kinase and limit our efforts to the EGFR gene and perhaps a few others? Or should we make fewer presumptions, take a more encyclopedic approach, and look at many more genes, using other lung cancer samples that had recently been stored in a more useful way (by quick freezing)? This would permit better DNA preparation and the sequencing of larger numbers of genes—at least those ninety encoding the tyrosine kinases. But we would be sacrificing helpful information—the responses of tumors to Iressa and Tarceva— since the frozen tumors were obtained at recent surgeries. These patients had not yet developed recurrent disease, and so had not been treated with drugs.

Provocatively, Rick Wilson's team had found an interesting, novel mutation in the EGFR gene in one of the three paraffin-stored samples of drug-responsive tumors that were initially tested. But the sequencing had been difficult, and the mutation was unusual and hard to interpret. So we convinced ourselves that it would be preferable to sequence more tyrosine kinase genes in more tumors with greater ease. This was a grievous error. It was not unlike the one I had made over twenty years earlier, when I encouraged Greg Payne not to presume that ALV proviruses in chicken lymphomas had inserted next to one of the few proto-oncogenes

---

* In some ways, this group resembled the multi-institutional group of virologists, molecular biologists, and others, the West Coast Tumor Virus Cooperative, which was so important for our much earlier work on RSV and proto-oncogenes.

we already knew about, like c-myc. It was another product of Thinking Too Much. And the outcome was similar. While we were scaling up to sequence many more tyrosine kinase genes from frozen tumor samples in the spring of 2004, I learned on a trip to Boston that two other labs, both at Harvard, were about to report that lung tumors responsive to Iressa had either of two unusual mutations in the EGFR gene.[22] One of these mutations was the same type that we had seen in a drug-responsive tumor several months earlier and had not adequately pursued.

Still, the Harvard findings were exciting, and a stimulus to get back on track. Within a few weeks, with help from many members of LCOG, we knew that what is true for one tyrosine kinase inhibitor (TKI), Iressa, is also true for another, Tarceva, the drug that is now commonly used in the United States to treat lung cancers known or suspected to have EGFR mutations.[23] As predicted from the clinical studies done earlier at MSKCC, the TKI-responsive lung cancers with mutations in the EGFR gene were especially common in nonsmokers; we found them in about half of the cancers in patients who had never smoked. In contrast, nearly all lung cancers with K-ras mutations arise in smokers, and those tumors do not respond to the TKIs.[24] Members of LCOG developed state-approved tests for the two most common EGFR mutations in lung cancers and started a clinical trial to seek benefits of TKIs in the early stages of lung cancer, at the time of surgery. Katie Politi, a postdoctoral scientist in my group, engineered mice that express either of the two mutant EGFR genes under the control of tetracycline.[25] As predicted, the mice develop lung cancers when the mutant receptors are turned on by tetra-cycline, and the tumors disappear when the mutant genes are turned off by removal of tetracycline or when the mutant kinases are inhibited by Tarceva.

Patients treated with Tarceva for EGFR-mutant lung cancers, unfortunately, do not fare as well as patients who receive Gleevec for treatment of CML. Patients feel much better and the lung cancers usually diminish in size; but they do not disappear and are likely to start growing again, within a year or two, despite continued use of the drug. Will Pao discovered why half of the tumors become resistant to the drugs: they acquire an additional mutation in the EGFR gene, one that makes the receptor's tyrosine kinase impervious to the inhibitory effects of Tarceva.[26] As in studies of Gleevec-resistant CML, drugs that appear to overcome the resistance are being tested against lung cancers in mice and in patients. This rational approach is a cause for optimism about controlling this subset of lung cancers in the reasonably near future.

These recent developments have come too late to offer hope to a colleague who seemed among the most unlikely to develop lung cancer: Howard Temin. Readers will remember Howard as the prophetic scientist who proposed the provirus hypothesis and codiscovered reverse transcriptase. He also encouraged our laboratory to undertake the search for proto-oncogenes, and later studied proto-oncogenes in his own lab at the University of Wisconsin. Although not medically trained, he was an outspoken proponent of public health practices. When he mounted the podium at his Nobel banquet in 1975 to offer thanks for his prize, he paused first to voice an objection: people—they happened to be Swedish princesses—were smoking, and he was about to speak about his work on cancer viruses. (At this point, Prince Bertil of Sweden gallantly and famously lit up.)

In 1994, at the age of fifty-nine, Howard succumbed to lung cancer. There was very little that medicine could offer him. Since he was a nonsmoker, his lung cancer may well have had one of those mutations I just described, in his EGFR gene, a proto-oncogene discovered by means of a chicken retrovirus. If this had been so, he would probably, for a while at least, have responded well, perhaps even dramatically, to TKIs. I am sorry that he did not live to see that the science he helped to forge now shows such signs of benefit for patients.

CHAPTER 8

Partnerships in Science

—

No READER OF THIS BOOK WILL HAVE BEEN OBLIVIOUS TO MY USE OF "we" rather than "I" in describing the work that led to the discovery of c-src. "We" is the pronoun most commonly used in many fields of science because most experimental work is performed—and subsequent manuscripts are coauthored—by teams composed of faculty members, postdoctoral fellows, graduate students, and technicians. Sometimes, my use of "we" has referred to such laboratory teams. But, at least as often, the "we" has referred to that uncommon relationship in science: a sustained partnership between faculty colleagues.

In the first part of the book, I described meeting Mike Bishop, compared our familial and academic histories, and explained why I decided to move to San Francisco to work with him and his colleagues. I had learned to do science at the NIH in an environment that encouraged full-fledged investigators to work closely together. (For instance, Ira Pastan and Bob Perlman became a harmonic duo for several years during their studies of the regulation of the lac operon by cyclic AMP. And much of what I needed to learn about the lac operon had been discovered by a famous duo at the Pasteur Institute, Jacques Monod and François Jacob.) I was drawn to the atmosphere of the UCSF laboratory I had chosen to join, in part, because Mike and some of his faculty colleagues, particularly Warren Levinson and Leon Levintow, were already operating as a small consortium.*

---

* Leon had been Mike's mentor at the NIH and, about fifteen years senior to Mike, was one

Within several months after my arrival at UCSF as a postdoctoral fellow, it began to seem likely that I would join this consortium as a full-fledged member. Because of my medical training, the department chairman, Ernest Jawetz, asked me to give some lectures to microbiology classes in the professional schools at UCSF and then proposed appointments for me, first as instructor and then, a year later, as assistant professor. In parallel, my source of salary moved from a fellowship sponsored by the California Cancer Society to a faculty development award that I received from the NIH.

At the same time, Mike and I increasingly recognized the synchronies of our views on scientific matters and other things, too: books, music, politics, and the people around us. Gradually, we offered joint supervision to technicians and later to students and fellows. The four faculty working on retroviruses (Mike, Warren, Leon, and I) pooled financial resources and shared research space, and we met together weekly with all of our trainees and technicians to discuss our scientific work at the eponymous "Rous Lunch" (an event that persisted as a group activity for over twenty years). The team spirit was also rooted in the intellectual engagement and dedication of our technical associates, some of whom worked with us for more than twenty or thirty years.

A particular intellectual camaraderie developed between the two of us during my first few years in San Franciso. As the more senior and better known, Mike had more grant money, more people already working with him, and more applications from prospective trainees. It was essential to the growth and success of our relationship that Mike was willing to share this bounty with a generous spirit.

For the years in which it prospered, the Bishop-Varmus partnership was a rare form of protracted collaboration in science. There are many examples of prominent scientific duets, but most of them are names linked by the famous experiments performed during brief times together

---

of those physicians who adopted biochemical approaches to the study of common pathologic viruses, like polio virus, in the 1950s. After twenty years in the Public Health Service, he left the NIH to join the UCSF faculty and helped recruit Mike. Warren had done graduate work with Harry Rubin after medical school, and brought tools and ideas about RSV into a group that was initially focused on polio virus.

or names also joined in matrimony. The most famous of all, Watson and Crick, was the product of Jim Watson's relatively short fellowship in Cambridge, England, during which he and Francis Crick proposed the DNA double helix; the duality of the helix (some like to refer to the Watson strand and the Crick strand) also helped to perpetuate and popularize the duet of names. Matt Meselson and Frank Stahl are forever united by the Meselson-Stahl experiment, which some have called "the most beautiful experiment in biology" and which validated one of Watson and Crick's crucial predictions about the duplication of DNA.[1] But Meselson and Stahl were together for only a few years as graduate student and faculty mentor, then lived and worked on opposite coasts of North America. At the other extreme, Marie and Pierre Curie in Paris, Carl and Gerty Cori in St. Louis, and, more recently, Pippa Marrack and John Kappler in Denver have had full-time, 24/7 partnerships as spouses and codirectors of eminent and highly productive laboratories. And a father-son pair, Laurence and William Bragg, shared a Nobel Prize in 1915 for collaborative work on x-ray diffraction.[2]

The intermediate version—two people working closely together for a decade or more without legal ties—is highly unusual. The best example I know is the partnership formed and sustained for nearly forty years at the University of Texas Southwestern Medical School in Dallas by two men of very similar age and training, Joe Goldstein and Mike Brown. Their shared passion for understanding cholesterol metabolism, blood lipids, and atherosclerosis brought them a shared Nobel Prize in 1985 and the sobriquet Brownstein, but they have maintained individual identities as a result of their different origins (South Carolina and New York), accents, cultural interests, personalities, and social relationships. David Hubel and Torsten Wiesel are another pair who shared a Nobel Prize (in 1981, for studies of the development of binocular vision). In a recent reminiscence, they talk about relishing the lengthy experiments they did together, intense marathons of animal preparation and oscilloscope viewing.[3]

I can't remember having this kind of experimental intimacy with Mike. We both maintained some semblance of laboratory work, despite the other duties of faculty life, until our early forties, but it usually involved taking care of cell cultures (an essentially lonely activity) or doing a more elaborate experiment with a technician or trainee. Still, the hours we logged together were lengthy, usually a string of hour-long meetings in which a single student, fellow, or technician, or sometimes little groups of two or three who happened to be doing a project together, would tell us about their latest findings or failures. Then we'd all try to plan the next step or figure out what went wrong. It seems to me now that, perhaps strangely, we had relatively little conversation involving just the two of us; most of what we thought and said got worked out in conversations in which one or more of our junior co-workers were also present.

Hearing the recollections of those meetings from our former trainees—most of them now senior scientists in academia, industry, and government—sheds interesting, although not always clarifying, light on the different roles Mike and I played. In the main, I am viewed as having paid the greater attention to experimental detail, Mike to the bigger picture. Those may or may not be flattering or accurate portrayals. But there is general consensus that our frequent gatherings were, in turn, good-humored, intimidating, unrelenting, productive, stimulating, and seemingly essential to our increasing productivity as a laboratory group.

Our collaborative arrangements within the lab also influenced patterns of behavior beyond it. This was most evident in the development of the West Coast Tumor Virus Cooperative, especially our relationship with Peter Vogt and his colleagues, without which we would probably not have discovered c-src. Those who were trained in this collegial environment became accustomed to sharing ideas and research materials, and usually maintained a generous attitude toward their colleagues in their careers as independent scientists.

Despite the successes of our partnership, however, the imbalance between our roles as the senior and junior member eventually led to its undoing. Although Mike and I continued to share research space, most of our projects, and supervision of many trainees until 1984, we knew as early as 1979 that we were ultimately going to separate our laboratories by eleven floors and to uncouple most of our research activities.

During the latter half of my London sabbatical, in the spring of 1979, I learned from Mike that he had been offered the directorship of a semi-independent and well-endowed research institute within UCSF, the Hooper Foundation, near the top of one of the UCSF research towers, and that I would be welcome to join him. This news triggered a number of reactions. On the one hand, the prospects of physically improved working conditions, with magnificent views and better financial support were attractive. (Gradually, over the preceding decade, we had acquired a rabbit warren of viewless and dilapidated laboratory space on a lower floor of the other UCSF research tower, and we were entirely dependent on external grants for research funding.) Our work together on proto-oncogenes, oncogenic proteins, retroviral replication, endogenous proviruses, and other things was going very well and attracting superb trainees.

But the uncomfortable sense that I was the junior member of a faculty partnership was made less tolerable by the prospect of a widening, rather than a lessening, gap in stature. Mike would always be four years older, but that would presumably become less significant with time. He was (at least, in my view) the more effective and popular teacher, but that did not affect our research relationship. Within our institution, however, the leaders (chairpersons, deans, chancellor) tended to deal with him as the senior partner almost exclusively. His elevation to an institute directorship would solidify this aspect of our relationship and make me feel even less visible within my home base. I did not desire autonomy, dominance, or greater resources of my own; I wanted parity. It felt as though I would be moving away from that if I moved with Mike to the better, endowed labs with the expansive views. So I said no.

The separation proved to be less difficult than I had expected. After many years of asking for improved laboratory space, I was rewarded with the chance to renovate our floor after Mike's group moved; this introduced me to the interesting new world of laboratory design.* I developed some new partnerships with other UCSF faculty, especially one with my neighbor on the fourth floor, Don Ganem, who had previously been a postdoctoral fellow with me. For several years, Don and I continued our joint studies of hepatitis viruses in our beautifully renovated labs. In the process of separation, my laboratory group was growing and flourishing,

---

* The instruction I received during this experience from our architect, Ken Kornberg, enlightened me about the importance of creating comfortable laboratory space and has strongly influenced my approach to the design of research buildings at the NIH and at MSKCC.

so there was little reason or time to mourn the loss of the intense and pervasive relationship with Mike. And he and I continued to codirect the work of a few people, to teach in the same courses, and to maintain the regular meetings, like Rous Lunch, that kept members of our groups interacting productively.

Soon, what had once been a single large team, became two independent groups that engaged in friendly competition (the annual Bishop-Varmus softball game), frequent collaboration (studies of proviral integration and certain oncogenes), and open exchanges of information and materials. Mike and I even seemed to become closer, once the new spheres of laboratory work achieved balance, through our increasing engagement in the politics of science. After I left UCSF in 1993, we remained in frequent contact, especially in recent years when he and his wife, Kathryn, come to New York on carefree cultural and culinary holidays or for scientific or political meetings. But the science on which our partnership was formed has, for the most part, given way to art and politics.

OUR NOBEL PRIZE: A FINAL WORD

In telling about the scientific work that led to our Nobel Prize, I have said almost nothing about the announcement and the award of the prize itself, parts of a scientific story that readers often relish. These events are strangely mythic in character—ritualistic and predictable on the one hand, but endowed with mystery and surprise in each case.

Like so many other laureates, I was called by reporters in the middle of the night—about 3 AM San Francisco time, on October 9. I was, of course, very pleasantly surprised, but not incredulous. (We had won other prizes along the way and suspected we were candidates.) Still, like others in this situation, I did want to hear from someone official. (Could this possibly be a practical joke?) Once reassured, my family and I were led, somewhat giddy and disoriented, through a day of press conferences, telegrams, celebrations, phone calls—even a special baseball game. For the announcement of our prize was distinguished by another kind of local excitement—the San Franciso Giants won the National League title on the same day. (We were given seats behind home plate by a San Francisco newspaper, and we shared the local headlines with the Giants on October 10.) Then, eight days later, a massive earthquake brought the Bay Area to a halt, just before the third game of the World Series. (Mike was in Candlestick Park; I was hosting a seminar at UCSF.) A month later, the Berlin Wall came down. (Neither of us was there.)

Again like so many others before and after us, we were charmed and entertained nine weeks later by several days of Nobel Prize events in Stockholm, in the spirit that W. B. Yeats, the 1923 laureate in literature, called "the bounty of Sweden."[4] Heading for Stockholm on an SAS flight a few days earlier than necessary (to get over jet lag and enjoy some family activities before the ceremonies), we were surprised when short film biographies of the new laureates on our flight appeared on the screen. Our days and nights in the city were filled with dinners, ceremonies, drinks, lectures, and museums, and Stockholm itself was ornamented by beautiful snowfalls that permitted cross-country skiing in the nearby Helles Garten. In a symbolic gesture, reflecting the new relations between the West and the Soviet Union, Boris Pasternak's 1958 Nobel Prize in literature was posthumously presented to his son. Even more memorably, Mstislav Rostropovich sat above the crowd at the Nobel banquet and played a Bach suite for the cello in Pasternak's honor. When we arrived for the awarding of our prizes at the concert hall, striking teachers were marching with picket signs in gently falling snow; as we passed them, mutually supportive messages were exchanged, as among faculty colleagues.

My most public moment at the festivities occurred when I took the podium at the Nobel banquet to offer our thanks, as Howard Temin had done fourteen years earlier. I had found a short passage from *Beowulf,* in a copy saved from my detour into English literature in the early 1960s, that described the honoring of heroes in a medieval mead hall, not unlike the events occurring in the Stockholm City Hall that night. I read the passage in incomprehensible Anglo-Saxon, translated it, then said, "[W]e recognize that, unlike Beowulf at the hall of Hrothgar, we have not slain our enemy, the cancer cell. . . . In our adventures, we have only seen our monster more clearly and described his scales and fangs in new ways—ways that reveal a cancer cell to be, like Grendel, a distorted version of our normal selves."[5]

Part Three

A POLITICAL SCIENTIST

CHAPTER 9

The Road to Building One

—

UNTIL THE MID-1980S, WHEN I WAS IN MY MID-FORTIES, I PAID RELA-tively little attention to the intersection of politics and science. This did not mean I was apolitical. I followed political events closely and had strong—largely left-liberal—opinions about them. Nor was I oblivious to the potential for engagement between politics and science. I recognized that science had become financially dependent on the federal govern-ment; federal agencies were (and are) the patrons that have largely dis-placed royalty, wealthy individuals, and foundations as our main source of financial support. But my UCSF colleagues and I seemed to have few or no difficulties in funding our research; budgetary growth for the agencies I depended on was generally healthy in the 1960s, 1970s, and 1980s; political support for science was bipartisan; and science seemed to be rarely controversial. Until the mid-1980s, it seemed to me that the use of tax dollars for biology and medicine was practically an entitlement: Why would anyone object to paying me to study cancer genes and viruses?

Over the next several years, the situation seemed to change. The gov-ernment's relationship to the scientific community became more com-plex, as contentious and even embarrassing issues—questionable spending of federal research funds by academic institutions, allegations of misconduct in science, concerns about the morality of using fetal tissue and later doing embryo research—became counterweights to the public's continued eagerness to see diseases controlled through medical research.

Perhaps more significantly for my own story, my stature in the scien-tific landscape changed, most dramatically by an event beyond my control: the award of a Nobel Prize in 1989. Combined with my growing involvement with the politics of science and my long-term interests in public service, the prize ultimately redirected my career. Although it did not lead me to abandon scientific work in my own laboratory and did not precipitate the steep decline in productivity that the sociologist Harriet Zuckerman described in her study of post–Nobel Prize careers,[1] it did significantly change the way I partitioned my time. After 1989, I was increasingly asked to voice opinions, to make speeches, and to join and even lead groups engaged in the politics of science. This new level of engagement with the forces that shape scientific life in this country led in a very short time, almost exactly four years, to the most important job I will probably ever have, the directorship of the National Institutes of Health (NIH).

My tenure as director of the NIH, from late in 1993 until the last day of 1999, has been a defining feature of my life in science. For this reason, I want to describe in some detail how it happened, what the experience was like, what I achieved, and how it has influenced my life subsequently. In a relatively short time, I was transformed from someone who was content to run a laboratory and teach, without any official authorities or responsibilities, into someone who was willing, even eager, to run a large federal agency, to represent the community of biomedical scientists, and to pursue the objectives of the public that looks to the NIH for advances against disease. Then, to my surprise and with some help and good fortune, I seemed to succeed at the task.*

An Apolitical Past

To talk about my path to the NIH directorship, I must begin at the beginning of my life in science. As told in an earlier chapter, I received my first significant training as a scientist at the NIH, in one small part of a government that was also waging war in Vietnam. So I was acutely aware of the potentially paradoxical relationship between NIH scientists

---

* I offer in support of this immodest assessment a profile by James Fallows that appeared in the June 7, 1999, issue of the *New Yorker* magazine, in the middle of my final year at the NIH. It is hard for a well-reviewed subject not to believe in such a welcome piece of reporting.

and the government that pays for their salaries and test tubes. When I sometimes worried that we might be spending government money extravagantly for new laboratory equipment during my first months doing science at the NIH in the late 1960s, a time when the nation's investment in the Vietnam War was escalating, my mentor, Ira Pastan, would place our modest laboratory requests in perspective by reminding me how much a new Air Force bomber cost. The unspoken assumption was not just that our laboratory needs were relatively trivial; we also believed that our work was a beneficial search for knowledge, whereas the most prominent activity of the U.S. government was brutal, based on a false reading of Asian history, and destructive to world harmony.

Indeed, none of our requests was ever denied, and I stopped worrying about them. In a very short time, I began to develop a sense of entitlement to government support of research. I set off from the NIH in 1970 for a career as a scientist in the academic sector, unlike most young faculty aspirants I know today, without serious concerns about financial support. I had been awarded what I considered to be a generous fellowship to continue my training in San Francisco,* and I was optimistic about the promise of medical science as a career. My anxieties had less to do with institutions, government, or society than with my own abilities and career choice: Would I be happy as a full-time scientist if I abandoned the medicine I had been taught to practice? Could I perform as effectively as other young scientists, especially those who had received Ph.D. degrees and sometimes had been working in laboratories since high school, not just during a two-year stint at the NIH?

With time and my growing success as a scientist, even these personal anxieties abated. As a faculty member at UCSF in the 1970s and 1980s, I never had much trouble finding research support from the American Cancer Society or the NIH, and I led a life that was generally full of responsibilities and pleasures at work and at home. So I didn't sense the need or have the time for efforts to ensure that the government and the public remained committed to the support of science. During those years at UCSF, I conducted and directed research on retroviruses and onco-

---

* My senior postdoctoral fellowship from the California Divison of the American Cancer Society paid $18,000 per year.

genes; taught infectious diseases to medical students and experimental virology to graduate students; guided the research strategies and career development of postdoctoral fellows; and wrote papers, delivered talks, attended many scientific meetings, and obtained grants to support further work, more or less as most of my colleagues did. Happily, these were things that I (and they) wanted to do; even better, we were paid by funding agencies and the state of California to do them. For the most part, the public and its representatives in Washington and Sacramento seemed to admire and support what we were trying to do. Science was a public good, not a political issue. Combative politics were about Watergate, the Vietnam War, civil rights, China, and the Soviet bloc. Science and politics didn't need to mix, and most of us thought it might be better if they didn't.

AN INSTRUCTIVE INTERLUDE:
THE RECOMBINANT DNA DEBATE

A notable hiatus in this idyllic state occurred in the mid-1970s. Federal and even local governments threatened to foreclose on the possibilities of using a powerful new technology—called gene splicing or recombinant DNA research—to study many complex biological problems, including my own research subjects: animal viruses and cancer genes. Since the new methods could be used to transfer into bacteria genes from any source— including human genes or genes from cancer viruses—some people imagined some frightening things, like newly engineered, cancer-causing bacteria running amok in human populations. I (and not a few others) thought the imagined dangers were remote and had been exaggerated in the press and in the political debate. But it seemed foolish to deny the existence of *some* risks—risks that could be rationally evaluated, intelligently explained, and minimized by reasonable guidelines and modification of the experimental methods.

In the summer of 1973, the risks were outlined in an influential letter written by several senior scientists attending one of those Gordon Conferences held at New Hampshire boarding schools.[2] The signatories and others—led by Maxine Singer, a prominent biochemist at the NIH, and Paul Berg, a Stanford professor and future Nobel laureate for work on recombinant DNA methods—then organized a now famous meeting in Asilomar, California, in the summer of 1975.[3] At the Asilomar Conference, the safety issues raised by recombinant DNA technology were openly addressed by a diverse audience, including journalists, government officials, and interested members of the public. For most of the scientists, the goal was to come up with a sensible set of guidelines that would allow the research to proceed without excessive government-imposed restrictions or legal sanctions of the sort that were already under consideration in places like Cambridge, Massachusetts, the home of MIT and Harvard University.

The participants at Asilomar found consensus on proposed rules for the governance of recombinant DNA research; the NIH has used the recommended approach successfully, with occasional modifications, for over three decades.[4] The importance of this achievement cannot be overemphasized. The world of biomedical science would be very different today if recombinant DNA methods had been prohibited, or severely limited, on the basis of the early scenarios. These methods are now the underpinnings of virtually all molecular research in biomedicine, and they are the essential tools employed by the biotechology industry for production of many components of modern medical practice, such as the hepatitis B virus vaccine, human insulin, monoclonal antibodies for treating cancer, and growth factors for promoting growth of blood cells. They have also been indispensable for the Human Genome Project and its sequels, and for many major discoveries in biology over the past thirty years.

The Asilomar meeting and its consequences taught scientists at least two significant lessons: our relationship with government and the public is sensitive to changes in the methods used for scientific work; and an active and open engagement with an anxious public can produce successful outcomes. The productive conclusion of the controversy over recombinant DNA continues to inspire current efforts to gain societal approbation of human embryonic stem cell research. But the stem cell debate has been complicated by the injection of religious convictions, not just concerns about safety, into the arguments opposing the new science, as further discussed in chapter 13.

Although I followed the gene-splicing debates closely in the science press and through colleagues who participated actively, I was not sufficiently established as a scientist in 1975 to have been invited to the Asilomar meeting; so my own interests and abilities in such negotiations were not tested. A decade later, however, I had my first direct experience with a political debate about science.

NAMING THE AIDS VIRUS

One day near the start of 1985, while working in my laboratory at UCSF, I received an unexpected phone call from Dani Bolegnesi, a virologist at Duke University. As an ally of one of the warring parties, he asked me to help resolve a contentious and increasingly public fight over the naming of the AIDS virus, the retrovirus that had been isolated from AIDS patients, grown in cultured cells, and partly characterized during the preceding two years. While narrower in scope and scientific impact than the recombinant DNA debate, this fight was closely followed in the scientific press, in part because of the elements of personal ambition involved, in part because resolution would ultimately determine how the entire world spoke about the cause of the greatest epidemic of our time. Although governments were not directly involved in the debate over the name of the virus, there were national issues at stake—reputation and revenue—and the affair had taken on some attributes of international strife.

One of the two principal combatants, Robert Gallo, was an American scientist at the NIH; the other, Luc Montagnier, was a Frenchman at the Pasteur Institute. They both had passionate supporters on their respective sides of the Atlantic, including attentive members of governments and those who worried about where the proceeds from commercialization of test kits (and any future therapies or vaccines) would end up. Because scientific tradition dictates that those acknowledged as discoverers can name their discoveries, the two were fighting about much more than nomenclature: hotly disputed claims for priority of discovery of the AIDS virus were at stake. Acceptance of a name for the virus by the scientific community could affect the outcome of debates over patents and distribution of royalties, and the decision could influence the award of important prizes, with implications for national stature. In addition, the names under consideration for the AIDS virus reflected different views about the nature of the virus, the manner in which it should be classified, and its significance as an agent of disease. These issues, as well as the lure of gossip and fights over priority, attracted the attention of scientists, physicians, AIDS activists, government officials, and the general public.

The situation boiled down to four basic options. Montagnier argued for lymphadenopathy virus, LAV, the name that he had given to the particles he had first observed in electron microscopic pictures of cells from the swollen lymph glands of patients who were in the course of developing AIDS. That name was unpopular in some quarters because it did not conform to the usual format and utility of retroviral names,* and, in other quarters, because it did not conform to what Gallo wanted. Gallo wanted to name the virus HTLV-III, the third "human T cell leukemia virus," putting the virus in a category for which he had appropriately received credit as chief of the NIH laboratory that discovered the first member of that group of viruses, HTLV-I. (Because the AIDS virus did not appear to cause leukemia, he proposed adding "lymphotropic," a term meaning that the virus preferentially infected lymphoid cells, as a more appropriate "L" word.) But this presented a serious problem for many virologists, regardless of their views of the disputed claims to priority: the AIDS virus seemed to be different from the HTLVs with respect to genetic content, shape of the virus particle, disease spectrum, and even multiplication strategy—too different to be classified with the HTLVs. The third camp was composed of compromisers, those willing to accept the cumbersome designation HTLV-III/LAV to try to satisfy the protagonists, both of whom claimed that they might accept the compromise. The fourth viewpoint held that a new name—more useful and more appropriate—should be sought. This fourth option had the added benefit of complying with neither of the two opponents and thus avoiding the suggestion that the priority dispute was going to be resolved by settling on a name.

A few years earlier, Peter Vogt had proposed my appointment to the International Committee on the Taxonomy of Viruses (ICTV). Having become head of the Retrovirus Study Group of the ICTV, I was given the

---

* The usual format for the name of a retrovirus includes the species in which the virus was found, the resultant pathology, and the term "virus," as in "feline leukemia virus."

charge by the ICTV's chairman to try to resolve the debate over the name of the AIDS retrovirus. To approach the problem in a balanced fashion, I convened an international panel of informed scientists, including Gallo, Montagnier, a couple of their well-known supporters, and a substantial list of senior, nonallied virologists interested in retroviruses, infectious diseases, and problems of virus classification. In addition, I solicited written opinions from many other virologists, clinicians, and various people engaged with the AIDS epidemic.

Members of the panel read the arguments for and against the names already being used (HTLV-III, LAV, and the combination compromise), generated a long list of other possibilities, most of which varied with respect to the one or two words between human (H) and virus (V), and then brokered an agreement for the consensus choice that was announced in May of 1986 and is now recognized everywhere: human immunodeficiency virus (HIV).[5]* However difficult this process was—with leaks to the press by Montagnier, belligerent letters to me from Gallo that were copied to most of our nation's leaders, surly and aggressive behavior by the two rivals, and refusals to sign the final statement by Gallo and his close colleague Max Essex, a virologist at Harvard's School of Public Health—it was interesting intellectually and socially. It also succeeded and it mattered. And the outcome has worked well for many purposes—scientific, political, economic, and medical.

POLITICAL ENGAGEMENT

During the years when I was negotiating the name of the AIDS virus, my status in the scientific community was changing. In 1984, I had been elected to the National Academy of Sciences (NAS).** This mark of respect from my colleagues was confirmed and accentuated by the several prizes that Mike Bishop and I received during the 1980s for the discov-

---

* It did not escape the notice of my laboratory colleagues that my own initials, HEV, might have formed a candidate name!

** The NAS is an "honor society" of mostly American scientists in all fields, elected by their peers through a complex nomination and winnowing process. But it also constitutes a crucial resource that the government is most likely to turn to for an authoritative opinion on virtually any scientific topic, as it has been doing since the founding of the NAS in 1863.

ery of proto-oncogenes. So, without my having to do much more than admit to an interest in fostering the good will of society toward science, when the next problems appeared—constrained budgets for federal science agencies, alleged misuse of government funds at universities, and accusations of misconduct in science—the NIH, the NAS, and science advocacy groups were likely to call upon me for opinions, talks, and committee work.

I first testified before Congress in about 1986 when I joined some better-known colleagues, including the Nobel laureates Jim Watson, Dan Nathans, and David Baltimore, to tell a special session of the House Appropriations Subcommittee, which finances the NIH, why it should greatly expand funding for research to combat AIDS and HIV.* Afterwards, Chairman Bill Natcher and other congressmen were eager to be photographed with Jim Watson, showing me that a scientist could be treated like a movie star. Furthermore, allocations for NIH-supported AIDS research were actually accelerated—something happened!— despite the Reagan administration's well-documented apathy toward the rapidly expanding and medically frustrating epidemic.

Especially after Mike Bishop and I received our Nobel Prize in 1989, my opportunities to work on behalf of the scientific community in the political arena increased sharply. But I wasn't dragged unwillingly into these activities. I enjoyed them, even before I entered the fray more fully in 1993 as NIH director. For one thing, they raised interesting and perplexing questions: How should the federal government allocate its science budget among competing disciplines and agencies—or the NIH budget among diseases or among the more than twenty separate institutes? What fraction of a research grant should be used to support the services provided by the investigator's institution—its administration and facilities—rather than the direct costs of the equipment, supplies, and personnel used in research? What constitutes misconduct in scientific research and how should allegations of misconduct be pursued? How

---

* As a result of this unusual hearing, I held an overly sanguine view of congressional hearings for several years: at that hearing, virtually all the committee members listened intently to the entire panel of experts for a full day. During my years as NIH director, I quickly became accustomed to much briefer hearings at which no more than a few committee members, and sometimes only the chair, were in attendance.

can scientists better inform the public and its representatives in government about the benefits and risks of sophisticated and potentially controversial or dangerous research?

In 1991, I spoke at an unusual public symposium staged at Stanford University on the ethical and societal implications of molecular approaches to human genetics. It was a revelation to find a large audience composed mostly of nonscientists become fully engaged in sophisticated talks about the social risks of genetic testing, molecular medicine, and other new technologies. The next year, I organized a similar weekend-long event at the Palace of the Legion of Honor in San Francisco, featuring a symposium, called "Winding Your Way through DNA," on the consequences of the recombinant DNA revolution.[6] To help the audience prepare for the scientific talks, the neighboring San Francisco Exploratorium developed exhibits that displayed the methods, principles, and products of modern biology, and high school students and their teachers were guided through the exhibits by UCSF trainees. Speakers at the symposium included Herb Boyer and Stan Cohen, reliving the moments of conception of the first recombinant DNA experiments; Jim Watson, describing the discovery and implications of the DNA double helix; and several other leading scientists, discussing medical, agricultural, economic, and ethical issues that emerged from the new technology. With over twelve hundred attendees and five thousand watching by satellite at twenty-seven sites, the symposium was accompanied by student workshops, videotaped interviews with speakers, and sales of coffee cups and T-shirts.

At about the same time that I was becoming more engaged in a wider world, I was also becoming a UCSF heretic. I began to wonder whether a scientific paradise was the right place to spend the rest of my career. Perhaps UCSF had become too comfortable, the pleasant routines too predictable, and my somewhat undemanding role there lacking in challenge. Although I had prestige and plenty of laboratory space, I had very little role in governance, in part because for many years I had avoided committee assignments and faculty responsibilities other than teaching, recruiting, or research.

For some of these reasons, late in 1991 I became a willing candidate to succeed David Baltimore as the director of MIT's Whitehead Institute, the place where I had worked during a second sabbatical in 1988–89. My biggest surprise was not learning that someone else was chosen.* Rather, the revelation was discovering my genuine disappointment that I would not be moving to a new and different kind of position. Apparently, I wanted a change and sought administrative responsibility and leadership.

Becoming NIH Director

Then, in the spring of 1993, another opportunity suddenly arose, one that seemed, at least superficially, to be even more of a departure from my established habits as a lab-oriented academic. Bernadine Healy, the Johns Hopkins cardiologist who had been appointed by George Bush Senior in 1991 as the first female director of the NIH, was being asked to leave the NIH by the recently arrived Clinton administration, despite having at first been allowed to stay on. (This change of heart is generally ascribed to her feisty relationships with some powerful members of Congress, especially the important Democrat John Dingell, who claimed to show his fondness for the NIH by watching it closely for improprieties and by investigating it vigorously and frequently.)

Bernadine Healy was unpopular with most of my colleagues, who bemoaned her lack of laboratory experience, her corporate approach to "strategic planning" for the NIH, her allegiance to the Bush-Quayle administration, and her own political ambitions. (She later made an unsuccessful run in Ohio for the Republican nomination for the U.S. Senate.) But I had had a few exposures to her and her job—once in Building One (which houses the NIH Director's Office on the NIH campus in Bethesda), as part of an advisory group on reimbursement for "indirect costs" of research, and once in a nearby hotel, as part of a large gathering of scientists asked to tell her how we would spend a $1 billion increment in the NIH budget (an unlikely event at that time). On both occasions,

* The new director, Gerry Fink, was a popular internal candidate and is a marvelous scientist and an old friend, with a background eerily similar to my own. The son of a Jewish physician and raised in Freeport, New York, my hometown, Gerry was a year behind me at both Freeport High School and Amherst College. He became a molecular geneticist, working on yeast and plants, who later discovered, among other things, how reverse transcription helps to move DNA elements called retrotransposons.

I was impressed by her command of information, her self-confidence, and her clear and forceful oratory, even when I was not in tune with her methods or her conclusions. Moreover, I was taken with the importance and complexity of the topics she had taken on, and could imagine why someone would interrupt an academic career to lead the NIH through bureaucratic, political, and financial thickets.

In view of my utter lack of administrative experience, I was surprised when I got a call from Bruce Alberts, my former UCSF colleague and the new president of the NAS, who was chairing an NIH director search committee, composed largely of leaders from academia and other "outside" constituencies and assembled by Donna Shalala, the secretary of Health and Human Services (HHS).* Bruce asked whether I would consider becoming a candidate and subjecting myself to a phone interview with his committee. I said yes.

The interview by conference call with the Alberts committee was not especially interesting or challenging. I had been supplied beforehand with a list of relatively predictable questions about NIH policies and funding. By that time—spring of 1993—I had made several visits to the NIH, the NAS, and Congress to discuss such questions, so I gave what were by then well-practiced answers to the search committee, and did not hear any negative reactions from its members. Soon thereafter, as evidence that I was on the "short list," I received an invitation from my prospective boss, Donna Shalala, to meet with her and others in the Clinton administration in Washington in June.

Aside from one discouraging chat with a functionary from the White House's Office of Science and Technology, who thought that I would be better placed as deputy director of the NIH in view of my limited administrative experience, my day in Washington increased my appetite for the job. Some journalists had portrayed Donna Shalala as aggressive, self-promoting, and egotistical, so it was a relief to find that she was warm, funny, and very smart. She quickly made me feel that the job was mine if

---

* I discovered much later that the government requires official search committees to be assembled mostly with federal employees; the fact that Donna did not toe that line was the first sign, invisible to me at the time, that she would treat the NIH just as she would have dealt with a program at the University of Wisconsin-Madison, where she had been a highly successful chancellor for several years before going to Washington.

I wanted it, and she allowed me to do what might have seemed impolitic to others—to meet with several of the directors of individual NIH institutes, who would later have to view me as their immediate boss. This proved to be a wise strategy, since it allowed me to see how very competent they were and also showed them (as several told me later) that I would care what they thought. By the end of the day, I called Connie in San Francisco and told her that I thought we might be moving to Washington soon.

After I returned home, press reports in science journals and even the *New York Times* reminded me that the president had not made his nomination and that there were other candidates, including some prominent women. Since Bernadine Healy's appointment as the first female director had attracted a lot of attention and her term had been very short (less than three years), the appeal of naming another woman was apparent. It was especially gratifying to learn in July that a long list of women scientists had sent letters of support for my nomination. As interest in the director's position mounted that summer, both locally and nationally, I began to appreciate the meaning of "Potomac fever," the infectious atmosphere of being under discussion and possibly slated for influence and authority in Washington. When the word finally arrived that I would be nominated by President Clinton, even though we had never met, I quickly accepted and began to reorganize my life and the lives of my family and laboratory members.

In a two-day trip, Connie and I found a private school (importantly, one without a dress code) for Christopher and placed a bid on a modest but attractive house in Woodley Park, in the District of Columbia, convenient to both the Metro's Red Line and Rock Creek Park. This offered public transportation as well as a bike route to the NIH, twelve miles to the north, in Bethesda. (Living on the NIH campus in the house earmarked for the NIH director never appealed to us: the décor was disturbing, the location was too visible to the NIH's more than fifteen thousand employees, and the setting was too pastoral for inveterate urbanites.) By Labor Day, we were temporarily installed in institutional housing on the NIH campus, while waiting to take possession of our house in Woodley Park, and attending an Orioles baseball game at Camden Yards, in Baltimore, while waiting for Senate confirmation.

Confirmation proved to be a frustrating experience. Even without any visible opposition and despite unexpected accolades from Republicans of a conservative bent, like Orrin Hatch, Strom Thurmond, and Judd Gregg, the process took entirely too long. Ted Kennedy, then the Chairman of the Senate Committee on Labor and Human Resources, conducted a confirmation hearing in early October, more than a month after I arrived in D.C. I delivered a brief statement of my goals for the NIH, basked in the approbation of my California legislators, Senator Barbara Boxer and Representative Nancy Pelosi, who sat briefly by my side, and then listened happily to flattering statements from the chairman and virtually every other member of the committee. The only cautionary comment came from Senator Daniel Coats, a Republican from Indiana, who quoted from *The Prune Book*, a handbook that describes major federal positions,[7] and wondered whether I had the "steel backbone" claimed to be required to run the NIH.

A few days later I experienced another spike of Potomac Fever when Ted Kennedy called me at home to say that the committee had approved my appointment unanimously. Still, their recommendation could not be acted on by the full Senate, as required before I could go to work, because some unnamed senator had used one of the less well-known and distressing privileges of the Senate, by placing an anonymous hold on my nomination for unknown reasons.

Days passed—many days. Press reports of my still unconfirmed appointment focused on my unusual but not entirely reassuring credentials for the job. On the one hand, I would be the first Nobel laureate to serve as NIH director, and the first director to run an active laboratory—which implied that I would be close to the real work of NIH-supported scientists and popular with the rank and file. On the other hand, would I have the time and the experience to do the real executive work of the NIH director? I was not shy about telling reporters that I had never run anything larger than my own lab group with about 25 members; the NIH had nearly 20,000 employees, and over 30,000 grant recipients. I had never managed a budget much larger than my own research budget of about a *million* dollars (and I wasn't always deft at managing that). The NIH budget was then just under eleven *billion* dollars, a difference of over four orders of magnitude.

The delay in my confirmation was frustrating, but it did provide my family time to get our lives in order. Our older son, Jacob, was by then a student at the University of Iowa; Christopher, who had agreed to move with us as a high school junior (no small sacrifice) was enrolled at Georgetown Day School. Connie had been working as a freelance writer after several years as editor of the book section of the *San Jose Mercury News* and a year as a Nieman Fellow at Harvard; now she was filling in at the *Washington Post Book World* for an editor who was on a sabbatical. We moved into that house we liked near the Metro and the bike paths in Rock Creek Park. And I began a commuting practice that gave me a kind of identity in Washington—the NIH director who rode his bike twelve miles to work.

After my picture on a bike in front of NIH's Building One appeared in the *New York Times*, an advance man for Clinton commented to Connie, "Who thought up the bike thing? Great image," and claimed that the young congressman Joe Kennedy kept a bike in his office but never used it. I did, nearly every day, in hot weather and cold, taking a morning shower in the third subbasement of Building One, the janitorial locker room, and trying to remember to have an ample supply of clean socks, shirts, and underwear at the office. This practice helped me handle the stresses of the job and also brought me an unexpected accolade—Montgomery County Commuter of the Year—the following year.[*]

Since I had still not been confirmed by the Senate, I was not really at work, just roaming the NIH campus as a "special volunteer." The time was useful for meeting many of the so-called intramural scientists and the administrators on the campus; visiting some of NIH's outlying sites throughout the Washington area, in Rockville, Poolesville, and off-campus Bethesda; learning some of the intricacies of the budget process and administrative procedures; and preparing to move about half a dozen members of my UCSF laboratory to Building 49 on the NIH campus, while finding suitable settings for the other twenty or so to continue to work in California.

---

[*] On summer days, especially when the government was in its doldrums, it was often possible to stop at the Potomac Boat Club to go out in a single scull on the way to work. Learning to row, largely in a double scull under the tutelage of my NIH colleague Ad Bax, was among the surprising pleasures of my years in Washington.

Someone in the NIH Office of Public Affairs suggested that I might benefit from a few sessions with a public speaking consultant, since I would soon be expected to make more public appearances than I ever had before. Despite my initial skepticism, this proved to be wise advice. In a series of three weekly sessions in her studio on Old Georgetown Road in Bethesda, Ms. Virginia von Fremdt gave me confidence as a speaker. She did this in two ways: by making short videos that allowed me to watch myself speaking from a podium and by encouraging me to depend on my natural style, rather than adopt a cautious bureaucratic voice. She praised my tendency to bound up the steps to the stage, told me not to slow the generally rapid pace of my oral delivery (lest I lose energy and enthusiasm), and convinced me that I could generally be more effective by talking naturally (even if a bit clumsily) from a few notes than by reading a verbatim text without error. This training also led me to recognize that I would be unlikely to find a speech writer who could capture my style effectively. In fact, I have never been able to use a talk composed for me by someone else—a situation that has restrained me from accepting too many invitations to speak.

Thanks to the sound advice I received from Ms. von Fremdt, I recognized that elements of style helped to attract favorable attention and get my message across. It also made me conscious of how other aspects of my behavior could help define me as an institutional leader—someone who was reasonably accessible, without pretensions, and slightly eccentric. I tried to dress for the occasion, not for my position: in a suit and tie to make my case at congressional hearings, but in khakis and an open collar to meet with colleagues on the NIH campus. Although I would have access to a car and driver once fully installed as director, I resolved to walk whenever possible, and without an accompanying retinue. Rather than drive my car to work (federal rules prohibited use of a driver to go between work and home), I would ride my bike or take the Metro. When I needed lunch, I would buy it (and be seen doing so) in one of the NIH cafeterias.

Still, these many efforts to prepare for the job, rather than do it, were becoming tedious. Finally, sometime in November, someone learned that Senator Charles Grassley of Iowa was responsible for placing the hold on my nomination. This news surprised me because I had already responded to a letter from him about my views on misconduct in science, an issue that he had taken up as part of his efforts to protect governmental whistle-blowers against reprisal. Having neither met him nor heard further from him, I assumed my response had been satisfactory. But, unknown to me and my colleagues, he expected an independent response from Secretary Shalala to a letter nearly identical to the one I had answered some weeks earlier. (We had presumed that my response would suffice, since letters to a secretary are often answered by the relevant agency head.) Once we understood the problem, repairs were swiftly made, the blackball was removed, and my confirmation took place, very early on a November morning just before the 1993 Thanksgiving recess, as part of a vote on a lengthy list of nominees, not unlike a mass wedding conducted by the Reverend Moon. For anyone watching on C-SPAN (I was not), it would not have been much of a show. I was sworn in the same day, surrounded by a small gathering of family members and colleagues, with Donna Shalala officiating. It was more like a common-law marriage than a coronation. In the process, I had learned something about the oddities of our government.

CHAPTER 10

Being NIH Director

—

We cannot be a strong Nation unless we are a healthy Nation. And so we must recruit not only men and materials but also knowledge and science in the service of national strength.

—PRESIDENT FRANKLIN D. ROOSEVELT,
AT THE DEDICATION OF THE NIH CAMPUS
IN BETHESDA, OCTOBER 30, 1940

IN SOME WAYS, THE EXPERIENCE OF RUNNING THE NIH IS NOT VERY different from that of running any government agency or large organization. But I was attracted to the job by its special features—the policy questions that affected the conduct of science, the opportunity to raise public support and government funding for scientific programs, and the historical significance of what had become the largest and arguably the most important source of funding in the world for biomedical research.

The origins of the NIH are generally traced to humble beginnings in a small federal laboratory of hygiene in New York in 1887.[1] After the laboratory moved to the District of Columbia early in the twentieth century, it gradually expanded. The first sign that the National Institute of Health (singular) might evolve into a more complex agency surfaced in 1937, with the founding of the then separate National Cancer Institute (NCI). The laboratories of the NIH and the NCI were given a remarkable opportunity to grow when Luke and Helen Wilson donated a large piece of land in Bethesda to the government. The dedication of the new Bethesda campus by FDR in late October 1940, in the midst of his third campaign for the presidency, was the occasion for the speech, cited at the start of this chapter and still available on an audio recording, that remains the source of some of most powerful justifications of the government's investment in health research.

After World War Two, inspired by the successes of government-supported, war-related science and by the rhetoric of Vannevar Bush's influential 1946 book *Science: The Endless Frontier*, the federal government began to establish new institutes, and the budgets for the health institutes grew at an intermittently rapid pace for at least the next four decades. At the same time, starting just after the war, the NIH began to distribute its funds in the form of grants and contracts to scientists working outside of government labs, throughout the nation and abroad. By the time I began my training in its laboratories in 1968, the NIH was already the largest supporter of biomedical research in the world, and its lead has only increased since then.

Given the NIH's history, significance, complexity, and size, the notion of running it was both compelling and intimidating. In most ways, the job did not disappoint: I helped make decisions about some of the most interesting and important issues of our time (AIDS, the Human Genome Project, global health, cloning and stem cells), I raised the profile and the fiscal fortunes of the NIH, and I enjoyed the company and sometimes the friendship of many of the leading political figures of my era in Washington. There were, of course, difficulties and disappointments, too. Overall, it was an experience that is best told thematically and episodically, not chronologically. The inevitable point of departure must be money.

THE NIH BUDGET

For the leader of any large organization, in government or out, month-to-month realities are dominated by one thing: finances. Early in my tenure as NIH director, the deputy director of one small institute said to me, "Appropriations is the lifeblood of an agency." Over the next six years, the truth of this was repeatedly brought home to me.

Just after I arrived at the NIH, Francine Little, the chief financial officer of the NIH during most of my time there, brought me an enormous loose-leaf notebook, sorted by month to provide a detailed timeline of the annual budget process. Francine was one of those lifetime civil servants who make federal agencies stay on track, even when directors come and go faster than electoral cycles. As a novice budgeter, I often did not fully grasp the nuances, arithmetic, and jargon that she used to describe the budget process. With time and her help, I learned.

In Francine's notebook, no month lacked its tasks. In principle, the fiscal year began on October 1 with two items: the delivery of U.S. Treasury money that congressional appropriators and the White House had agreed in the prior year that the NIH should spend in the coming year (that was the easy part), and the first steps in planning the president's budget proposal for the following year.* At this early point in the forthcoming funding cycle, all HHS agencies aimed to position themselves for as large a slice of the departmental budgetary pie as might be within reason, recognizing that the overall size of the HHS pie would be determined later by the administration and the congressional budget and appropriations committees. Because NIH spends so much of its funds on grants and contracts to outside (extramural) scientists, routinely turns down the majority of applicants, and can envision a limitless landscape of opportunity, the NIH's idea of what might be a reasonable increase over the prior year's budget tends to be grander than what would be expected at an agency that is thinking mainly or solely about its own employees and their salaries and equipment.

The justification for our estimates would ultimately depend on the plans and ambitions of each of the institutes and centers, nearly all of which are authorized by Congress to receive directly an amount of funds determined by the Appropriations Committee, with guidance from the administration. (For example, in the first year of my directorship, the NIH received $10.9 billion overall, distributed in amounts ranging from $21 million to $2.1 billion among about twenty-five institutes and centers.) Even at this early phase of the fiscal year, each institute is planning a proposal to the NIH director and the secretary that would help it

---

* During the past ten years, because of partisan bickering over appropriations, the fiscal year has usually begun with a series of "continuing resolutions" rather than a new appropriations bill. Continuing resolutions allow agencies such as the NIH to continue spending at the preceding year's rate, pending conclusion of the appropriations process, which has sometimes occurred as long as three months or more into the fiscal year.

gather as large a piece as possible from whatever is slated for the NIH in the next cycle.

The planning process is constrained by an essential feature of the NIH budget. The NIH spends all of its dollars each fiscal year—this is simple Micawber economics: for every dollar received, a dollar (perhaps a little less, certainly no more) will be spent each year.* But the NIH starts each year burdened with very large commitments made in prior years, when it awards multiyear grants that are paid one year at a time. Since the average duration of a grant is about four years and about 80 percent of the budget is used for external grants, about 60 percent of each year's appropriation is already promised to existing grantees. Furthermore, the NIH normally expects to increase the size of its grants, including the previously awarded ones, in accord with the rate of inflation of research costs (usually about twice the national rate of inflation). Much of the rest of any request must support the salaries and expenses of the intramural research program and administrative staff, leaving only a modest amount, generally less than 20 percent, to support entirely new projects and competitive renewals of old ones. For these reasons, opportunities to move in new directions are highly dependent on annual increases that at least equal or, preferably, exceed inflation. The alternative methods for generating new funds—decisions to reduce existing programs or to pay grantees at less than the inflationary rate—are painful and unpopular.

After the agency heads made their budget requests to Secretary Shalala—and, in some years, even voted on budgets we thought appropriate for other agencies!—she and her closest advisers would determine the department's budget request to the administration. (At this stage, in the late fall, the NIH budget was represented by a single number, although we knew that eventually it would need to be broken down into institute-sized pieces.) The size of the department's allocation in the president's budget would then be influenced by the secretary's success in negotiating with the Office of Management and Budget (OMB) and ultimately the

---

* In Dickens's *David Copperfield*, the amiable Mr. Micawber delivered his formula for economic success: "Annual income twenty pounds, annual expenditure nineteen nineteen six, result happiness. Annual income twenty pounds, annual expenditure twenty pounds ought and six, result misery."

White House, including, finally, the president himself. (Donna Shalala took special pride in remaining in town during the Christmas holidays, when the final decisions were often made; no doubt, this increased the proposed allocations for her department.) In early January, a more detailed breakdown among agencies (and, for the NIH, its institutes and centers) would be made to create the massive document known as the president's budget proposal for the next fiscal year, which still remained about nine months in the distance.

THE PRESIDENT'S BUDGET REQUEST

The elaborate unveiling of the president's budget proposal to Congress in January is a significant indicator of an administration's priorities, a reflection of the nation's economic health, and usually an inaccurate harbinger of final allocations, since Congress generally has the upper hand in making those decisions. This has been so especially for the NIH, which has traditionally received more from Congress than the president requested. Increases above the president's request for the NIH are particularly likely to occur at times when the party in the White House does not control the Congress, as was true for five of my six years in Washington. Medical research is politically popular, and the opposition party can score points by saying that the president is not doing enough for it.

Of course, even if not the final arbiter, the president's proposal is highly influential, especially when specific measures are requested. For example, inclusion of requests for funds for a new building, like proposals in the mid-1990s for a grand new NIH Clinical Research Center, was an important sign to Congress that the department, the OMB, and the president were supportive of this major investment, one that already had congressional proponents, including Senator Mark Hatfield, the chairman of the Senate Appropriations Committee and the person for whom the Clinical Research Center was named.* Similarly, the $1 billion increase that President Clinton requested for the NIH for fiscal year

* The Mark O. Hatfield Clinical Research Center opened its doors on the NIH campus in 2003.

1999 triggered the bipartisan plan for doubling the NIH over the next five years.*

To signal its support for the NIH in 1998 during the State of the Union address, an event that nearly coincides with the unveiling of the president's budget proposal, the White House used another traditional device: I was accorded the seat of honor next to Hillary Clinton in the House of Representatives gallery on January 27.** Bill Clinton's State of the Union speech received special attention that year, because the early revelations about Monica Lewinsky's relationship with the president had just appeared; in fact, Mrs. Clinton had made her famous remarks about "a vast right-wing conspiracy" on morning television that very day. My appearance by her side that evening was equal to anything Woody Allen's Zelig ever did.

THE CONGRESSIONAL APPROPRIATIONS PROCESS

After the annual announcement of the president's budget proposal, the budget committees go to work in the House and Senate; their critical task is to determine the sizes of the money pots available to each of the appropriations subcommittees. My focus was on the HHS-Labor-Education Subcommittees, which oversee the appropriations for the NIH and all the other components of these three major departments. Thus the NIH inevitably competes with other health agencies and with the Labor and Education Departments, not with other science agencies, for its annual funds. Happily for the NIH, traditionally and throughout my tenure, the chairmen of these subcommittees and the ranking members from the minority party were firm and generally passionate supporters of medical research and of the NIH specifically. These people, both Democrats and

---

* By 2003, the NIH budget had risen to nearly $27 billion, from a 1998 level of about $13.5 billion.
** I learned about the invitation to sit among Mrs. Clinton's guests for this speech a day earlier in London, on my way to the World Economic Forum in Davos. The prospect of flying back to Washington, then turning around to return to Europe, was not appealing, especially if I were to be seated out of sight in the upper part of the gallery. But I said I would do it if I could sit next to the First Lady. To my surprise, this request was granted; I even had Tipper Gore seated on the other side.

Republicans, form an "honor roll" of NIH benefactors, and they are often the people whose names are perpetuated on the entrances to buildings on the NIH campus. Prominent among these leaders during my time at the NIH were Representatives William Natcher and John Porter and Senators Mark Hatfield, Arlen Specter, and Tom Harkin. Buildings are already named for the first three.

Because the subcommittee members enjoyed listening to the usually upbeat reports on the advances in science and medicine that their appropriations bills paid for, the hearings on the NIH budget could be very long—extending on the House side for up to three weeks, with hearings twice a day for three days a week, until every institute and center director, and sometimes a few others, were heard from. Despite their length, these hearings were warmly welcomed, because they afforded all components of the NIH an opportunity to advertise both its accomplishments and its prospects in a public forum. (Unfortunately, in recent years, the time allotted for hearings on the NIH has shrunk dramatically.)

Each year of my tenure at the NIH, I sat at the hearing table with every one of the institute directors, in part to demonstrate my support and interest, in part to be there in case anything unexpected happened, like an unplanned appeal from a director for more funds or more personnel than the agreed-upon budget proposal allowed. The temptations to make last-minute requests were considerable and often fueled by advocacy groups that would provide subcommittee members with questions intended to provoke deviations from administration policy. The effects were generally minimal, but as the agency head I prized discipline among the directors of individual institutes at these long sessions, so that the institute budgets remained synchronized. I also welcomed opportunities to make my own heretical appeals for more than the president had requested for the entire NIH. Of course, neither the president nor the secretary had the time to police my behavior at these hearings, although the department always had its agents in the audience to report any significant deviations from budget policy. (I often exercised the old government adage in seizing opportunities to depart from policies I did not like: it is better to apologize later than to ask permission first.)

Appropriation hearings in the Senate were usually much more efficient and superficial than those in the House, sometimes too much so.

The first time I testified before Senator Specter's Appropriations Subcommittee, I was given just five minutes to present my proposal for the coming year for the entire NIH. This was among the few times Connie came to one of my hearings, and, as the red light on the tribunal began to blink, she was stunned to hear the chairman bark, "Sound bites, Dr. Varmus, sound bites," in an effort to move quickly to the question period.

In either setting, regardless of the size of the president's budget request, the game was basically the same: getting the witnesses for the NIH—me and the institute directors—to admit that we could use more funds than the president was requesting, without compromising our position as witnesses on behalf of the administration. It was a game everyone understood—Bill Clinton joked with me about it more than once, acknowledging that he should be asking Congress for more, but was constrained by desires to submit a balanced budget. But he also knew that, whatever he did, Congress would likely do more for us. Usually the questioning took a friendly turn, especially when it came in the form of a Republican attack on the president's budget: "We understand that you need to conform to the president's proposal, Dr. Varmus, but how much could you productively spend at the NIH if there were no other competing concerns?" And so forth.*

A REVERSAL OF BUDGETARY FORTUNES

The success of an NIH director is often (unfairly) appraised by the agency's budgetary history, and I became the lucky beneficiary of the good financial times created by the economic policies of the Clinton administration. As the nation's fiscal deficit shrank and the budget became balanced in the mid-1990s, appropriators were willing to increase spending on projects and agencies they favored. Few government agencies have the reputation, promise, and political appeal of the NIH. Everyone, in government or the electorate, is worried about one disease, or all diseases.

---

* Unfortunately, this encouraging line of questioning is rare in the current era, in which the budgetary fortunes of the NIH have been declining at an unprecedented pace.

When I arrived in Washington in 1993, the situation was not so favorable. The federal deficit was large, and the budget was unbalanced. Many leaders and pundits were speculating about across-the-board cuts to all agencies, as much as 5 to 10 percent, as part of a "share the pain" effort to restore fiscal responsibility. I tried to make the case that the NIH was a different kind of agency and that cuts of this kind would put medical scientists out of work, break up strong research teams, and significantly slow progress against disease for a period longer than the budget reduction. The research community would get by, I argued, during a short period of budgetary stringency as long as we received inflationary increases—even if we were not given the major increases that we could productively use and many wanted to argue for.[2] This moderate position seemed to work, and the NIH was spared the budgetary cuts that had been threatened. Then, as the economy thrived, so did the NIH budget, beginning with modest but steady increases for a couple of years, thanks to the work of our congressional champions, who did what the president probably expected by overriding his more modest proposals for the NIH.

Then, in 1998, the stars seemed to align for the NIH. There was confidence throughout the executive and legislative branches in the competence of the agency. There was excitement about the science we were doing, and strong expectations among disease advocacy groups that discoveries in research were going to improve health. John Porter, as chairman of our Appropriations Subcommittee and an enthusiast for medical science, took a small group of leaders of science-based industries to lobby Speaker Newt Gingrich and others on our behalf. Testimony by many of us at the NIH and by leaders of the scientific community had further persuaded Congress and the administration that inflationary growth of the NIH budget was not enough, especially during good times for the federal budget. As a result of these converging events, several important members of the congressional leadership, Republicans and Democrats alike, supported a proposal to launch a plan to double the budget over five years.

This launch was made easier by the president's decision to highlight a proposed $1 billion increase in the NIH budget (then about $13.5 billion) in his State of the Union address in 1998, the occasion for my night in the

1942, my parents, Bea and Frank, and I were living near a lake in Winter Park, Florida. A couple years later, we were joined by my sister, Ellen, and I had outgrown my sailor suit.

I tagged along with my Amherst classmate Art Landy (right) when he won a college prize to attend the International Congress of Biochemistry in Moscow in August 1961; here we are sightseeing in Leningrad.

Peyton Rous, the Rockefeller Institute physician-scientist who isolated the eponymous chicken tumor virus, Rous sarcoma virus, nearly a century ago.

Howard Temin, the iconoclastic virologist who proposed the provirus hypothesis and then discovered reverse transcriptase in 1970.

David Baltimore (right), who also discovered reverse transcriptase, photographed thirty years later at my sixtieth birthday party at the Cold Spring Harbor Laboratory, talking with Ira Pastan, my mentor at the NIH in the late 1960s.

Peter Vogt, the viral geneticist with whom Mike Bishop and I collaborated for many years, at a Bishop-Varmus group reunion at UCSF in 1990 with Suzanne Ortiz, my lab manager at UCSF, NIH, and MSKCC for over thirty years.

Mike Bishop (left) and I co-organized the annual RNA Tumor Virus Meeting at Cold Spring Harbor in May 1978.

Connie and I lived at 35 Cross Street in Islington, with Jacob, then five, and a very young Christopher, during my 1978–79 London sabbatical.

The announcement of our Nobel Prize was co-featured on the front page of the *San Francisco Chronicle*, in a somewhat smaller typeface, with the San Francisco Giants' victory in the National League Championship series.

A few days later, we posed in the refurbished laboratories at UCSF where our Prize-winning work was done over a decade before.

In this "obituary photo," I am receiving the Prize from Swedish King Carl Gustaf, in the Stockholm Concert Hall on December 10, 1989.

Colleagues in our two laboratories gathered after an annual Bishop-Varmus softball game in the early 1990s. Mike and I are wearing our official San Francisco Giants uniforms.

After the Presidential election of 1992, the UCSF Gang of Four—Bruce Alberts, me, Marc Kirschner (standing, left to right), and Mike Bishop— wrote an open letter to the incoming Clinton-Gore administration about federal science policy.

While waiting for Senate confirmation in November 1993, I rode my bike in front of NIH's Building One for a photographer from the *New York Times*.

Fifty-three years earlier, FDR dedicated the expanded NIH campus in Bethesda. (Note the singular "Institute" on the building's cornice.)

In the spring of 1997, the NIH's Tony Fauci briefed Bill Clinton and Al Gore on HIV and AIDS in the Oval Office. (The balding pate on the lower left is mine.) A post-briefing chat with the President accelerated plans for the NIH Vaccine Research Center.

On January 27, 1998, I appeared between the First Lady and Tipper Gore at the State of the Union address in which Bill Clinton announced an unprecedented request for a one billion dollar increase in the NIH budget.

Unveiling a bust of the late House Appropriations Chairman William Natcher, a notable NIH champion, at the new conference center named for him on October 3, 1994. The other string-pullers, all NIH loyalists, are HHS Secretary Donna Shalala, Representatives John Porter and David Obey, and Phil Lee, Assistant Secretary of Health.

In January 1996, NASA Chief Scientist France Cordova (left) and I made the requisite stop at the South Pole marker during a trip to assess America's scientific work in Antarctica.

In January 1997, I visited the Bancoumana field station of the NIH-sponsored Malaria Research and Training Center in Bamako, Mali. The Center's Director, Ogobara Doumba, is seated in front at the left, with his colleagues and trainees.

An enjoyable form of fund-raising: rowing down the East River to Pier 13 in lower Manhattan in a lifeguard boat with Rick Shalvoy, a former Jones Beach lifeguard, during one of his annual Row for a Cure events.

In May 2008, celebrating the fifth anniversary of the opening of the Ralph Lauren Center for Cancer Care and Prevention in Harlem, with the designer Ralph Lauren (middle), Center director and surgeon Harold Freeman (left of Ralph), cyclist and cancer survivor Lance Armstrong (right), and public health advocate and New York City Mayor Mike Bloomberg (far right).

gallery with the First Lady. As a percentage of the NIH budget, his proposed increase (about 8 percent) was more modest than what would be required to double the budget in five years (about 15 percent)—he was proposing a doubling over ten years—but it was still historically unprecedented as measured in dollars.*

SPENDING THE MONEY: SCIENTIFIC PROGRAMS

Seeking strong budgets for the NIH is a central task for the NIH director, but guiding the way the funds are spent is a more delicate and complex job. Some of the guidelines are simple. Under normal conditions, when the agency receives at least an inflationary increase in its budget, each of its institutes and centers must honor the commitments made to grantees who received multiyear awards in prior years. The roughly sixteen thousand employees of the NIH need to receive at least cost-of-living salary adjustments. The pool of funds available for "investigator-initiated" grants, the mainstay of NIH's successes over the decades, must be maintained. And the intramural research program should receive at least an inflationary increase. But deciding how individual institutes should fare in the appropriations process, determining whether to favor intramural or extramural research, choosing among competing topics for special emphasis, responding to the burdens of individual diseases (like AIDS, cancer, or diabetes), or expanding certain kinds of research (on genomes or animal models) in the light of technical advances—all of these issues are difficult and often contentious.

Still, the NIH has a great advantage over many other agencies: its appropriations bill rarely contains the kinds of "earmarks" that direct an agency to spend its funds on a favored project at a specific institution in

---

* This bipartisan effort, also later endorsed by George W. Bush during his presidential campaign in 2000, led to the now famous "doubling over five years," that ended in 2003. Since then, however, NIH has received only subinflationary or negligible increases and its purchasing power has decreased by about 13 percent as of 2008. Combined with increases in numbers of grant applicants and the average sizes of grants, the budgetary slide has reduced the success rates for applicants to disturbingly low levels and created an unprecedented sense of stress in our research community, especially among younger investigators. The absolutely flat budget proposed by President Bush for fiscal year 2009 has further demoralized and mobilized NIH advocates.

a member's district or state. Appropriators have opportunities to promote research on certain topics by influencing allocations to individual institutes or centers. They can also introduce nonbinding recommendations in "reports" that accompany the bills. These recommendations might ask the NIH to give special attention to certain diseases or to monitor progress in certain research areas, but they fall short of telling the NIH what projects to fund and where.

These earmark-free appropriations bills represent votes of congressional confidence in the NIH's system of peer review. Since the late 1940s, the NIH has judged the merit of applications for financial support of research by impaneling experts from the extramural research community to evaluate and rank grant applications. No one believes that the method is perfect, and the procedures for writing and reviewing the applications are frequently reexamined and changed, but peer review is generally acknowledged to be superior to other methods—such as administrative review or congressional earmarks.*

Because the NIH director has much more influence over the distribution of funds to institutes than over their distribution among initiatives within the institutes, I sometimes felt frustrated by my lack of authority to become engaged in the scientific programs. But the position does come with some power over program development, even if the influence seems indirect and bureaucratic, exercised through the formation of panels, persuasion, political debates, or the shaping of budgets. In the next sections, I discuss some of the ways in which I used that influence in the domains of major scientific initiatives.

(1) The Research Program for HIV and AIDS

Even before I arrived at the NIH, the manner in which decisions would be made about funding research on AIDS had become the subject of a

---

* In financially good times for the NIH, success rates for grant applications generally averages about one in three, a situation most seasoned observers agree is appropriate. When times are tough, as is the case now, success rates can fall as low as one in six or one in seven on average, and even lower for new investigators. Under these conditions, it is common to argue that peer review is not working well, in part because it is difficult to make choices among excellent applications, not all of which can be funded under adverse circumstances.

public debate, and I had joined a number of colleagues in support of a position that caused difficulties for me during the nomination process. Many AIDS activists, troubled by the nation's slow response to the epidemic, had argued that AIDS research should be carried out by a new NIH institute, not simply managed within existing institutes, such as the National Institute of Allergy and Infectious Diseases (NIAID), which had naturally assumed primary responsibility for directing AIDS research.

The NIH is traditionally (and, in my view, appropriately) resistant to the formation of new institutes. When many NIH leaders opposed the idea of an AIDS institute, a compromise was brokered with the help of Congress: there would be no new institute, but AIDS research across the NIH would be coordinated by an Office of AIDS Research (OAR). Importantly, the OAR would be authorized to receive a budget for AIDS research that would be distributed among the various institutes and centers that studied different aspects of AIDS through their intramural or extramural activities. To many of us on the outside, this seemed like an unnecessary complication in the budgetary process and a potentially confusing way to lead the AIDS research effort, so we signed a public statement objecting to the new office and its authorities.

In retrospect, we'd had a naïve response to a political compromise that spared the NIH from the creation of another institute. Although the solution has not always worked smoothly, it has served at least adequately; the NIH has adapted to the budgetary complications; and the OAR has served the cause of trans-institute program coordination reasonably well. But, at the time, my earlier public opposition to the OAR caused some AIDS activists to be skeptical about my appointment or even loudly opposed to it—despite my research credentials as a retrovirologist and my political support for increased funds for AIDS research. By meeting with all of the prominent activists, both supporters and opponents, during the nomination process, to assure them that I would work effectively with the OAR (which by then had become established in law), the controversy gradually abated.

But the central scientific issues remained. With inhibitors of reverse transcriptase as the only (and not very effective) drug therapy, with a still poor understanding of the mechanisms by which HIV causes AIDS, and with no evident prospects for a vaccine against HIV, the AIDS research program needed reevaluation. In 1994, on the advice of some distinguished scientists,* I commissioned a full review of the NIH's research program on HIV/AIDS. An impressive committee of mostly external investigators, headed by the virologist Arnold Levine, produced a remarkable report that served as a blueprint for the AIDS program for several years—years in which the world was also benefiting from the earlier investments that led to better drugs (especially the protease inhibitors), the development of multidrug antiretroviral therapy, prevention of mother-to-infant transmission of HIV, and a dramatic reduction in AIDS death rates in the developed world.

Included among the report's recommendations was one that helped reshape the NIH's approach to vaccines. The outside committee had stressed the need for greater attention to the failures of the immune system that might explain earlier unsuccessful attempts to develop an HIV vaccine. Soon thereafter, Bill Paul, a prominent NIH immunologist and the person I had selected to direct the OAR, suggested that the NIH intramural program, already well staffed by virologists and immunologists, should form a targeted HIV vaccine program on the NIH campus. This would entail a dedicated facility, recruitment of additional personnel, and budgetary increases—a large effort that would normally not be undertaken easily.

But, in this instance, the government proceeded with unaccustomed speed. Shortly after Bill Paul's suggestion, a few of us were coincidentally invited to the White House to brief the president, the vice-president, and some of their senior advisers on the status of HIV/AIDS. On that day in the spring of 1997, President Clinton had laryngitis, so he asked fewer questions than usual but listened intently. Part of the presentation addressed the lack of significant progress toward a vaccine, and I brought up the proposal to build a vaccine research center at the NIH. As we were breaking up, the president took me aside and said that he'd like to support the center concept as best he could in the budget process.

A few days later, one of his speechwriters called to say that the presi-

---

* This advice came, most forcefully and notably, from Phillip Sharp, a virologist at MIT, who shared a Nobel Prize in 1993 for his discovery of RNA splicing.

dent would like to include the proposal for a new NIH vaccine center in a commencement speech he was soon to deliver at Morgan State University, a historically black institution in Maryland. After some predictable exchanges over what we thought the speech could legitimately promise— not "a vaccine in ten years," but instead "progress toward a vaccine in ten years"—the talk was written and given. Happily, it attracted attention. Appropriators still at work on the fiscal year 1998 budget for NIH added the new Vacccine Research Center as a separate item on the buildings-and-facilities line, with expectations that the rest of the funds would be forthcoming in subsequent years. They were. The building, now called the Dale and Betty Bumpers Vaccine Research Center, was dedicated by the president and other dignitaries in the fall of 1999.*

Now, of course, ten years have come and gone, and we still lack an effective vaccine against HIV. Still, I view the Vaccine Research Center as a valuable investment. An enormous amount has been learned at this NIH center (and elsewhere) about the properties of viral proteins on the surface of HIV, about the receptors that allow HIV particles to enter cells, about the ways in which the two prominent arms of the immune system—B cells (antibody forming) and T cells (cell killing)—respond to HIV, and about ways to deliver HIV proteins to components of the immune system that recognize foreignness.[3] Unfortunately and unexpectedly, despite this new knowledge, the most promising candidate vaccine, formulated by Merck, failed miserably in a clinical trial.[4] In the wake of this revelation, debates have resurfaced about whether a vaccine against HIV is possible and whether efforts to make one should be abandoned. But it seems unconscionable to walk away from this enormous biological challenge in view of the magnitude of HIV's human toll.

(II) GENES AND GENOMES

As the fortunes of the NIH improved in the mid to late 1990s, the budgets of individual institutes and centers tended to rise, more or less in syn-

---

* The name honors the president's Arkansas friend and senator, one of his strongest supporters during his trial in the Senate after the 1999 impeachment. Senator and Mrs. Bumpers are also active proponents of universal childhood vaccine programs.

chrony. I fostered this egalitarian concept in my conversations with our appropriators largely to acknowledge that new opportunities were evident in all fields of medical research, but also to avoid the loss of enthusiasm for the NIH among advocates for any particular component. Still, each institute needed to justify its budgetary increases with new programs; these plans were formally presented to Congress as Areas of Research Emphasis. Using this advertising device, it was possible to ratchet up funds a bit more swiftly for some institutes than for others.

Funding for the National Human Genome Research Institute (NHGRI), which was the lead agency for the Human Genome Project (HGP), was among the few exceptions to the generally uniform rise of budgets across the NIH. To insure that the HGP moved as quickly as possible, the NHGRI budget grew at an especially rapid pace. This was made possible by the popularity of the project, the applicability of its findings to all areas of medicine, its performance ("ahead of schedule and under budget," the NHGRI liked to boast), the eloquence of its chief advocate, NHGRI Director Francis Collins, and, of course, the country's healthy fiscal situation overall.

Already long before the sequencing of the human genome had commenced in a serious way, the project had brought favorable publicity to the NIH and helped create a sense of optimism about the importance of genes in the study and control of disease. An early stage of the project, mapping of landmarks on chromosomes, had been highly successful and was very helpful to scientists looking for specific genes implicated in familial diseases, such as Huntington's disease, familial forms of breast and other kinds of cancer, several rare hereditary diseases, some forms of diabetes, and others. Completion of parallel genome projects on simpler organisms—single-cell organisms like bacteria and yeast, or more complex experimental animals like the roundworm and the fruit fly—also generated excitement and anticipation. And new technologies, including methods for assessing the activity of all of an organism's genes simultaneously, illustrated the power of genomic information to transform the way experiments in biology are performed.

While other directors could not dispute the wisdom of moving with full speed toward completion of the genome project, the growth of the NHGRI's budget provoked envy and concern. Knowing that institute budgets are rarely, if ever, reduced, some asked what the NHGRI would do with such large budgets after the project was finished. And the genome project was not devoid of political problems. There were occasional conflicts with the NHGRI's partners—the U.S. Department of Energy, which had initiated the effort many years before and had begun to feel overpowered by the greatly enlarged NIH component; and the Wellcome Trust in the United Kingdom, which sometimes felt isolated from decision-making on this side of the Atlantic. Then the Celera Corporation, headed by the sometimes pugnacious, unpredictable, but indisputably clever Craig Venter, issued a highly publicized challenge to the publicly funded HGP from the private sector.*

Because the HGP was generally managed superbly, I had little involvement in its day-to-day activities, but was brought in to help with these conflicts, to participate in the many press events to announce the isolation of new genes or the achievement of the HGP's major milestones, to advocate for the steep budgetary increases, to organize a "Millennium Night" on genomics at the White House, and to plan for genomic research after the HGP was completed. These were welcome diversions from my usual tasks, since they were firmly grounded in the science itself and since they were part of a dramatic transformation of medicine and biology.

Science before genomes was different from science after genomes. Moving as rapidly as possible into the age of genomics was the right thing to do—important for those of us working on cancer and for everyone else too. It was also essential for the genome project to be undertaken in the public domain, so that everyone could make efficient use of the new information, setting a standard for the sharing of research findings via

---

* Numerous accounts of the "race" between the public and private genome projects provide different perspectives on the outcome and meaning of the confrontation.[5] But there is widespread agreement on several important points: both efforts were accelerated dramatically by improvements that had recently been made by the manufacturers of sequencing machines; the private side was the beneficiary of enormous earlier investments in technology, mapping, and sequencing by the public players; and the openness of the public project—with all information rapidly, easily, and freely available to all on the Internet—continues to dominate the culture of genomics. That final point represents the ultimate and important victory.

the Internet. Escalating financial support for the NHGRI was an important part of the strategy to make the HGP as beneficial as possible.

(III) CLINICAL RESEARCH

When I became NIH director in late 1993, the entire scientific community was in a somber mood as a result of recent declines in the success rates for grant applicants. No sector of that community was in a bleaker mood than clinical investigators, those who worked directly with patients or with human tissues. Some of the complaints were directed at academic institutions, which were said to provide too little time or incentives for clinicians to do research. Some were directed at the system for training clinical scientists, a system that encumbered physicians with enormous debts, did not provide formal instruction or adequate mentoring in clinical research methods, and ultimately discouraged them from participating in research. And some complaints were directed at the NIH, which was accused of not allocating enough funds for patient-oriented projects, of lacking sufficient numbers of clinical scientists on grant review panels, and of generally overvaluing laboratory research at the expense of patient-oriented studies.

I was surprised by the vehemence of these arguments. In response, I attempted to assess their claims and to try to fix what needed repair by establishing a panel of esteemed clinical investigators, headed by David Nathan, from Harvard Medical School. (Readers will, by now, recognize that knowing when and how to assemble such panels is among the major skills demanded of an NIH director!) Some of the panel's first actions were simply to clarify the situation—to define the forms of clinical research, to determine the (very substantial) fraction of the NIH budget devoted to these categories, to show that significant declines in that fraction had not occurred, and to trace the career development of clinical investigators (which was indeed troubling). The Nathan panel, as it came to be known, did more than a simple assessment.[6] It also proposed remedies, many of which have been adopted: new awards for the training of clinical investigators; career development awards to provide new clinical faculty members with more time for research; development of curricula in clinical research; and changes in composition of review panels. Now, at a time when collaboration between laboratory and patient-oriented scientists is so important, these efforts to boost clinical research can be judged to have been unarguably timely, even though clinical investigators are no better protected than anyone else against recent budgetary declines.

(iv) The Intramural Research Program

The intramural research program is carried out by government scientists employed by the NIH, principally on the main campus in Bethesda, but also at satellite facilities in Rockville, Maryland, Tuscon, Arizona, Hamilton, Montana, and elsewhere. Most of the institutes and centers have established their own intramural components. The laboratories are headed by faculty-level scientists and staffed by technicians, postdoctoral fellows, and visiting students from other universities and medical schools. Funds for these laboratories are part of each participating institute's annual budget, allocated to individual laboratories by a scientific director, according to their size and perceived value. Intramural NIH scientists are only rarely eligible to apply for grants, but virtually all are assured of sustained funding, unless performance is persistently inadequate; in that case, they leave the NIH or, commonly, transfer to an administrative position that does not include the conduct of laboratory research.

The history of the intramural program reaches back to the earliest days of the NIH, when it was simply a collection of small government laboratories. (Recall that the now dominant activity of the NIH, the awarding of extramural grants, was a post–World War Two invention.) The history of intramural science is not only long; it is also rich. Several Nobel laureates have worked for most or all of their careers at the NIH; among them is Marshall Nirenberg, whose discovery of the genetic code was described in part 1. The more than one thousand independent NIH laboratory heads also include about fifty members of the National Academy of Sciences and many others who are prominent in their fields. Furthermore, the intramural program is renowned for its success in training young scientists, including those physicians (like me) who fulfilled their service obligations at the NIH during the Vietnam War, many medical students who come to the NIH for a year or two under the auspices of a joint program with the Howard Hughes Medical Institute, thousands of foreign scientists who work as postdoctoral fellows at the NIH and return home, and university graduate students who conduct their thesis projects in laboratories on the NIH campus.

Still, the intramural program has been a repeated target for criticism, especially when times are tough for NIH grantees. When I arrived at the NIH as director, at a time of declining success rates for grant applicants from the external academic community, criticism of the intramural research program was rampant. Many extramural scientists who were having trouble obtaining or renewing grants, or were watching colleagues terminate their research careers, began to ask why intramural scientists were protected from budgetary vicissitudes. Was the work of the NIH scientists really different? More valuable? Of higher quality? Were outside advisers to the individual components of the program encouraged to make the kinds of critical judgments that would restrict or terminate funds for labs that were underperforming? When sanctions were recommended, were those recommendations followed by the scientific directors of the intramural program? Was it right to devote about 11 percent of the NIH budget to the intramural laboratories consistently, when external scientists were struggling to renew their grants?

This debate had been given a prominent airing in the pages of *Science* magazine,[7] and one of my first responsibilities was to confront it, in hopes of restoring the program's reputation as a haven for superlative science and as the training ground for many of the country's leading scientists. The dominance of the intramural program in American biomedical science had declined since the 1960s and 1970s, in large part because of the rising success of many medical schools, research universities, and independent institutions, which had built strong programs, often headed by former NIH trainees and scientists (as I knew from my own experiences at UCSF) and funded by the then rapidly expanding NIH budget. So it was legitimate to ask: Did the nation still need a large intramural program? Did it serve functions that could not be provided by the external research community? Had the quality of its performance declined? If so, were there ways to reverse the decline?

These questions and others were posed to a study group of leading scientists and physicians from the outside research community, headed by Paul Marks (then president of MSKCC) and Gail Cassell (then a professor at the University of Alabama Medical Center). Their report was a milestone in efforts to return the intramural program to a respected position in American science.[8] It stressed the need for a more rigorous review process. It acknowledged that the intramural research could not be different in all respects from research at other places, such as academic medical centers, but ought to be different in some ways because of its size, its capacity to respond more quickly to public health emergencies, its ability to recruit patients from around the world for clinical research, its emphasis on experimental work rather than classroom teaching, its budgetary stability, and the diversity of its technical capacities. But the report also noted that the intramural research program was less competitive than many academic organizations in recruiting outstanding scientists, because of the relatively low government salaries, the limited opportunities to consult for industry or perform other "outside activities," the several aging laboratory buildings, and a declining reputation.

One of the most rewarding aspects of my job at the NIH was to put into action much of the advice offered by the Marks-Cassell committee. Even before the committee began its work, I had persuaded one of the finest scientists in the intramural program, Michael Gottesman, to take over as its new leader (with the status of a deputy director of NIH). Michael, who is still in that position nearly fifteen years later, proved to be a remarkably effective partner in pursuing the charge we were given by the Marks-Cassell report, and much more. We began by strengthening mechanisms for stringent review of individual laboratories and for enforcing unfavorable recommendations concerning budgets and space. We pledged that the budget for the intramural research program would grow less rapidly than the budget for extramural grants; that policy remained in place for at least a decade. We worked successfully with the administration and the Congress to obtain funding for a new Clinical Research Center, the physical and thematic focus of the main campus, and the centerpiece of a national effort to foster research that requires the direct participation of patients (often called patient-oriented research). We found ways to increase salaries for the program's leading scientists, using existing statutes that permit payment of government experts at rates that are nearly competitive with salaries at academic institutions, if not at for-profit companies. And we lowered restrictions on participation in outside activities, including consultation with medical industries. As a result of these changes, our ability to recruit superb scientists increased, as did our ability to retain them, aided no doubt by the continued appeal of stable research budgets and by the improving quality and reputation of the program and its facilities.

These changes, especially the limit on the intramural program's relative rate of growth, were easier to achieve in an era in which the NIH budget overall was growing. In the past few years, with the loss of the NIH's spending power overall, the internal program has also faced serious funding shortfalls, so its attraction as a place where nearly all investigators have some resources for research projects is offset by the difficulty of undertaking new initiatives within a restricted budget. Furthermore, the intramural program has taken heat from some congressional critics because of accusations that a few senior investigators had engaged in paid consulting arrangements with industry that were not appropriately reported to or reviewed by ethics officers at the NIH. As a result of congressional hearings, investigations, and negotiations, the NIH was forced to rescind many of the opportunities that its scientists had become accustomed to pursue with nongovernmental organizations, and this may have diminished the program's attraction for job candidates.

In a series of articles published in the Los Angeles Times, the alleged conflicts of interest were traced, in part, to my decision to allow NIH scientists to engage in some of the kinds of consulting arrangements that their colleagues at extramural academic institutions were permitted to have.[9] I felt stung and inappropriately chastised by the claims in those articles. There was no recognition of the fact that I had acted on the recommendation of the Office of Government Ethics (OGE) to ease earlier excessive restrictions, or that the OGE had approved my proposal to change the policies. Moreover, the OGE had been unwilling to consider a more nuanced policy, in which our most senior scientists might be more restricted than others, because even the most senior (such as institute directors or heads of major programs) were of lower rank than people in other agencies or departments who were allowed a significant range of outside activities. Moreover, violations of NIH policy, such as failures of individuals to report consulting activities, should not have been grounds for reprimanding the entire agency or for rescinding, rather than refining and more vigorously enforcing, policies that had clearly improved one of the government's most effective scientific programs.[10]

CHAPTER 11

Priority Setting

—

ONE OF THE MOST DIFFICULT ASPECTS OF THE JOB OF RUNNING THE NIH, or of directing any individual institute, is the designation of research priorities. This is an emotionally and politically sensitive part of the job because it is closely watched by some of NIH's strongest supporters, who often advocate for the NIH because of a passionate interest in a small fraction of what the NIH does. That fraction is almost always a specific disease or even a subset or facet of that disease.*

SETTING PRIORITIES BY DISEASE

Shifts in funds assigned to the mechanisms for supporting research, such as the intramural versus the external grant programs, or differential growth of budgets for individual institutes, are often easier to absorb than changes that affect the dollars devoted to specific diseases. Directives to alter allocations for disease-oriented programs are especially problematic if they occur abruptly or come at the expense of research on another disease. The situation may be further complicated if the directives are demands from powerful people rather than consensual decisions.

One of my first exposures to this problem occurred soon after I arrived

* Any past director of the National Institute of General Medical Sciences, a major source for support of basic biological research, will say, "There aren't many patient groups advocating for general medical sciences." So support for the NIGMS depends on an enlightened understanding of the benefits of basic research; on the other hand, this institute is spared the internecine battles among disease groups that plague some of the other institutes.

at the NIH, when I received a call from my own former congresswoman, Nancy Pelosi, asking me to add $50 million to the budget for AIDS research. As the representative from one of the districts most heavily affected by the epidemic, her wishes were understandable. Since she was a member of the House Appropriations Subcommittee for the NIH, she was in a position to try to increase funds for AIDS research when the subcommittee was debating the size of the NIH budget, without taking the money from some other research program. But, in that period of spending caps, she had presumably been unsuccessful in negotiations with her fellow committee members and was now trying to fulfill a promise to her San Francisco constituents by asking me to shift funds from some other budget categories into the OAR account. I declined as politely as I could.

Sometimes it was not so easy to say no. Late one afternoon in May of 1996, as I was walking on the NIH campus, my driver pulled up with an urgent expression and asked me to take an emergency call on the car phone. A senior member of the administration—Jack Lew, then deputy director, later director, of the Office of Management and Budget—told me that the president had just met the recently paralyzed actor Christopher Reeve for the first time that afternoon and had promised in the presence of the press to increase spending on spinal cord research by $10 million. I started to explain the difficulties of doing this, when the phone was passed at the other end to a more junior person, who said, basically, just do it, don't argue, or you won't get the money. Of course, the White House was not in a position to send us any additional funds directly. But the president's wishes are always obeyed. When the next accounting was made of disease-specific spending at the neurology institute (formally known as the National Institute for Neurological Diseases and Stroke, or NINDS), the funds for spinal cord research were accordingly higher, and funds for other purposes were proportionately lower.*

---

* Soon after the phone call, I was asked by the president's advisers to go to Bedford, New York, to help Chris Reeve prepare for his appearance at the 1996 Democratic National Convention. Chris and I had a long and wonderful day together, talking about science, literature, movies, NIH, and other things. He subsequently visited the NIH and became, as is well known, a passionate and effective advocate for medical research generally and for stem cell research in particular. In his convention speech, he quoted the passage from FDR's dedication of the NIH campus in 1940 that opens chapter 10, always remembering how much FDR accomplished despite his paralysis.

Advocacy narrowly focused on a single disease is often problematic for leaders of the NIH, because such advocacy is likely to be inconsistent with the ways science works best. Furthermore, the goals of such advocacy are often spending levels that are difficult to measure accurately. For example, research on a specific neurological disease, like ALS (amyotrophic lateral sclerosis, or Lou Gehrig's disease), should, in principle, include basic studies of nerve cells and mechanisms of cell death, in addition to clinical trials in ALS patients, which are readily classified. The basic work may be impossible to classify by disease category, since it could help to understand many neurological diseases or others. This is where the concept of scientific opportunity comes into play: spending funds to seize a chance to understand a fundamental principle in biology is often a more effective approach to disease than mandating funds for research on a specific disease. Furthermore, efforts to understand another disease, even one that does not affect neurons, might prove to be a more valuable means to understand ALS than work on ALS itself.

My favorite examples of such serendipity come from the world I know best, cancer research. In the 1980s, as I described in part 2, our studies of retrovirus-induced breast cancer in mice led to the discovery of a class of genes, the wnt genes, which work in concert with several other genes that make components of what is called the wnt signaling pathway. Although there is still little evidence that this pathway plays a major role in human breast cancer, virtually every case of colon cancer is now known to be attributable to a defect in some part of the wnt pathway. Conversely, studies of a rat neuroblastoma (a brain tumor) in Bob Weinberg's laboratory revealed a new cancer gene (called neu, or HER2) that is often aberrant in human breast cancer. Today, an antibody (called Herceptin), formed against the protein made by the neu (HER2) gene, is used successfully in many thousands of women to prevent and treat metastatic breast cancer, as mentioned in chapter 7. So studies of breast cancer have helped with colon cancer, and studies of brain tumors have helped with breast cancer.

Apart from the difficulties of predicting where and how discoveries will arise, the priority setting process can be ugly—for instance, when advocates refuse to recognize, or to care, that funds for their disease must come from funds being spent elsewhere, including funds used for a disease important to another group of advocates. To justify their desires for more targeted spending, advocates will often claim that support for their disease has been historically inadequate or will focus on selected features of a disease that make the distribution of funds seem inequitable. Of course, very different impressions can be produced by the use of different criteria—the number of people living with a condition, the number who die from it each year, the age-adjusted death rate, the number of healthy individuals at risk, the number diagnosed each year, the annual medical expenditures, the annual costs to society, or the degree of pain and suffering. These are all legitimate aspects of the nation's burden of disease, but they are crude tools for deciding how to spend research dollars appropriately.

Nevertheless, such numbers are used, often to the discomfort of NIH and its institute directors. For much of my time at the NIH, I was castigated by advocates for research on heart disease because the NIH was spending about as much on AIDS research as on studies of heart disease, even though there were about twenty times more deaths from heart disease than from AIDS in the United States each year. The arguments tended to ignore other important facts: that AIDS was a new and expanding disease, that it is infectious, that it is devastating large parts of the world, or that age-adjusted death rates from heart disease have fallen by two-thirds in the past fifty years.

The passion behind such perceived injustices could produce some very unpleasant episodes, even when the NIH was making a genuine effort to expand research in disease areas where need and opportunity were clearly growing. For instance, I recall sitting through vituperative rants against the NIH by a Connecticut physician named Abraham Lieberman from the National Parkinson's Foundation, with his patient, a silent Muhammad Ali, by his side, while I was waiting to testify at a hearing about priority setting held by the House Commerce Committee in March 1998.*

Dr. Lieberman had (perhaps understandably) misconstrued an

---

* The fact that I was waiting suggested that the committee chairman, Mr. Bilirakis, had been persuaded to allow other witnesses to precede the government witnesses, who are usually heard first. But the transcript reveals that I had won Mr. Bilirakis's favor by listening to the multiple panels that preceded mine.

authorized level of funding for NIH research on Parkinson's disease, $100 million, to be a mandate to spend that much. Indeed, by our measure, the NIH was spending at least $100 million, but we judged that some was spent on studies that directly affected patients with Parkinson's disease (such as clinical trials or diagnositic tests) and some on the underlying disease mechanisms (such as nerve cell death or dopamine metabolism) that might also apply to other neurological diseases. This did not make Dr. Lieberman happy:

> What we're telling you is set up specific goals, conquer Parkinson's disease, and then you know you've spent the money well. To just give the National Institutes of Health additional moneys to do more and better science, you're going to be in the situation of saying to yourself, how do I know that I really did something. . . . [T]he scientists at the NIH have different priorities than the advocates of patients.[1]

It was not easy to listen to this from the back of the room.

In the same year, some advocates for diabetes research, responding to perfectly legitimate concerns about rising rates of diabetes, especially type 2 diabetes, adopted an unusually militant approach, openly criticizing my management of the NIH and even picketing the Illinois home of John Porter, the chairman of our House Appropriations Subcommittee. (The attack on Porter was ill-conceived: his wife was a diabetic, his concerns about the disease were evident, and his support for the NIH was unsurpassed.)

Responding to attacks of this kind is never easy, especially when the rhetoric becomes personal, the demands are excessive, and the budget isn't very flexible. In most instances, we designed a public hearing on the topic—often a workshop or (as for diabetes research) a larger symposium at the NIH, followed by a formal report from an outside advisory group—to review the current state of the disease and discuss new opportunities for studying it. Even when these conferences succeeded in defining areas that deserved a greater effort by the NIH and its grantees, it was often difficult to determine the numbers of dollars that should be shifted in the direction of the new efforts. After all, most of the extramural scientists who participated were already working in the contested area and had a vested interest in budget proposals that were as large as possible. At the same time, NIH staff felt an understandable obligation to moderate programmatic shifts and to protect current expenditures in other promising areas of work. These conflicting goals meant that plans could not easily satisfy all parties.

These comments are not meant to imply that advocacy for research on specific diseases is necessarily wrong, or that NIH leaders can simply divide up the funds according to the quality of grant applications, regardless of the research objectives. NIH must be (and it is) attentive to subject matter, and it must ensure (and it does) that at least some work is going on in all important areas. It should (and does) stimulate work on relatively neglected problems, especially when new opportunities arise, by advertising that funds are available for such research. One of the potential strengths of the NIH is its ability to encourage scientists throughout the country to pay greater attention to underserved and deserving problems, even when the new opportunities may not be obvious. Simply by encouraging attention to such problems—autism, rare neurological diseases, imaging methods, emerging infections, or bioengineering, to mention a few areas promoted during my tenure—new ideas may emerge to create those opportunities. In this regard, the NIH must walk a narrow line: to respond responsibly to public health needs and yet to provide the freedom for investigators to exercise their imaginations as fully as possible.*

Whenever the NIH tries to assign funds to defined categories of research, it enters a land of uncertain criteria and subjective judgment, and it risks undercutting the use of its resources for the best kind of unfettered research. The failure of other national research systems— most flagrantly, the Soviet system—is often attributed to excessive direction from a scientific hierarchy.

One of the by-products of the repeated debates about priority setting at the NIH was a 1998 report by the Institute of Medicine (IOM), entitled *Scientific Opportunities and Public Needs: Improving Priority Setting and Public Input*

---

* Some of these principles are set forth in a pamphlet on priority setting that the NIH published in 1997.[2]

at the NIH. While the study group recognized the inherent difficulties of allocating funds by disease category and acknowledged that the NIH generally made fair decisions, it was also critical of the limited avenues for redress that the NIH was said to provide.[3] One solution offered by the IOM report was especially useful—one that I wished I had conceived myself: the creation of a Council of Public Representatives (COPR). We swiftly established a group composed of thoughtful, well-known advocates for specific diseases who would agree to relinquish their individual loyalties when they entered a meeting room in order to give the NIH balanced advice about how to spend its money. After a complex nominating and vetting process, my staff and I brought together a truly remarkable group of individuals to serve on the COPR.* The council provided excellent advice on a wide variety of topics, not just on priority setting; as a result, we generally included some members in virtually all major relevant activities, such as the annual retreat of institute directors and various kinds of workshops. The COPR also offered safeguards against partisan attacks by disgruntled advocacy groups and showed that the NIH was open to public inspection and comment.

BALANCING GROWTH OF INSTITUTE BUDGETS

One of the strengths of the NIH is the fierce support it receives from members of the public, especially from those who are eagerly awaiting progress against disease. This kind of support is often focused on individ-

---

* Among the original members were David Frohnmayer, the president of the University of Oregon, who had three daughters with Fanconi's anemia; Robin Chin, a pharmacist, breast cancer survivor, and advocate for people with diabetes and HIV/AIDS; Lydia Lewis, the Executive Director of the National Depressive and Manic-Depressive Association; Pam Fernandes, a diabetic who lost her vision at age twenty-one, then became a championship bicyclist following a renal transplant; Roland McFarland, a broadcast executive with strong interests in diseases that disproportionately affect African-Americans; Rosemary Quigley (now deceased), a University of Michigan–trained lawyer and expert in health policy, with cystic fibrosis diagnosed at the age of six months; Debra Lappin, a public advocate on health and science policy and the former chair of the Arthritis Foundation; Barbara Lackritz (also now deceased), a speech pathologist who had battled chronic lymphocytic leukemia for a decade, cared for a husband with Parkinson's disease, wrote a book about adult leukemias, and established online services for leukemia patients; and several other extraordinary people.

ual institutes and centers by patient advocacy groups and professional societies. These groups can limit the possibilities for adjusting the distribution of funds across the institutes, since annual changes in each institute's budget are scrutinized carefully, to one hundredths of a percentage point, and any downward deviation from the NIH average is likely to result in appeals to influential congressional or administration advocates. This has the sometimes stultifying effect of keeping institute budgets in approximate lockstep, simply to avoid the inevitable outcry if one of them doesn't do well.

For these reasons, intense favoritism for one institute, especially a large one, can be problematic. Still, steep changes in the fortunes of a couple of institutes and centers were not deeply controversial. In the latter half of my time at the NIH, I was able to accelerate the growth of budgets at the Fogarty International Center, where the total was so low that a high growth rate to boost investments in global health had no significant effect on others, and at the National Human Genome Research Institute, which was understood to be funding the Human Genome Project, an enterprise highly valued by the entire NIH and by the worldwide scientific community.

But Vice-President Al Gore posed a potentially serious dilemma for the NIH late in 1997 when he proposed that the National Cancer Institute (NCI) should receive a much larger share than the other institutes in the record-breaking $1 billion budget increase that the president was going to request for the NIH for fiscal year 1999. Possibly as a result of promises made to cancer research advocates, possibly because of his personal concerns about cancer (his sister had died of lung cancer at an early age), possibly because cancer research was popular politically, Gore asked that the cancer institute's budget grow at twice the rate accorded the others.

I was very unhappy about this. The differential rates of growth were not in accord with clearly defined medical needs or with carefully considered scientific opportunities. No major changes in disease rates or outcomes and no sudden developments in cancer research made the needs for the NCI any greater than those for brain disorders, metabolic diseases, or infections. By any measure, the NCI was already the largest institute by a considerable margin, and Gore's plan would further accentuate the differences. And, of course, there would be a strong negative reaction from the supporters of the other institutes when the plan was announced. But he was the vice-president, and conceivably the next president, so the idea of arguing with him about this issue on my own was not appealing.

Fortunately, Donna Shalala strongly supported my position, and she insisted that we take up the matter directly with Gore. To his credit, he agreed to see us late one afternoon in early January of 1998, then listened stonily to our point of view. It was apparent that he felt committed to the goal of favoring cancer research in some fashion and that he needed a way to show that he had done so. To try to convince us that his formula would benefit the entire NIH, he speculated that rapid growth of the NCI would "act like an engine" to pull the other institutes up the budgetary hill. This idea was not persuasive. But we were able to reach a rapprochement when I pointed out that many institutes did cancer research, not simply the NCI, and he was surprised and pleased to learn this. That gave us an opening for a compromise: we would ensure a relatively large increase for cancer research, but it would be spread among all the institutes that could legitimately be said to work on cancer. Cancer research would have a short-term boost in funding, but discrepancies in the sizes of institute budgets would not increase in the long run. The percentage increase in funding for the NCI during the eventual doubling of the NIH budget would not—and ultimately did not—exceed the increases at other institutes. Of course, this was true, in part, because the pace of the doubling set by Congress exceeded the administration's plan. In those five years of bounty, no one needed to be pulled along by anyone else.

ENLARGING THE DIRECTOR'S POWERS

One of the limiting factors in my own efforts to respond to complaints about how the NIH spent its money was the lack of significant fiscal authority in the Director's Office. Of course, I had a role in determining the annual increase in budgets for individual institutes, and I tried to exercise this role by asking the institute directors to provide me with lists of new and expanded initiatives for the coming year. This allowed me to describe our budget request in a coordinated and appealing fashion by grouping the initiatives into Areas of Research Emphasis, which spanned the institutes, and it helped me to justify increases with substance, not simply with a vague or self-serving need to maintain budgetary growth. I also had, in most years, a very modest discretionary fund (usually no more than about $10 million, not enough to do much more with than fund a few grants that were scored just below the funding level) and the author-ity to transfer a limited amount of funds, usually up to 1 percent of the total, between institutes. Still, the Director's Office lacked the personnel required to plan and oversee research programs, so (without funds to build such staff) it was unrealistic to think about issuing contracts or grants from the central office, even if that was a desirable option.

The transfer authority, however, offered an opportunity for me to get more involved in the substantive work of the NIH, the awarding of grants. But the transfer of funds between institutes was also a mechanism that made institute directors anxious. Understandably, they did not wel-come the thought of losing control over any of their appropriated dollars. Nonetheless, they recognized that the transfer authority could be useful to the agency, as a mark of its flexibility, and that it was better to use it, even if sparingly, than to lose it. So, in most years, we would identify some projects that interested several institutes. Then, usually with the advice of some senior extramural investigators, we would move money from one or a few institutes into the pockets of another to allow such projects to be adequately supported.

The use of the transfer authority allowed me to see how the institutes could sometimes work more effectively together to achieve things that even the larger institutes could not easily do on their own. (Remember that the budgets of the institutes and centers ranged from under $50 mil-lion to more than $2 billion.) As I became more comfortable with my role as director—and sometimes frustrated by my limited options for involvement in scientific program development—I began to propose "trans-NIH" research initiatives that would benefit all parties without creating new institutes or centers.

For example, in the mid-1990s I learned that rapid progress was being made through studies of zebra fish, a versatile animal model that was a vertebrate (unlike fruit flies and roundworms) with relative rapid embryonic development and a short generation time, compared with mice and rats. I invited Leonard Zon, an especially articulate leader of zebra fish research at Harvard Medical School, to speak to a meeting of the institute directors. With Zon's help, I was able to persuade them to contribute to a fund, administered by one institute, that would accelerate the analysis of the zebra fish genome, isolate and characterize mutants, and study development and disease with this model organism.

Subsequently, similar successful initiatives were launched to study the genome of the laboratory mouse and the expressed genes of the laboratory rat. But, with time, the institute directors, even those with whom I was particularly friendly, became resistant to these efforts, seeing them as incursions on their turf and claiming that the initiatives complicated their budgets and oversight mechanisms. The message I took away from these discussions was that the NIH needed some reorganization to allow the director to have a stronger hand in program development. I will say more about this possibility later.

THE NIH'S ORGANIZATIONAL DILEMMA

Anyone who looks at an organizational chart of the NIH will be immediately struck by its complexity, especially by the multitude of institutes and centers, now twenty-seven, then twenty-four, each with its own authorities, leaders, and (nearly always) appropriated funds.

This, of course, is not the way the agency was initially designed. The individual components have been created over the past seventy years, in a fashion that reflects one of the most appealing things about the NIH— its supporters' passionate loyalty to the idea of using science to control disease. Each of the centers and institutes was legislated into being by members of Congress, commonly working together with citizen advocates, who believe that some aspect of biomedical research—a specific disease (like cancer or arthritis), a specific organ (like the heart or lung), a time of life (like aging or childhood), or a discipline (like nursing or bioengineering)—can benefit from the creation of a unit of the NIH devoted to it.

But the resulting proliferation of institutes and centers has not been healthy in every way. It has doubtless helped to drive budgetary growth for the NIH as a whole, but it has also created administrative redundancies. (Some of these were partly reversed during my time at the agency by the creation of inter-institute administrative centers.) The multitude of institutes has helped to focus attention on many important diseases and conditions and to sustain public advocacy for the NIH. At the same time, it has placed some topics at a disadvantage, because they are overseen by relatively small institutes that may lack the capacity to conduct large-scale efforts, like major clinical trials. Most plainly, the diversity of institutes complicates the central management of the NIH by the Director.

Despite my efforts to restrain further proliferation, three new centers and institutes were created during my tenure as director or shortly thereafter: the National Center for Complementary and Alternative Medicine (NCCAM), the National Institute of Biological Imaging and Bioengineering (NIBIB), and the National Center on Minority Health and Health Disparities (NCMHD). Each of these three new entities illustrates the same problem: their activities are pertinent to the studies of virtually all diseases, organs, and stages of life. For that reason, in my view, the research activities overseen by the new organizations would have been more properly assigned to the many preexisting institutes and centers, then monitored and coordinated by offices under the NIH director or by coalitions of representatives of the relevant institutes. Indeed, such coordinating bodies—the Office of Alternative Medicine, the Office of Minority Health Research, and the Bioengineering Consortium— preceded and gave birth to the new centers and institute. But passionate advocacy for the creation of these new organizations, by congressional leaders (such as Senator Tom Harkin for NCCAM), by congressional groups (such as the Congressional Black Caucus for NCMHD), and by leading academics (bioengineers and radiologists for NIBIB), proved too difficult to resist.

Resistance to these developments is especially difficult because the advocates are among the agency's best friends, so the legislation that creates a new unit is unlikely to be something over which an NIH director wants to take an unalterable stand. I well remember receiving a phone call from Tom Harkin, one of the NIH's strongest supporters, during the period when Congress was considering his proposal to convert the OAM into the NCCAM. We discussed my concerns about concentrating research on alternative medical practices in a new and separate center and my efforts to create a coordinating body that included representation from the CDC and FDA, as well as from most of the existing NIH institutes. But Harkin was not convinced. Then he said that if I didn't agree with his position and he got his way in Congress, I could simply resign. I was surprised by this proposal, since I was quite sure that he didn't really want me to leave, and I didn't perceive the issue as one that would compel me to fall on my sword. I told him that I was unlikely to change my views if he prevailed, but that I'd do my best to comply with the law by finding an outstanding leader for the NCCAM and helping the new center prosper. Needless to say, he did prevail, and I did not quit. Instead, I was able to recruit an extraordinary scientist, Steve Straus, to run the center,* and the center has done well. But the episode reveals how deep these passion may run.

During my final year at the NIH, I expressed my anxieties about the continuing proliferation of autonomous units at the NIH in public talks and extended the discussion in an essay published in *Science* magazine shortly after I left the agency.[4] In these presentations, I argued that, unless proliferation was stopped, the NIH would become an unmanageable collection of over fifty units within a decade or two at its current rate of growth. I then took the argument a step further, and proposed that the current organization of the NIH be reconsidered and redesigned, creating six centers of approximately equal size, including one for the director, giving him or her increased authority over coordinated programs, new initiatives, and budgets. Although this might have been the right way to build an NIH if it had been newly created, I did not expect my proposal to be adopted, given the strength of the advocacy for many of the existing components of the NIH. But I did hope to stimulate debate and find some measures adopted.

In 2001, at least in part in response to my published comments, the Institute of Medicine brought together a distinguished group to reexamine the structure of the NIH. While not subscribing to my more radical proposals, the IOM report did suggest an experiment with coalitions of institutes with related purposes (e.g., those devoted to studies of the

---

* Steve was a remarkable virologist, teacher, and leader, who unfortunately succumbed to a brain tumor in 2007.

brain and other parts of the nervous system), and it endorsed means for providing greater powers to the NIH director.[5] When the NIH was reauthorized in 2006, for the first time since 1993, barriers were installed against the creation of additional institutes and centers, and the NIH director was awarded new means for assessing the research portfolio and for initiating new programs.[6] The long-term effects of these changes on the NIH will be interesting to watch.

CHAPTER 12

Bad Times and Good Times as NIH Director

–

Some of the worst moments in the career of any agency or department chief are those in which he or she feels utterly powerless. There were for me at least two versions of these moments. In one category, I simply had to take the blame in front of a congressional committee for something bad that had happened at the NIH. In the other, political power overwhelmed any effort my colleagues and I had made to do the right thing.

TAKING THE BLAME: THE NSABP

Blame taking was one of my first experiences at a congressional hearing, in April 1994. Before I had arrived at the NIH, one of the NCI's largest clinical study groups—the National Surgical Adjuvant Breast and Bowel Project (NSABP), which conducted clinical trials on breast and bowel cancers—was under fire. One of the investigators in the network of study sites (this one, in fact, in Canada) had included a couple of ineligible patients in a trial, the consortium had been slow to correct the public record, and it had continued to use data from the same site, with the negligent investigators as coauthors, in subsequent studies. This prompted an extensive congressional investigation of the NSABP, its leaders, and the NCI's oversight and corrective measures. While it was clear that some wrongdoing had occurred at the Canadian site, it was also apparent from the NCI's analysis that the inclusion of data from the ineligible patients did not materially affect the conclusions of the study. Still, public apologies were in order.

The chairman of the oversight committee, John Dingell, did not make this easy or without drama. He opened the hearing with testimony from three young women who had recently been treated for breast cancer and were understandably frightened or outraged by irregularities in the conduct of studies they would be depending on.[1] This did not make my appearance, as part of a second panel composed entirely of male government officials, any easier. To try to ease the transition, I made a short impromptu speech "to say a word or two about the transition in mood," instead of launching immediately into my carefully prepared statement of contrition and explanation.

> We've just experienced an emotionally trying discussion by three women who have all been affected by . . . breast cancer studies. . . . We're going to now move into a more analytic mood to discuss the process by which the current events unfolded. . . . As we do that, I think it's important to realize that although we are five men at this table responsible for some of the events . . . we too have a deep passionate involvement in these issues.

I went on to mention my family's history of breast cancer, my own laboratory work on breast cancer, and the fact that our responsibilities at the NIH affect all people with disease, not just women with breast cancer, so that we are all subject to the consequences of slow or inadequate action by the NIH. Still, this did not appreciably reduce my discomfort or the chairman's eagerness to press his points home.

And there were more points for him to make. He had learned that the medical school at which some of the senior researchers in the NSABP worked, the University of Pittsburgh, was benefiting from a donation made to the school by the manufacturer of a drug that the NSABP was testing. I acknowledged my "concern about engaging in that kind of relationship," but Mr. Dingell pressed on, and this odd colloquy occurred:

Mr. Dingell: I wonder. Does it pass the Aunt Minnie Sniff Test?

Mr. Varmus: What test? I'm sorry.

Mr. Dingell: If Aunt Minnie were to sniff this, what would she say?

Mr. Varmus: Can you explain the test to me, sir?

Mr. Dingell: Well, Aunt Minnie is somebody we use around here because she has a sensitive nose. What we're trying to figure out is would she like the smell of this or not.

Mr. Varmus: Probably not.

Nonetheless, by the end of the day, the chairman seemed satisfied with our answers, stated his admiration for me and Sam Broder (then the director of the NCI), and offered his "expression of sorrow and apology . . . if things have happened here today which cause you distress." He also offered me a subtly threatening, backhanded compliment, noting that our efforts had been "significantly different and better than [those of] your predecessors, including one of your most immediate predecessors, Dr. Varmus," a barely disguised reference to Bernadine Healy, whose departure as NIH director had been attributed to Mr. Dingell's complaints about her.

Taking the Blame: Illegal Research at the NHGRI

Another moment of extreme discomfort on the congressional stage occurred a few years later, in 1997, when the staff members of Representative Joe Barton's Oversight and Investigations Subcommittee of the Committee on Commerce learned that an intramural investigator at the National Human Genome Research Institute (NHGRI), Mark Hughes, had violated the ban on the use of federal funds for human embryo research. Hughes was a talented young scientist who had served on the NIH Human Embryo Research Panel (see chapter 13), had developed a technically demanding method for genetic diagnosis by sequencing DNA from single cells, and was applying that method to tests of eight cell embryos produced by in vitro fertilization.*

---

* The strategy was to remove only one of the eight cells to test DNA for mutations like those that cause cystic fibrosis; the remaining seven cells would suffice to form an embryo that would develop into an apparently normal human being after implantation in the uterus.

Hughes had been told directly, by me and by others, that such work could not be done on the NIH campus or with federal funds, and was relocating his work to other places, including the nearby Suburban Hospital and Georgetown University. Unfortunately, he had conscripted NIH fellows to participate in projects that could not be performed by trainees on government salaries; even more problematic, he had apparently done some genetic diagnostic tests on human embryos in his NIH laboratory, and he had sent about a million dollars worth of government equipment to his new off-site laboratories, without notifying his superiors at the NHGRI.

Needless to say, this was a mess, and just the kind of mess that committee chairs belonging to the opposition party like to expose under the limelight. The problem was further compounded for me because Hughes's misdeeds had been discovered, and he had been subsequently fired, a few months before I learned about the situation. My awakening occurred when the story was reported in the *Chicago Tribune*, while I was at a malaria conference in Dakar. Unfortunately, my deputies in Building One and the head of the NHGRI, Francis Collins, had not determined who would inform me about the Hughes fiasco; as a result, no one did.

I was the sole witness at Barton's hearing and was understandably distressed when this embarrassing gap in communications surfaced after more than an hour of questioning:[2]

Mr. Burr: Let me ask you one additional question, if I may? When did you personally know that Dr. Hughes was conducting this illegal research at NIH?

Mr. Varmus: The full outline of what had been done and the equipment issues were laid before me when I returned from a trip to Africa in January of this year. . . .

Mr. Burr: Let me rephrase my—let me reask my question.

Mr. Varmus: All right.

Mr. Burr: When were you personally informed that Dr. Hughes was or had conducted illegal research at NIH?

Mr. Varmus: In January of this year.

Mr. Burr: . . . From the period of August to January, nobody at NIH told you?

Mr. Varmus: That's correct.

I might have thought that my admission was pretty clear, but my next questioner did not let go:

> *Mr. Klink:* . . . I can't figure out for the life of me why they fired him in October and you didn't find out until January that this had occurred. That is just incomprehensible to me that somebody doesn't e-mail or pick up a phone or send a memo or a letter or something in that whole period of time, October, November, December, January.
>
> *Mr. Varmus:* This is, again, a very unusual circumstance. We have a fairly open communications system and we have asked ourselves this question. Apparently, many people assumed that someone else had done it but it hadn't occurred. It is rather unfortunate given the circumstances.

This was not a pleasant experience, but the outcome could have been worse. Because Francis Collins and I did not try to hide anything and came to the hearing equipped with a plan to correct deficiencies, the reprimands were mild, given the circumstances. Barton and I had not had difficulties before, and he seemed to have more than a little respect for me and the NIH. So, aside from some bruised feelings, danger was averted.

ERGONOMICS

A seemingly innocuous request to the NIH to commission a study of repetitive stress injuries in the workplace proved to be a much more grueling experience than a violation of embryo research rules. Henry Bonilla, a conservative Republican member of our House Appropriations Subcommittee from San Antonio, had requested the study during discussion of the fiscal year 1999 NIH budget early in 1998, on behalf of small-business owners belonging to the Chamber of Commerce. The intent, however, was not to protect workers from injury; it was to delay implementation of regulations that had been recommended by a recent, large-scale report from the CDC's National Institute of Occupational Safety and Health (NIOSH) and strongly endorsed by leading Democratic members of Congress.[3] I was being asked to use funds in the NIH budget to pay the National Research Council (NRC) at the National Academies for a two-year study of the issues, on the assumption that no regulations would be issued until the new study had been completed.

This put me—a nonexpert, sympathetic to the NIOSH report, but also protective of the NIH budget—in an unenviable position. If I refused to commission the study, the Republicans (then in control of Congress) were likely to hold back on proposed increases in the NIH budget. If I agreed to pay for it, my Democratic allies in Congress would be angry, and my colleagues at NIOSH and elsewhere in the Public Health Service would accuse me of selling my soul for NIH funding when a consensus among experts had already been published by NIOSH. I proposed a compromise, one that was ultimately adopted, but one that won me no friends. The NIH would ask the NRC to hold a workshop of experts to reevaluate the field and review the findings of the NIOSH study in about six months, rather than two years, but before regulations were issued.*

Some Republicans accused me of asking for a shoddy study, and my patron, John Porter, was obliged to assemble a small group, which included Mr. Bonilla, the Speaker of the House at the time, Robert Livingston,** and the Whip, Tom DeLay, to lecture me severely about the weakness of my compromise. David Obey, the ranking Democrat on the House committee and a strong friend of both labor and the NIH, called to decry my willingness to sell out workers for NIH dollars. The head of NIOSH called to say that she was disturbed by the NIH's willingness to allow another study of what their report had so thoroughly evaluated. And NRC staff, who had been promoting the project with Republican members, were disappointed not to have the more lucrative contract for a larger study. Like all things, this situation passed, but for several weeks I was unpopular on all sides.

---

* A report of the findings of this workshop was published by the National Academies Press in 1998.[4]

** The report ultimately included answers to seven questions provided by Mr. Livingston.

Needle Exchange

The ergonomics debacle was a clearly partisan issue, pitting Democrats against Republicans over my poor body. But bad times could be had without going outside the Clinton administration.

Congress had given the secretary of HHS the authority to declare that federal funds could be used for needle-exchange programs, provided that she ascertained that needle exchange protected health and did not promote drug use. In view of the persistent transmission of HIV and hepatitis viruses among drug addicts, the limited number of state and city needle-exchange programs, and the need for further study of such programs, the leaders of the Public Health Service agencies and Secretary Shalala herself were motivated to lift the ban on the use of federal funds for needle exchange. Early in 1998, with help from investigators at the National Institute of Drug Abuse (NIDA), I assembled the published studies on the relevant topic and was convinced that there were strong data favoring reduced transmission of lethal viruses by needle-exchange programs and at least acceptable evidence that needle exchange did not foster drug use. My colleagues at the FDA and CDC, David Kessler and David Satcher, also provided information that supported the secretary's proposal to lift the ban on funding.

Of course, a step of this magnitude could not be taken without presidential approval, and we knew there was reason to be concerned about whether the president would subscribe. His decision was going to be conveyed to us on a Monday morning, April 20, 1998. We then learned that General Barry McCaffrey, the head of the White House office on drug control, was going to spend the preceding weekend with the president, flying to and from Santiago, Chile. McCaffrey had been generally supportive of NIDA's efforts to approach drug addiction as a disease state rather than a criminal act, but he was adamantly opposed to needle exchange, which he saw as an inducement to drug use. So it wasn't a complete surprise, just a terrible disappointment, to the several of us gathered with Donna Shalala at department headquarters that Monday morning, when we learned that the White House had ruled against Donna's proposal to lift the ban.[5]

By coincidence, that very night Connie and I had a long-standing date for dinner with Rahm Emanuel, then a domestic policy adviser in the White House.* I was mourning the defeat of our needle-exchange proposal, but Emanuel was not sympathetic. In his view, the policy change would have opened the administration and the Democratic party to charges that they were soft on drugs. Since Carol Moseley Braun, an African American senator from Illinois, was running for reelection and had already been damaged by other revelations about her time in office, Emanuel was convinced that a lenient policy on needle exchange would further impair her chances of reelection and the Democrats' chance of regaining control of the Senate. As it turned out, everyone lost: we didn't get our policy change, drug abusers didn't get help from the federal government, Moseley Braun lost her seat, and the Democrats remained the minority party in both houses of Congress. The only satisfaction we received was the later admission by Bill Clinton, speaking at an international AIDS conference in Spain, less than two years after he left the White House, that his failure to lift the ban on funding needle exchange was wrong and one of the worst decisions he made during his presidency.[6]

TOWN-GOWN RELATIONS

Like any other large organization embedded in a community of residents, the NIH and I were potential targets for complaints about our effects on the quality of local life. Sometimes these were relatively trivial, as when some neighbors, accustomed to walking across our campus to the Metro station, objected to the mending of the holes in our fences, their points of entry onto the campus. (We left the holes open then. But now, in an era of tightened security, the entire NIH campus is ringed with an impenetrable barrier.) Sometimes the concerns could be mollified with information, as when the NIH built a secure facility for working with potentially dangerous microorganisms, such as drug-resistant strains of the bacterium that causes tuberculosis. By offering tours of the facility and explanations

---

* The dinner had been arranged through Rahm's brother, Zeke, an oncologist and Amherst College graduate, who had recently been recruited to head the bioethics program at the NIH Clinical Center.

of its safety features, the community reaction subsided. At other times, though, the conflicts escalated.

One of the first disagreements I encountered after becoming director was a long-standing feud between NIH and its neighbors over allegations that incineration of medical and laboratory waste on campus was polluting the neighborhood. Experts had been brought in to support the claims of both sides, debates had occurred over the best ways to perform decisive tests, and the rhetoric from some community members had become nasty. I thought it might help to have a discussion with some neighbors critical of the NIH, so I arranged a dinner meeting with a few of the more prominent ones at a Bethesda restaurant. The event was congenial and informative, but a local newspaper blasted me in banner headlines for violating the First Amendment when I excluded its reporter from the dinner group.

I agreed to hold an open forum on the incinerator issue in the small auditorium in Building One on a weekday evening. The room was full, local television stations broadcast the event live, and the exchanges were heated. At the end of the evening, I surprised the audience by announcing that we would close our campus incinerator. By then, I had learned that we had other, better ways to dispose of our waste, that incineration technology had improved, and that our facility was no longer state-of-the-art and was beyond simple renovation. Still, not everyone was happy. For some, it seemed that my decision eliminated what had become a full-time occupation. For others, closure of our incinerator meant that certain kinds of tests, with the unit in operation, could no longer be performed. We did carry out extensive testing of soil samples to examine claims that safety standards had been violated in the past, but never found evidence of that. Still, I suspect that some neighbors remain unconvinced. But the public debates ended long ago.

GOOD TIMES

Given the unpleasant aspects of the NIH director's job—the predictably tedious and repetitive steps in the appropriations process, the vagaries of priority setting, the occasional criticisms from Congress or advocacy groups or fellow scientists—what were its redeeming qualities, and why did I like it? For I did enjoy it.

Above all, there was the pride, excitement, and (at times) historical significance of being the leader of the largest funding agency for medical research in the world. The position represents medical science and the good things it does for the country, if not the world. I felt this when working within the administration, when speaking to members of Congress, when talking to reporters, and when addressing the public at commencement exercises and elsewhere. In this symbolic capacity, when giving ceremonial talks, I enjoyed citing FDR's ringing phrases at the dedication of the expanded NIH campus in Bethesda during his third election campaign in 1940, a year before the U.S. entry into World War Two:

> The total defense, which this Nation seeks, involves a great deal more than building airplanes, ships, guns and bombs. We cannot be a strong Nation unless we are a healthy Nation. And so we must recruit not only men and materials but also knowledge and science in the service of national strength. . . . All of us are grateful that we in the United States can still turn our thoughts and our attention to those institutions of our country which symbolize peace—institutions whose purpose it is to save life and not to destroy it.

In 1997, I became the first scientist in fifty-one years to deliver the Harvard commencement address. As a representative of medical science, I tried to explain the importance of what had been done to improve health during the past century, NIH's current role as a defense against disease, and the parts that graduates might play in the future.[7]

I enjoyed participating in administration politics, negotiating for the NIH when leaders of the other federal science agencies were called together by the Office of Management and Budget or by a congressional committee. Often the best way to support the NIH and science in general was to make a magnanimous gesture toward the other agencies, emphasizing their importance in an increasingly interdisciplinary world of science and hoping that the gesture would be reciprocated. This strategy was appreciated by my colleagues in the other disciplines, helped to dispel jealousies about our fiscal success, and is remembered as a hallmark of my time at the NIH.

I learned that the NIH director also had sufficient convening power to help bring together the leaders of research organizations in several countries. In the latter half of my tenure, the heads of some governmental and private funding agencies in the United States and Europe began to meet regularly to talk about shared issues, such as intellectual property, research ethics, public support for science, peer review, and other things. I found gratification in the prospect of making research a more interactive, international activity, one in which values and approaches and information were shared.

VISITORS TO THE NIH

I also enjoyed bringing influential members of Congress and the administration to the NIH campus to show them some of the most visible aspects of biomedical science (such as methods for imaging brain and heart functions, other research involving patients, or microscopic views of chromosomes) and to tell them about progress in deciphering genomes, treating AIDS, or understanding cancer or neurological diseases. Most frequently, our visitors were members of our appropriating or authorizing committees seeking such show-and-tell to improve their ability to legislate. Sometimes a congressional leader, like Richard Gephardt, the House Democratic leader, would turn up and talk with a few of us about science policy for an hour or two out of an unalloyed interest in what the NIH does.

To interrupt the cultural dominance of science on the NIH campus at least once a year, I initiated an annual cultural lectureship by inviting the actress Jane Alexander, who was then serving as administrator of the National Endowment for the Arts, to give the first talk. Robert Pinsky, the U.S. poet laureate, was among the subsequent lecturers, and he later returned the favor by inviting me to participate in his imaginative Favorite Poem Project at the Library of Congress. To prepare, I spent a pleasant weekend at home reading aloud from old anthologies, seeking a poem of moderate length that would be both entertaining and fun to read. Given the venue, I was delighted to discover that the poem I selected, Andrew Marvell's "To His Coy Mistress," had been an essential part of the circumstances that first brought Jesse Helms, a leading senator during my years in Washington, to public attention. Helms, a radio commentator in North Carolina in the 1960s, had aired a story about a college professor who assigned his students the task of writing a letter that captured the seductive argument of Marvell's poem. The incident, with a picture of Helms, was reported in *Life* magazine; the teacher was reassigned to nonclassroom duties.

Of course, no visitors to the NIH were more important than members of the First Family. Only a few days after taking my oath of office near the end of November 1993, I was invited to a small party at the White House for that year's crop of American Nobel laureates. Hillary Clinton greeted me like a long-lost friend, the start of what remains a relationship of mutual admiration. We agreed that she'd soon pay a visit to the NIH campus. A few months later, on February 17, she came to Bethesda for a full day of meetings with NIH and university scientists, a tour of the campus, visits to patients participating in research protocols, and a speech to an enthusiastic crowd of NIH employees. Her wide interests and penetrating comments amazed the scientists who spent the day with her. She clearly understood the basic principles of genetics. When told about germ line mutations that confer risks of breast cancer, she asked why those mutant genes had been preserved, not eliminated, during human evolution. When we talked about retroviruses and AIDS, she told me that she had recently been helping her daughter, Chelsea, prepare a high school report on the retrovirus life cycle. And she promised to get the other members of her family to the NIH campus soon.

Chelsea, then contemplating a career in medicine or genetics, came first, in the last week in June of 1994, to work for a week in the NCI laboratory of a bacterial geneticist, Susan Gottesman, and to visit other laboratories each afternoon. She, too, seemed remarkably talented. In the course of the week, she isolated three bacterial mutants (called CC1, CC2, and CC3, and no doubt carefully preserved in the Gottesman laboratory). When she visited my laboratory, she wanted to know what we, as retrovirologists, thought was the explanation for the resistance shown by some Kenyan sex workers to infection by HIV. (This topic remains an area of active investigation.)

The president's first visit, on August 5, 1995, during a relaxed summer weekend, began with the broadcast of his Saturday morning radio address, given from the Children's Inn at the NIH, on the topic of the recently passed Family Leave Act.[8] Following his performance (and after shaking many hands on the campus's North Drive), we drove to the NIH Clinical Center for an unpublicized tutorial on the science of AIDS, cancer, and the human genome. Like his wife, the president was a quick study. When told how kidney cancer cells in a petri dish could be returned to normal by introduction of a certain gene, he expressed appropriate doubt that that could be done to a kidney cancer growing in a patient. He seemed to understand, absorb, and enjoy some complex ideas about the location of breast cancer genes in chromosomes, hormonal and drug treatments for AIDS, and progress on the Human Genome Project. Still, when he recalled that day in his autobiography,[9] I was disappointed to find no mention of the science briefing we had provided, only an account of visiting and joking with Sam Donaldson, the television host, who was then a patient in the Clinical Center.

I also enjoyed sharing the success of NIH-funded science, usually by participating in press conferences when NIH scientists had some exciting discovery or other milestone to announce: the cloning of the breast cancer gene BRCA-1; the demonstration that an antiviral drug can reduce maternal transmission of HIV to newborns; the complete sequencing of an animal genome (the first was the genome of the roundworm, *C. elegans*); the outcome of studies showing that tamoxifen reduces the rate of appearance of breast cancer; and many others. I enjoyed representing our science at the White House, both on celebratory occasions (as when the Clintons invited new batches of Nobel Laureates each November or when they orchestrated a millennium event in the East Room to talk about the science of genomes and computer science*) or on more routine occasions (as when the president asked for briefings on AIDS, global health, or the human genome). Because I was nearly always conscious of the symbolic value of my position, I also felt a pleasurable seriousness when asked to comment on contentious issues by the press,

---

* The evening featured a lively discussion among the head of the largest U.S. sequencing center, Eric Lander; the Internet codeveloper Vint Cerf; and the two Clintons.

when called to testify even on unpleasant topics by Congress, or when asked to help resolve an internal disagreement over budgets or some international or interagency unhappiness over aspects of the Human Genome Project.

Representing the NIH in interagency discussions was sometimes less a pleasure than an act of self-defense. But a willingness to be involved did bring occasional dividends. A commonly used platform for convening these discussions was the National Science and Technology Council (NSTC), an amalgam of the leaders of principal departments and agencies that conducted or depended on scientific work. When I first arrived in Washington, I had fought to be included on the NSTC, since the only position assigned to the Department of HHS was occupied by Donna Shalala; but she had been happy to campaign for my inclusion. As I soon learned, the NSTC principals rarely met, and, if they did, it was generally within the context of an NSTC subcommittee. Meetings of the subcommittees were normally attended by lower-ranking representatives of the agencies, so little business was transacted. But the NSTC subcommittee on basic science that I cochaired with the director of the National Science Foundation (initially Neal Lane, later Rita Colwell) and an associate director of the White House Office of Science and Technology Policy (initially Ernie Moniz, later Artie Bienenstock) often had significant issues before it. To make better progress, I suggested that the three of us meet unofficially at the Firehook Bakery on Connecticut Avenue, near my house in Woodley Park, and this efficient, nonbureaucratic practice continued for several years.

One of our topics on the NSTC subcommittee was the status of American research efforts in Antarctica. Senator Ted Stevens of Alaska had questioned the tenfold difference in budgets for science in the Arctic and the Antarctic, a difference that might be further increased if the South Pole Research Station received an expensive proposed overhaul. So the NSTC assembled a study group to evaluate the multiagency efforts being made in Antarctica. As a member of the Antarctica study group, I enjoyed what were doubtless my best few days in government.

In January of 1996, just as the failed negotiations between Speaker Gingrich and President Clinton over the fiscal year 1996 budget were shutting down the federal government, Washington experienced its biggest snowstorm in years.* A few days later, with the U.S. government closed and melting snow leaking into our house in Woodley Park, I boarded a plane to Christchurch, New Zealand, and then connected to a Navy C-130 cargo plane that flew a few passengers and abundant cargo to the McMurdo Station in Antarctica. Over the next few days of astral summer, the sun never set and I rarely slept as we toured the large lab at McMurdo, roamed through excavations of glaciers, took helicopter trips to the Dry Valleys, and flew another C-130 to visit the South Pole Station's physics and meteorological projects. There was also time to meet penguins, see the Shackelton cabin, try ice fishing, climb the hills around McMurdo, take a cross-country ski trail toward Mount Erebus, and learn to build snow houses. If this were typical of government service, everyone would want to do it.

THE NIH DIRECTORSHIP IN RETROSPECT

As the preceding anecdotes illustrate, I had both good days and bad days as NIH director. But, looking back on the experience, I take some pride in my accomplishments as an agency chief. I believe that I effectively promoted the idea that public service as director of one of the NIH institutes could be a desirable and gratifying job—indeed generally more interesting and decisive than the NIH director's position—despite the low pay and governmental rules. During my term, I recruited many outstanding people to run individual institutes,** encouraged the idea that

---

* The three-foot blanket of snow allowed me to fulfill a pledge to myself to ski from home to NIH before my tour of duty was over. Setting off in blizzard conditions and breaking a trail through drifts in Rock Creek Park, I arrived on the NIH campus exhausted about four hours later, just as the sun was breaking through the clouds and plows were beginning to clear the streets. My secondary goal was to persuade Steve Hyman and his wife, Barbara Bierer, both Harvard faculty members, to accept job offers at the NIH on a day when the snow had trapped them in Washington. I succeeded with this mission too. Steve, now the Provost at Harvard, did a remarkably effective job as director of the National Institute of Mental Health.
** Among the most notable were Zach Hall and Gerry Fischbach as sequential directors of NINDS, Rick Klausner (officially recruited by Donna Shalala and appointed by the president) as director of the NCI, Alan Leshner as director of NIDA, Jim Battey as director of the National Institute of Deafness and Communications Disorders, and Allen Spiegel as director of the National Institute of Diabetes, Digestive, and Kidney Diseases, as well as Steve Hyman at NIMH, and several other directors, scientific directors, and deputy directors.

these were not lifetime appointments, established five-year evaluations of directors by outsiders, and emphasized opportunities for institutes to work collaboratively on behalf of the entire agency. My ability to do these things and others was enhanced by budgetary success, crowned by the agreement between the executive and legislative branches to double the NIH budget over five years. Budgetary growth improved the mood of scientists in the external sector when success rates for grant applicants returned to reasonable levels (about one in three), after having fallen to about one in five earlier in the decade. The intramural research program also flourished, with the improved management recommended by the Marks-Cassell report and with the funding and construction of several new buildings, especially the Mark O. Hatfield Clinical Research Center, the Louis B. Stokes Research Building, and the Dale and Betty Bumpers Vaccine Research Center.

Now that I have been doing another job, as president of the Memorial Sloan-Kettering Cancer Center (MSKCC), in New York City, for longer than I served as NIH director, I am often asked how the jobs differ and whether one is easier than the other. These are revealing questions. In some ways, MSKCC is a smaller and simpler organization. It operates solely in the New York metropolitan area, not throughout the world; it has less than half as many employees as the NIH, and no grantees; it is composed of only two major institutions (Memorial Hospital and Sloan-Kettering Institute), not twenty-seven institutes and centers; and the annual budget is about fifteen times smaller than the NIH budget. The administrative organization is also simpler, with only three critical people reporting to me (the heads of the hospital and the institute, and the senior vice-president for administration), whereas at the NIH I was responsible for the heads of all twenty-four institutes and centers, my several deputies, and the heads of all the offices in the central administration.

But in other ways, my current job is more complex. At NIH, the funds came through only one route, congressional appropriations, and the only objective—admittedly simple in concept, if not in execution—was to spend all of it wisely before the last day of the fiscal year. At MSKCC, the money enters through many different doors (payments for patient care, donations, grants from a multitude of sources, royalties and licensing fees, returns on investments), in varying and unpredictable amounts, at any time of the year. And the scheduling and goals of spending are similarly diverse, carried out with much greater independence. At the NIH, we were always conscious of working on an open stage, subject to the views of the public and interrogation by the press. I was always vulnerable to the oversight of all 535 members of Congress, many senior members of the administration (including anyone at or above the rank of assistant secretary in the Department of HHS and several people in the White House, the OMB, and OSTP).

In contrast, MSKCC has the advantage of being not only a private, nonprofit institution, free of requirements to do our business according to federal rules, but also a free-standing cancer center, without a need to coordinate with other departments or schools, as would be necessary at a university-based center. Thus, beyond the obvious need for the most senior leaders to work with common purpose, the only immediate source of governance is our Board of Overseers and Managers. The board is composed of nearly sixty successful, intelligent, well-connected, and usually wealthy individuals who joined the board with the intention of helping the center succeed in its aspirations to care for cancer patients, to study biological systems, to discover better ways to treat and prevent cancer, and to train clinicians and scientists for the future. Dealing with Congress and the administration, with their many responsibilities and various ambitions, was (and is) a much more difficult endeavor.

There is no simple answer to the question of which job I prefer on operational grounds. But government jobs like the one I held can grind you down, because of their importance, the public exposure they afford, and the incessant and inevitable conflicts. Just rereading, for the composition of this book, the calendars that list my scheduled meetings, talks, and travels during more than three hundred weeks at the NIH has induced wonder, weariness, and (frankly) self-admiration.

After six years, I had had enough, and was ready to fulfill my promise to Connie that we'd remain in her hometown, a place she had come to dislike, for no more than that. News that I had accepted the presidency at MSKCC began to leak to the newspapers in August and was announced officially in October. The latter half of December was a tumultuous time of celebrations—a farewell ceremony at the NIH Clinical Center, a sixtieth birthday party that featured a reunion of many of my laboratory trainees and older colleagues at Cold Spring Harbor Laboratory, and a night of revelry with friends in D.C. to celebrate the arrival of the year 2000. On January 1, we decamped for New York, MSKCC, and the new millennium.

Part Four

CONTINUING CONTROVERSIES

CHAPTER 13

Embryos, Cloning, Stem Cells, and the Promise of Reprogramming

—

OVER THE PAST DECADE, STEM CELL RESEARCH HAS BECOME THE MOST visible and contentious manifestation of the promise of biological science, akin to the Human Genome Project in the 1990s or recombinant DNA research and biotechnology in the 1970s and 1980s. The term "stem cells"—shorthand for the controversial type, human embryonic stem cells—is now widely recognized, and it represents a defining issue for candidates in national and local politics.

To a biologist, "stem cells" has a precise meaning, encompassing more than the human embryonic type that attracts political attention. All of the many specialized cells in animals and human beings have developed through an orderly process in which cells divide and differentiate. At the beginnings of these developmental pathways are immature cells with the capacity to produce two types of daughter cells when they divide: one daughter cell is indistinguishable from its parent (and has the same capacities), while the other has taken a step toward specialization. These immature cells, which both renew themselves and produce differentiated offspring, are called stem cells. Many stem cells reside in adult tissue and have restricted abilities to differentiate, becoming cells only in a particular organ, such as the skin, the liver, the brain, or the blood system. But stem cells with much greater potential are abundant much earlier in animal development, in the first stages, the early embryo. These early embryonic stem cells can serve as precursors to all of the cells that form the tissues and organs of a mature animal; because of this "plural" potential, they are called pluripotent.

Embryonic stem cells have achieved prominence in part because of the still unsubstantiated hopes that therapies that use them can ameliorate a variety of human ailments. They have attracted controversy mainly because the cells are obtained from human embryos, linking stem cell research to historical battles over abortion and over the legal and moral status of the human embryo and fetus.

The current debates about stem cells and the policies governing their use were influenced by three pivotal events that occurred during my tenure as director of the NIH in the 1990s: an NIH panel's prophetic report in 1994 about the prospects for research on the early human embryo; the birth of the lamb named Dolly, the first animal cloned from an adult cell, in 1997; and the isolation and growth of pluripotent stem cells from very early human embryos in 1998. To understand the nature and history of the debates, it is helpful to consider how these three topics—embryo research, reproductive cloning, and embryonic stem cells—are interwoven, both biologically and politically. It will also be important to describe newer methods, less controversial than those involving the use of embryos, that can also produce pluripotent cells. Together, these developments have changed our concepts of biological systems and driven political discussions of science to new levels of complexity.

Each of the three events in the 1990s had a defining characteristic. The 1994 report on human embryo research, inspired by scientific opportunities arising largely from then recent work with mouse embryos, recommended that many (but not all) of those opportunities be pursued by the NIH with human cells and embryos. The report also anticipated important advances in mammalian biology that might allow embryo-related research to be applied beneficially in clinical settings. Although written in response to a new and potentially permissive political environment, changes in the political climate soon led to prohibitions that continue to limit much of the research recommended in the report. The birth of Dolly in 1997 was a remarkable scientific accomplishment, which fundamentally altered the way that biologists view the control of genetic information in animal cells. It revealed a greater than expected capacity to "reprogram" cells—to reset the genetic program that guides development. But Dolly's birth also unleashed fears about human reproductive cloning, and these have restricted the pursuit of a promising method for reprogramming cells for therapeutic purposes. Finally, the advent of research on human embryonic stem cells, following the growth of the first lines of such cells in 1998, moved the ethical debates about the use of human embryos from speculation to pragmatic immediacy, with clear implications for the pace at which such research would proceed in this country.

THINKING ABOUT RESEARCH WITH HUMAN EMBRYOS

Any account of recent developments in embryo research, cloning, and stem cells must begin at least a few decades before animal clones and human embryonic stem cells were announced, with brief descriptions of two underlying accomplishments: the successful development in the United Kingdom of in vitro fertilization (IVF) procedures in the late 1970s and the flowering of genetic engineering with experimental mice in the 1980s.

The birth of Louise Brown, the first child conceived by IVF, in England in 1978, fundamentally changed the perspectives of society toward the early stages of human development.[1] The idea of manipulating life, by allowing fertilization of an egg by a sperm cell to occur in a test tube, and then implanting a tiny embryo into a receptive uterus days later, met with expected resistance. But the initial resistance has by now been overwhelmed by the success of IVF procedures to treat reproductive failures, allowing many thousands of infertile couples to enjoy the satisfactions of bearing and raising children.

In the years immediately following the initial successes of IVF, the U.S. government established a requirement that any proposed research on human fertilization, embryos, or the later fetal stage of development must be reviewed by an ethics advisory board before federal funds could be used to support it. From 1980 until 1993, in the administrations of Ronald Reagan and George H. W. Bush, no board was ever assembled and no federal dollars were ever spent on such research. Consequently, IVF work in this country was largely confined to clinical use, often in the private sector; improvements in IVF methods came largely from research done abroad. Furthermore, no federally supported research was performed to explore the use of cells or tissues from aborted fetuses or from unused early embryos to treat human diseases, such as Parkinson's disease, that were caused by loss of normal cells.

In 1993, Bill Clinton's arrival in Washington reactivated the possibility of supporting research on the developing forms of human beings—embryos and fetuses. Among the new president's first actions was to sign a new NIH reauthorization bill that removed prior constraints on the use of federal funds for research with human fetal tissue and embryos.[2] Soon thereafter, NIH began to fund fetal tissue research—for example, clinical trials of fetal brain cell treatments for Parkinson's disease—under guidelines that already existed for the ethical acquisition and use of fetal tissues.*

But no administration had considered the prospects of research on human materials from a much earlier stage of development, the preimplantation embryo. This stage normally begins with the fertilization of an egg by a single sperm cell, forming a one-cell embryo, also called the zygote, that divides several times during the next ten to fourteen days, after which the embryo normally implants in the wall of the uterus. At that point, the embryo begins to form the three basic tissue layers that are precursors to many types of cells present in mature organs, even though no recognizable nervous system or other organs are yet discernible.

Preimplantation human embryos had been produced commonly for many years by IVF, the union of a donated egg and sperm in a test tube, with the intention of producing offspring for otherwise infertile couples. A few days after IVF, embryos that appear viable are placed in a woman's birth canal in hopes that one or more will implant in the uterine wall and develop into a normal baby. However, not all embryos produced by in vitro fertilization are actually used in efforts to produce new offspring, either because the embryos do not appear normal or, more commonly, because the IVF clinic has generated more embryos than were needed to achieve a couple's reproductive goals.

Because research on the IVF process or the resulting early embryos had never been conducted with federal funds in the United States, either

---

* Such tissues are usually obtained, with parental consent, after medically supervised abortions, performed about two to four months after conception.

before or after the birth of Louise Brown, there were no guidelines or regulations for such studies. This meant that the federal funding of human embryo research in any of its aspects—in vitro fertilization, formation of the zygote (the fertilized egg), the early cell divisions, and first steps in differentiation of these tiny clumps of human cells—would have to be deferred until the various types of embryo research could be more carefully evaluated and guidelines proposed.

There were good reasons to examine the prospects. During the preceding two or three decades, biologists had made enormous progress by studying the early development of embryos of mice, the most widely studied mammal. It is relatively easy to obtain fertilized eggs from laboratory mice and then observe the subsequent cell divisions until the embryos comprise fifty to one hundred cells or more and are ready for implantation into the female reproductive tract. At this stage, disaggregated cells from the mouse embryos can grow and divide indefinitely in petri dishes when fed appropriately. These cells are also able to develop into all kinds of organs or tissues. For instance, if they are injected into an intact embryo, which is then allowed to mature into a newborn mouse, descendants of the stem cells can contribute to any part of the mature animal. Thus they meet the definition of a pluripotent stem cell: they divide to yield daughter cells that are indistinguishable from the starting cells ("self-renewal"), and they differentiate into a wide variety of types ("pluripotency").

Over the past couple of decades, work with early mouse embryos—and with stem cells derived from them—has been dramatically enhanced by some powerful new methods that allow genetic modification of the mouse germ line and rigorous study of mammalian gene functions. DNA mapping and sequencing—features of the Mouse Genome Project—have defined the genetic composition and organization of mouse chromosomes and identified genes that are involved in the formation and function of specific tissues. Genes that govern normal development and produce disease are now routinely studied in mice by altering the genetic makeup of the early embryo. This can be done in either of two ways. First, genes can be added to the mouse germ line, putting them directly into fertilized eggs, and the genes will then be transmitted to mouse progeny.[3] Before this maneuver, the genes can be mutated to mimic genetic alterations observed in human diseases or engineered to be expressed as an investigator wishes. In the second approach, any gene in a cultured embryonic stem cell can be specifically targeted to make mutations that explore normal functions of the gene or recapitulate mutations found in human diseases.[4] Again, by appropriate manipulations, these mutations can enter the germ line of mature mice. These two methods have been extraordinarily important for studying normal functions and many diseases in a mammalian species, but they are currently, and appropriately, forbidden in human beings.*

By 1993, work with mouse embryos had stimulated many provocative and testable ideas about how early cells differentiate to form mature tissues and about how diseases arise. These ideas are pertinent to analogous human events, in part because of the great similarities observed between mice and human beings when their genomes, biochemical properties, and cell functions are compared. By the early 1990s, it was also widely appreciated that many human embryos were stored in freezers and destined for destruction at IVF clinics in the United States and elsewhere, because they had been kept in a frozen state too long for efficient implantation in a uterus or because the sperm and egg donors had either already achieved parenthood or had abandoned attempts to reproduce for other reasons. Thus, many kinds of work on human embryos would be feasible without creating additional embryos for research purposes.

But what work ought to be pursued? Late in 1993, after legal constraints on federal funding of human embryo and fetal tissue research had been eased, my NIH colleagues and I assembled a group to think about this question. The Human Embryo Research Panel was asked to survey the experimental possibilities in the realm of human embryo research and recommend the ones that deserved to be pursued with federal funds, on the basis of scientific merit, possible medical applications, and ethical implications.**

We were fortunate to attract a wide range of eminent people, from

---

* Three scientists who developed the methods for making targeted mutations in mice received the 2007 Nobel Prize in Physiology or Medicine.

** It is important to note that the panel was not asked to rule on whether or not certain kinds of experiment should be done at all, as might be the case in the United Kingdom and other European and some Asian nations. In those countries, government policies that guide the conduct of research apply to all work, regardless of the source of funding. In the United several fields of medical science, jurisprudence, and ethics, to serve on the panel, including, as chair, Dr. Steven Muller, a former president of Johns Hopkins University. The group met repeatedly over the next year, in both open and closed sessions; commissioned reports on several ethical, medical, and scientific aspects of embryo research; and debated each decision with vigor and intelligence.* As requested, the panel offered thoughtful judgments about the kinds of studies that should be supported with federal funds, which should not be supported, and which should be postponed for consideration until more information was available or further discussion had occurred.

Looking back on the panel's lengthy report today,[5] with our much deeper knowledge about embryos, cloning, and stem cells, I find its prescience truly astonishing. The panel anticipated by a few years several major developments, including the derivation of stem cells from human embryos and the use of cloning methods in embryo research. And it made prophetic observations about how those developments might be used for medical benefit. In particular, the panel foresaw in 1994 the prospect of growing human embryonic cells from early embryos, even though no stem cells from any primate embryo had yet been grown in the laboratory. From earlier work with mice, members of the panel knew that embryonic stem cells were likely to have the potential to develop into many specific tissue types; if so, they could be used to repair damaged tissues or to treat chronic degenerative diseases of the brain or spinal cord, endocrine organs (such as the pancreatic islets), muscles, joints, or other tissues.

But the panel also recognized the biological difficulties such therapies might pose. For example, cells from preexisting embryos would likely be different genetically from the patients who received embryonic stem cell

---

States, tradition dictates that scientific work is generally not deemed forbidden or illegal; only rarely has scientific work been outlawed and subjected to civil or criminal prosecution. Instead, certain kinds of controversial work may be deemed ineligible for use of taxpayer's funds, usually federal. Despite the restrictions on public funding, such work can be pursued with private money or with nonprohibited public funds, as has recently occurred with human embryonic stem cell research.

* The panel members—and I—also received literally thousands of nearly identical postcard messages, telling us not to encourage research on early embryos, because they were innocent human beings.

therapies. If so, the immune system of the patient would reject the transplanted cells as foreign. For this reason, the panel argued that it might sometimes be acceptable to create embryos that more adequately represent the full range of human genetic diversity. This would be done using IVF, with sperm and eggs donated by adults from varied ethnic origins. Stem cells derived from these embryos would increase the likelihood of good matches between the cells used in therapy and the recipients (patients). But the generation of immunological diversity in this fashion would also cross an ethical line that a couple of panel members were unwilling to cross: the creation of human embryos for purposes other than reproduction—in this case, medical research and treatment.

In considering other ways to overcome the problem of immune rejection in the imagined use of human stem cells in medicine, the panel also discussed an especially prophetic strategy, one that depended on the possibility of "reprogramming" the genes in mature (adult) cells so that the resulting cells would behave like embryonic stem cells. This strategy was based on the only method then known to "reprogram" cells to an earlier phase of development: somatic cell nuclear transfer. This method, later used in the course of producing Dolly, involves the transfer of a cell nucleus, with the full repertoire of an individual's DNA, from a somatic cell, such as skin cell from an adult, to an unfertilized egg from which the nucleus had been removed.

Nuclear transfer was not an entirely new idea, even in 1994. More than three decades earlier, British developmental biologists, led by John Gurdon at Oxford University, had electrified the scientific community when they transferred nuclei from mature frog skin cells into a frog egg deprived of its nucleus.[6] The reengineered cells divided repeatedly and ultimately gave rise to tadpoles, implying that the genes in the transferred skin cell nuclei had been "reprogrammed" to direct many steps in the early development of frogs. Each tadpole was a clone, genetically an identical twin, of the frog from which the skin cells were obtained. But mature animals—full-fledged frogs with reproductive capacity—never emerged after the tadpole stage; presumably the reprogramming was incomplete. Analogous experiments with mammals were so uniformly unsuccessful that many biologists had come to think that the kind of reprogramming of genes required for true cloning of animals by nuclear transfer might be impossible.

Still, the panel recognized, a few years before the advent of Dolly, that if nuclear transfer could be made to work in mammals—even just to get development started, not necessarily to produce a mature animal—the impact would be large. For example, if the nucleus of a patient's cell could be transferred into an egg to generate an early embryo from which therapeutically useful stem cells could be derived, the stem cells would have a genetic makeup identical to that of the person to be treated. Then immune rejection would be unlikely to occur. In the absence of any evidence that reproductive cloning of mammals, yielding full-fledged progeny, was possible, the panel thought about nuclear transfer simply as a means to generate cloned embryos and useful stem cell lines for study and therapy—a strategy now called therapeutic cloning.

The panel astutely noted that nuclear transfer, unlike IVF, is an asexual process, generating embryos (and embryonic stem cells) genetically indistinguishable from cells in the nuclear donor, the prospective patient—not embryos (and cells) with entirely novel combinations of genes. This was sensibly viewed as more acceptable on ethical grounds than creating new embryos by fertilization. In other words, nuclear transfer would use an already existing combination of genes, the combination present in the donor, to make an early embryo through which pluripotent stem cells would be derived. In contrast, the production of genetically varied embryos and stem cell lines would mix genes from many different pairings of sperm and eggs, yielding embryos with *unique* combinations of genes—new biological entities that warrant greater ethical concern.

These speculations led to the panel's most controversial and politically difficult recommendations. Citing the potential clinical benefits, the panel approved (with a couple of dissenters, and only under defined conditions, ethical guidelines, and careful supervision) the use of federal funds in special situations for two controversial methods to generate pluripotent stem cells likely to be useful in therapy: IVF to create genetically diverse embryos from which stem cells could be derived, and reprogramming by somatic cell nuclear transfer to make pluripotent cells immunologically compatible with prospective patients. The panel approved these recommendations even though neither growth of human embryonic stem cells nor nuclear transfer with mammalian cells had yet been accomplished.

POLITICAL CONSEQUENCES OF THE
HUMAN EMBRYO RESEARCH PANEL REPORT

Although well received by scientists who were watching its work, the panel's report ignited a storm of government opposition, even within the liberal Clinton administration. I had made several visits to the Old Executive Office Building to brief White House staff well in advance of the planned presentation of the panel's formal report in early December 1994. At these sessions, I explained the methods and goals of embryo research, showed pictures that displayed the amorphous, undifferentiated character of the tiny early human embryos, and outlined the panel's forthcoming recommendations, some of which had unexpectedly appeared in the press as early as August.

Despite my efforts, the president's senior advisers remained uneasy. We had planned to release the report officially following the meeting of my advisory council on December 2, but the White House was in shock from the Democratic Party's loss of control of both congressional chambers in the midterm elections held a month earlier. Democrats across the nation, especially those at the highest ranks of the Clinton administration, were concerned about a shift in the electorate toward the conservative policies of Newt Gingrich and his Republican revolutionaries, and already anxious about the presidential election of 1996.

I remember getting a call from Leon Panetta, then the White House chief of staff, telling me that I was expected to repudiate some of the panel's recommendations, in particular any that might permit the use of federal funds to create embryos for research purposes. I refused to reject the recommendations of my panel summarily. I was not fired, as the tone of Panetta's call had threatened. But on December 2, a few hours after the panel's report was approved by my advisory council and officially released, the White House issued an executive order, signed by the president, prohibiting the NIH from supporting any studies that entailed the creation of embryos for research.*

---

* A more detailed account of these dramatic events can be found in *Merchants of Immortality* by the distinguished science historian Stephen S. Hall.[7]

Many people thought (and still think) that the executive order was more prohibitive than it was, perhaps because it came so suddenly and from such high authority, and because it was then followed by more severe restrictions imposed by the newly Republican Congress. In fact, the studies that the president ruled ineligible for federal funding made up a very small part of the panel's recommendations, and the executive order did not oppose the vast majority of the recommendations in support of embryo research. Most obviously, it did not limit the many experiments that would use donated embryos originally created for reproductive purposes but slated for disposal. For instance, it would have been possible to proceed with nearly all of what is now called stem cell research, including the derivation, study, and use of new lines of stem cells from human embryos donated by infertile couples treated at IVF clinics.

Now, nearly fourteen years later, federal funding of research on human embryos remains stalled by a twelve-year-old congressional ban, and President George W. Bush's six-year-old policy limits funding of human embryonic stem cell research to work on cells derived before August 9, 2001. So viewed from the current perspective, Clinton's executive order of 1994 seems relatively mild and even permissive. Still, the directive had a strong impact. Our subsequent deliberations at the NIH were tinged with fear that any rapid movement toward funding any of the permitted embryo research would be attacked by the newly powerful Republican right wing and might adversely affect the agency's budget, which, as always, was the major concern for the NIH and its constituency. The administration was certainly not urging us to initiate embryo research. And those of us in charge of NIH policy were strongly advised by knowledgeable people, both inside and outside government, to move cautiously in this contentious arena. So we were cautious. No guidelines were drawn up, no applications for funds were solicited, and no grants were issued for human embryo research of any kind.

Given this atmosphere, conservative members of Congress who were eager for broader restrictions may have been emboldened by the executive order. Indeed, several months later, early in 1995, during negotiations over the 1996 budget for the NIH, two Republican members of the House Appropriations Subcommittee for HHS, Labor, and Education, Jay Dickey of Arkansas and Roger Wicker of Mississippi, wrote an amendment to that year's spending bill to prevent any use of funds under the committee's jurisdiction for experiments that would create, damage, or destroy a human embryo. This prohibition included many types of research acceptable to the Clinton administration, including work with donated embryos, and was written to make the definition of an embryo as broad as possible. The so-called Dickey-Wicker amendment has been attached as a "rider" to every subsequent NIH appropriations bill. It continues to prohibit federal funding for essentially any kind of work with human embryos.

THE BIRTH OF DOLLY AND THE SPECTER OF HUMAN REPRODUCTIVE CLONING

One weekend in the winter of 1997, as I was preparing for my annual hearings on the NIH budget before the House Appropriations Subcommittee, I was stunned by a story on the front page of the Sunday *New York Times* by Gina Kolata. Her article described a report, soon to appear in *Nature* magazine, in which Ian Wilmut and his colleagues at the Roslin Institute in Scotland announced the birth of Dolly, the first well-documented case of an animal (a Finn Dorset lamb) cloned from an adult cell.[8]

Even before getting my hands on the actual report in *Nature,* I could see that this news was explosive. For those familiar with biological research, the feat of making a cloned animal by transferring a nucleus from an adult cell to an egg would reverse a long-held presumption: that it was not possible to "reprogram" a cell so completely. The Human Embryo Research Panel had noted John Gurdon's partial success in reprogramming nuclei from frog skin cells, and it had recommended using nuclear transfer to make cloned human stem cells. But Wilmut had gone much further than Gurdon. His team had fully reset the program of a single, highly specialized, mature cell—a cell derived from the breast tissue of an adult ewe—so that the nucleus could direct formation of a complete, complex organism with its many varieties of mature cell types. For the general public, however, the birth of Dolly would raise a troubling issue: the prospect of human cloning—the generation of new individuals with genetic constitutions essentially identical to those of the person who had provided cells for the cloning process. This possibility would engender a wide range of questions about the purposes, applications, and ethics of modern biological research.

All of these issues were rapidly and publicly aired in the few weeks following the publication of Wilmut's paper—in countless news reports, columns, and letters in the press; at the White House, where the president asked his recently formed National Bioethics Advisory Commission (NBAC) to consider the implications of the new experiments; and at congressional hearings, both those I had been preparing for in the course of NIH's appropriations cycle and others.

We were not very far into the usual to-and-fro regarding the president's proposal for the NIH's 1998 budget before John Porter, the chair of the Appropriations Subcommittee, brought up the very recent news from Scotland. Pointing out that the story "shocked many in the scientific community because they said it couldn't be done," Porter then asked "whether this is valid science, whether it would lead to cloning of adult human beings, what the implications are, both positive and negative, for science itself, and what are the ethical implications . . . for all of society." This was a very good summary of what well-informed people were wondering. I asked, "How much time do I have, Mr. Porter?" He said, "As much as you'd like."

Given this unprecedented liberty, I spoke at unprecedented length, in an answer that took up nearly six pages of the published transcript of the hearing.[9] (After I was done, Porter said, "Dr. Varmus, that's probably the longest answer ever not interrupted by a member of Congress.") I told the subcommittee about Gurdon's classic experiments on nuclear transfer with frog cells; about Wilmut's earlier work, showing that nuclei from very early lamb embryos (not yet from sheep cells) could be transferred into enucleated sheep eggs, producing embryos that matured into full-fledged lambs when implanted in a uterus; and, finally, about Wilmut's latest success, doing the same kind of experiment with nuclei from older embryos, from fetuses, and, most dramatically, from adult sheep breast cells growing in tissue culture.

I didn't stop there. I then talked about the significance of cloning, making new animals with nuclei derived from existing adult animals. While acknowledging the inevitability that public attention would be given first to the "sensational aspects"—the possibility of making clones of mature human beings—I also pointed out the potential benefits in agriculture and in medicine that could result from cloning animals or making cloned human cells. I placed the greatest emphasis on the prospects for "a much deeper understanding" of development, of the process that determines whether a cell behaves like a nerve cell or a liver cell. The birth of Dolly, I said, demonstrated that "a cell derived from an adult mammary gland has been reprogrammed to become . . . fully potent . . . to make every component of a sheep." Learning the rules of reprogramming, I argued to the subcommittee, could provide unexpected opportunities in medicine—for making skin cells, bone marrow, or neurons from a patient's normal cells to treat burns, to replace blood cells destroyed by chemotherapy, or to counteract degenerative brain diseases.

In the final part of my answer to Porter's questions, I summarized the arguments against human reproductive cloning that had been developed by the NIH panel on human embryo research. In addition, I pointed out that congressional restrictions (the Dickey-Wicker amendment) and Clinton's executive order already prevented the use of federal funds to clone human beings. In response to a follow-up question by Representative Nita Lowey, I said there was reason to be "concerned about the rush to legislation in this arena. We have a new finding. It needs to be absorbed and discussed. . . . (The) National Bioethics Advisory Commission . . . is very well suited . . . to discuss these issues and to make some recommendations."

Mine may have been a temperate, reasoned statement, but the immediate response to Dolly in Washington, and throughout the country, was a political impulse—to use persuasion, moral authority, and legislation to discourage or prevent the creation of cloned human offspring, even if the possibility of human reproductive cloning was likely to be at least years away. The White House quickly issued an executive order to reduce the likelihood of human cloning by prohibiting federal funding to pay for it and by urging scientists with access to other sources of support to respect a moratorium on cloning.

The president's announcement to the press of this new executive order was accompanied by a directive to the recently formed NBAC, asking it to recommend how to respond to the new developments in the longer run.

The press event was preceded by a short briefing with Harold Shapiro (the chair of NBAC and the president of Princeton University at the time), several presidential advisers, and me. I was seated next to the president and, as the discussion was drawing to a close, began to explain to him why the methods that led to Dolly had potential importance for understanding basic principles of biology and for producing therapeutically useful cells, without ever allowing an early embryo to grow past very early stages in a petri dish. For these reasons, I maintained, any effort to legislate should be treated with caution, lest we cut off worthwhile avenues of investigation.

Overhearing my colloquy with Clinton, perhaps thinking I was trying to undermine the president's resolve about the executive order, Vice-President Al Gore broke in, saying that he didn't want to be harsh, but time was short and the cloning matter needed urgent resolution. Then, to my amazement, he said that human cloning was already likely being performed elsewhere and that, when he was in the House of Representatives, one of his committees heard testimony about the successful cloning of human beings in India. It was neither necessary nor prudent to challenge him in front of the others. But as we reassembled for the press briefing in the Oval Office, he came up to me, apologized for his abruptness during the briefing, and, recognizing my skepticism about his claims, said he'd ask his staff to send me the transcripts from the hearing. I wasn't surprised that they never arrived.

The president's new executive order and attempts to legislate a ban on the cloning of human beings were more useful as means of public reassurance than as necessary or effective deterrents. We knew at the time that reproductive cloning from adult animal cells was a low probability event—Dolly was the only success out of 277 attempts in the reported experiments with sheep. We know now that the success rate is also low (if sometimes a bit better) in other species and that animals generated by cloning are rarely, if ever, entirely normal: they may age rapidly and die early, and their DNA bears marks of the cloning process.[10] Thus the utility of a legislated ban on the cloning of human beings has remained unclear. Responsible scientists would not undertake human reproductive cloning, because of its safety, ethical concerns, and difficulty. Determined outlaws would simply break the law or go to one of the many places where such laws did not exist. Still, most scientists favor a legislated ban (which still does not exist at the federal level), if only to put the issue to rest and to show support for a reasonable ethical position.

In the immediate aftermath of the Wilmut paper and the executive order, several congressional committees held hearings to show legislative concern, and many ethicists, public figures, and other talking heads filled the airwaves and newspapers with anxiety about cloning human beings. Exactly two weeks after the House appropriations hearings (which had followed by days the announcement of Dolly's birth), Senator Bill Frist organized a hearing of the Senate Committee on Health and Human Resources to debate the news, discuss possible legislation, and take advantage of Ian Wilmut's coincidental visit to Washington.[11] I appeared as a witness with Wilmut and delivered another lengthy discourse on the biological meaning of his work. For this occasion, I had had enough time to prepare drawings that illustrated the normal processes of fertilization and early development and to enlarge photographs that showed the delicate process of nuclear transfer and the amorphous appearance of early embryos. Again, I reviewed the potentially beneficial uses of nuclear transfer and reprogramming, described the safeguards already in place against efforts to misuse the new technology, and urged that public discussion precede "efforts to legislate in areas where the issues are complex."

But my efforts to hold off legislation seemed mild compared with a speech given later in the hearing by Senator Tom Harkin. Although I sometimes sparred with Harkin about the funding and oversight of research on alternative medical practices, he has been a consistent supporter of basic research and the NIH budget. On this occasion, he took his defense of research to an unexpected plane:

> I do not think there are any appropriate limits to human knowledge—none whatsoever. . . . Now some would have us believe that Dolly is a "wolf in sheep's clothing," but I do not think so. I think there is enormous potential for good in this kind of research. . . . To those like my friend, Senator Bond [who had introduced a highly restrictive bill that would ban all human nuclear transfer], and President Clinton [who had issued the exec-

utive order to block federal funding of human reproductive cloning and to request a moratorium in the private sector], who are saying stop, that we cannot play God, well, I say, okay, fine. You can take your side and your ranks alongside Pope Paul V who, in 1616, tried to stop Galileo.

Before concluding his defense of the free play of science, he stepped the argument up another notch:

> I will make a statement right here. Cloning will continue. The human mind will continue to inquire into this. Human cloning will take place, and it will take place in my lifetime, and I do not fear it at all. I welcome it.*

DOLLY'S SIGNIFICANCE: GENETIC REPROGRAMMING

Dolly is now the most famous sheep in history, and her birth is viewed as one of the most dramatic moments in the history of science in the twentieth century. The experiment that produced her upset existing dogma, which argued that mature (differentiated) cells in a complex organism could not be "reprogrammed" to behave like a fertilized egg (the zygote), the primordial embryonic cell that gives rise to a complete organism. The birth of Dolly convinced most scientists that a new organism, genetically identical to a previously existing individual, could be produced by means of the full set of chromosomes derived from a specialized adult cell. In Wilmut's experiment, the genetic program that directs a cell to behave like a breast epithelial cell was replaced by a genetic program responsive to cues present in the egg's cytoplasm. In this way, the cell newly formed by nuclear transfer generated daughter cells that ultimately led to the formation of a complete, complex organism.

What does reprogramming mean? In earlier chapters, I introduced the idea that individual cell types make use of only a subset of the genes

---

* This extraordinary moment was later incorporated into an episode of a popular television series, *The X Files*. My cameo appearance boosted my standing with friends and relatives under the age of twenty-five.

in the genome to produce RNA and protein; the pattern of expressed genes is often called the program. During normal differentiation—in development of an embryo or in formation of specialized cells in an animal after birth—successive patterns of gene expression are observed. Generally, the sequence of patterns occurs in only one direction. The possibility of reversion to an earlier stage of development ("dedifferentiation" or "reprogramming") has been a perennial topic of debate. It has long been acknowledged that a dramatic reprogramming must occur without experimental intervention during reproduction, when two specialized cells, a sperm cell and an egg cell, combine to produce the zygote, a single cell from which all subsequent cells in an organism arise. The cloned animal called Dolly showed that such dramatic reprogramming can also occur when the nucleus of a fully differentiated cell is moved into a new environment, the cytoplasm of an egg.

So what are the molecular events that control the genetic program, determining whether a region of DNA, a gene, remains silent or is read out to make RNA and, usually, protein? And what triggers those events? Although we are far from knowing the answers to these questions in satisfying detail, a few things are evident. For any cell type, there is a characteristic pattern (or program) of gene expression, with some of its roughly twenty-two thousand genes silent, some turned on at low levels, some at higher levels. To change from one cell type to another, the activities of many thousands of genes would have to be altered. How this happens is not fully understood, but part of the answer involves master regulators, proteins affecting the behavior of large numbers of genes, in a kind of hierarchy.

To envision how this happens, imagine the consequences of pushing ("expressing") some of the keys on a twelve-key piano. One combination produces one harmonic sound; another combination produces a different sound. A change in sounds would require a change in programming, something that would be relatively easy to do with such a simple piano. But if the instrument had a much larger number of keys, perhaps thousands, it would be more efficient to control changes in sound by designing a hierarchy, with some keys as regulators of large sets of other keys. If the regulatory keys governed partly overlapping rather than distinct sets of keys, the situation would be similar to what appears to occur in animal cells.

We now know what some of the regulatory genes are, we know something about what genes they regulate, and we even know a bit about how they are themselves regulated, especially in normal development. Dolly's birth and other experiments tell us that it is possible to reset the program without resorting to the usual process of fertilization—observations that are fundamentally exciting and rich with possibility. But what components of the egg's cytoplasm triggered the critical changes in gene expression to convert a breast cell nucleus into the nucleus of a one-cell embryo? Could the same effect be achieved in an adult cell without laboriously manipulating the cell's nucleus into a new cell? Or without requiring an egg cell as recipient? Could this be done with chemical triggers (hormones or drugs)? By some kind of physical shock? Or by delivering a few master regulatory genes into the cell?

Dolly's birth inspired additional efforts—increasingly successful (though still relatively inefficient)—to clone several other kinds of animals (mice, cats, dogs, horses, cows, and even nonhuman primates). The extent to which the cloning of animals has succeeded can be gauged by the current debates over the use of cloned animals for food in Europe and the United States.[12]

These successes have encouraged efforts to recapitulate reprogramming by other means. Most dramatically, a small number of labs have used retroviruses carrying regulatory genes to reprogram mature cells, mostly skin cells, from mice and, more recently, human beings.[13] The infected, reprogrammed cells have many features of embryonic stem cells, including the crucial ability to form a variety of differentiated cell types, such as muscle and nerve cells. The "induced pluripotent stem cells" (iPS cells) have opened exciting new prospects for understanding and treating disease, as will be noted near the end of this chapter.

AVOIDING LEGISLATION TO CRIMINALIZE NUCLEAR TRANSFER

In response to the continuing debates about the reproductive cloning of human beings—Is human cloning possible? Is it safe? Could it ever be justified ethically?—most scientists have taken a conservative stance and remained receptive to a legislative ban. This is based in part on evidence that cloned animals are not entirely healthy, in part on the inefficiency and expense of the process, and in part on the complex ethical and political issues raised by reproductive cloning. But the birth of Dolly also raised a question on which most scientists take a position that diverges from public policy in the United States. Should the government support therapeutic cloning, by means of nuclear transfer into an egg to produce embryonic stem cells for treatment of serious medical conditions?

Seen in this context, the announcement of Dolly's birth had a special poignancy. Dolly's existence showed that it was possible, after all, as speculated by the Human Embryo Research Panel, to "turn back the biological clock"—to reset the program of the genome of an adult mammalian cell so that it would behave like the genome of a fertilized egg. This new cell could lead to the complete development of a complex organism. But nuclear transfer could also be the first step toward a different, beneficial and much less contentious, outcome: the production of cloned early embryos from which cloned, pluripotent stem cells could be derived. Even in 1994, it was apparent to the embryo research panel that such cells might be among the best prospects for cell-based therapies, as well as important tools for the study of normal and abnormal development, for understanding diseases, and for screening for new drugs to treat disease.

But could the distinction between reproductive and therapeutic intentions be preserved? My colleagues and I hoped that any legislative efforts to prohibit reproductive human cloning, by making it a criminal act, would be flexible enough to allow nuclear transfer for creation of cloned pluripotent cells. Initially, only a few in Congress seemed concerned about preserving the option of reprogramming the human nucleus by nuclear transfer as a method that would promote discoveries and therapies. The embryo research panel's view—that nuclear transfer to generate embryonic cells from adult nuclei is an asexual, therapeutically beneficial, and ethically more acceptable method than IVF—was generally ignored. A bill introduced in 1997 by Senator Kit Bond of Missouri and endorsed by Senator Frist would have made nuclear transfer illegal, as part of an effort to ban the cloning of human beings. They viewed the method as the first step down the "slippery slope" to reproductive cloning. But with orchestrated lobbying by scientists and help from a bipartisan coalition of legislators—including, prominently, Senators Orrin Hatch, Arlen Specter, and Tom Harkin—the bill was blocked by a modest margin, an effort that demonstrated how scientists could beneficially influence debate on complex issues.

Still, because the public's introduction to nuclear transfer occurred in the context of Dolly's birth, the method became inextricably linked to cloning in the most dramatic sense—the making of cloned human beings. Efforts to emphasize that nuclear transfer was just an early step in an elaborate method that *could* lead to reproductive cloning, but that it was also essential for achieving the more acceptable objective of "therapeutic cloning," has not fared well. For instance, it is still not possible to use federal funds to support research on nuclear transfer, because the method is considered a means of creating an embryo and thus federal support of it would violate the Dickey-Wicker amendment.*

Not surprisingly, nuclear transfer has been pursued more actively in countries in Asia and Europe, especially the United Kingdom. American scientists have used funds from industry, state initiatives, and private philanthropy to support work on nuclear transfer, but progress has inevitably been slowed by the exclusion of the NIH, our major source of funding for research and training and the predominant influence on research trends in the United States. Still, reproducible success with human nuclear transfer has yet to be achieved in any country. Furthermore, the procurement of human eggs for the procedure remains difficult for ethical and medical reasons. Newer approaches to reprogramming seem likely to overtake nuclear transfer as the preferred method for making cloned pluripotent stem cells.

GROWING HUMAN EMBRYONIC STEM CELLS

When Dolly appeared on the scene in 1997, scientists still did not know how to grow embryonic stem cells from early human embryos, despite the repeatedly successful cultivation of mouse embryonic stem cells. So

---

* No penalties are associated with such research conducted in the United States with other sources of funds.

the potential medical utility of nuclear transfer and other kinds of human embryo research remained theoretical in the first year or two after Dolly's birth.

But debates about cloning and embryo research became much more sharply focused on the prospects for treating human disease late in 1998, when Jamie Thomson, at the University of Wisconsin, reported the prolonged growth in culture dishes of human cells derived from early embryos.[14] For those following Thomson's work closely, this step might have been anticipated, since a couple of years earlier he had reported a method for growing pluripotent stem cells derived from embryos of non-human primates.[15] But to most of the scientific community and to the public at large, Thomson's announcement about human embryonic stem cells was stunning.

To make his embryonic stem cell lines, Thomson and his colleagues disassembled early human embryos that were provided by sperm and egg donors at IVF clinics.* Suddenly it was possible to learn the rules of normal human development—the recipes required to turn the early embryo cells, not yet committed to any particular tissue type, into specialized cells of virtually any type—in simple experimental systems. It also meant that medical scientists could focus on making large numbers of differentiated human cells that could be used to repair many kinds of injured or diseased tissues: the deficient pancreas in a diabetic patient, the paucity of dopamine-producing cells in the brains of patients with Parkinson's disease, the exhausted cardiac muscle cells in patients with congestive heart failure.

Thomson's success in developing human embryonic stem cell lines, his interest in promoting their widespread use, and the generation of other similar lines elsewhere in the United States and abroad created an

---

* To circumvent the Dickey-Wicker amendment, which prohibited federal funding of research that destroyed human embryos, Thomson's group used money from two nonfederal sources: the Wisconsin Alumni Research Fund, a state resource fed by philanthropy and by royalties from earlier research at the university, and the Geron Corporation, a privately financed company focused on the disorders of aging. These funding strategies presaged the pattern that now prevails in the face of continued severe restrictions on federal support of research on human embryos and stem cells—funding from philanthropy, commercial investments, private research organizations, and state budgets.

important opportunity. Now that such lines had been created without the use of federal funds, there didn't seem to be any obvious obstacle to the use of federal funds to support studies of the lines themselves. Since no further damage would be done to human embryos by working with the newly produced stem cells, there was no reason to think that federal funding of the research would violate the Dickey-Wicker amendment. Still, there was reason to fear that spending federal money to study cells that had been derived by destroying human embryos would incite a congressional backlash against the NIH.

For this reason, early in 1999 I asked Harriet Rabb, then the general counsel of the Department of HHS (now head of legal affairs at Rockefeller University), for a detailed legal opinion. In a widely known brief, she argued that since stem cells themselves were not embryos, research on them could legitimately be supported with NIH funds.[16] No embryos would be damaged by doing so; the damage had already been done, legally, by use of nonfederal funds. This provided the basis on which to proceed to finance human embryonic stem cell research with NIH dollars. But we needed other kinds of assurances as well. So I recruited a panel, headed by Shirley Tilghman, the molecular biologist and mouse embryologist who is now president of Princeton University, to write guidelines for regulating the ethical use of such cells in NIH-funded research. However, by the time her panel had completed its report, sought and responded to public comments, and posted the rules, the presidential campaigns of 2000 were in full swing, and the political sensitivities to the issue were acute. (I was, by then, gone from the NIH.)

Stem Cells in the Era of George W. Bush

Whatever the explanations, no NIH money was used to pay for human embryonic stem cell research until President Bush gave his famous speech of August 9, 2001. It is a measure of the importance the stem cell debate had achieved in the political arena that this was the topic of the new president's first televised address to the nation, nearly eight months after he assumed office. The speech was well written, and its effort to make all sides happy was clever in conception; but its apparent benefits were doomed to

be relatively short-lived.* Rather than close the door on any federal funding of stem cell research, as many had predicted, Bush agreed to allow funds
to be used to study only those lines that existed before he began speaking
at nine that night. This policy allowed him to say to his right-wing supporters that the prospect of federal funding could not be an incentive for deriv-
ing additional lines from additional embryos, while also saying to medical
scientists that he was allowing federal support of research with existing
lines of human embryonic stem cells for the first time.

The Bush policy unarguably permitted the first federal funding of
human embryonic stem cell research. Coming from a conservative president, the policy was less prone to attack from the right wing than similar
actions from a Democrat; still, many of his supporters voiced disappointment. But, predictably, his compromise quickly passed the limits of usefulness. The number of cell lines eligible for funding was always much smaller
than the sixty or more claimed to exist. This was true, in part, because the
speech conflated truly established cell lines that exhibited reliable properties with frozen samples of disaggregated embryo cells that had yet to
show reproducible growth patterns in culture. In addition, some lines
were difficult to obtain because of the licensing requirements of those
who had filed for patent protection of their cell lines. Furthermore, none
of the existing cell lines was likely to be useful for the ultimate goal of therapy, because they had been initially propagated on "supporting" layers of
mouse cells that might produce viruses dangerous to patients. In the
meantime, new and better stem cell lines have been generated with funds
from nonfederal sources, principally the Howard Hughes Medical Institute, private philanthropies, laboratories abroad, and industry. But these

---

* According to an article that appeared in the January 2008 issue of *Commentary* magazine by
Jay Lefkowitz, one of Bush's policy advisers at the time, the president devoted a large portion
of his first months in office to discussions of this issue with many physicians, scientists, ethicists, patient advocates, and others. However, Lefkowitz's claim that I "sat down" with President Bush at Yale to talk about stem cells is an exaggeration that raises doubt about other
claims in the article. In fact, I met the president in a receiving line at the 2001 Yale graduation, where we were both receiving honorary degrees. When I surprised him by saying that
I'd like to talk about three things, one of which was stem cells, he looked uneasy and called out
to Andrew Card, his chief of staff, "Andy, Andy, come on over here and talk to the doc!" Card
and I then chatted briefly about my views. I never sat down with President Bush to discuss
stem cells or anything else.

lines cannot be studied with NIH grants unless legislation to broaden the repertoire of eligible cell lines—legislation that has twice been passed by the U.S. Congress and twice vetoed by President Bush—is enacted into law. This seems unlikely to happen until after the election of 2008.

During the years of adjustment to the Bush stem cell policies, the landscape has been altered by the emergence of knowledgeable and committed stem cell advocacy groups, by important discoveries about the behavior of embryonic stem cells, and by new strategies for engaging state governments and philanthropists in the pursuit of stem cell research. As a result, stem cell research has not fallen drastically behind similar efforts in other countries, as some had feared, although progress has surely been compromised by legal and bureaucratic obstacles. In this area of research, a traditional strength of American science policy—a centralized, well-coordinated, and openly competitive process for making grants at the NIH—has been replaced by an uneven patchwork of state-based programs and other, nongovernmental funding opportunities. Some wealthy institutions have been able to pursue human stem cell research through philanthropy, while many others lack access to such resources. Some states have enacted bans on both cloning and the methods used for cloning (e.g., somatic cell nuclear transfer), while others, most famously California, have passed measures to finance many kinds of human stem cell research handsomely.

More Californians supported the state's bond initiative for stem cell research in 2004 than voted for the Democratic presidential candidate, John Kerry. The bill provides $3 billion in bonds over ten years for stem cell research. Nevertheless, roadblocks thrown up by legislative dissents and legal challenges significantly delayed the spending of taxpayers' funds. Other states, notably Connecticut, New Jersey, Wisconsin, and Michigan, have passed progressive policies that provide financial support for stem cell research. In 2007, following the election of Eliot Spitzer as governor, my own state, New York, allocated at least $600 million for stem cell and related research over the next decade, without attracting significant attention or objection.* Meanwhile, private monies, such as

---

* In September 2007, I was appointed as a commissioner on the funding subcommittee of the New York stem cell program.

the $50 million given by the Starr Foundation to support collaborative work on stem cells at MSKCC, Rockefeller University, and Weill Cornell Medical College, are supporting broad programs of stem cell science at many leading U.S. research centers—at least, at those with the good fortune to have wealthy, enlightened donors.

Still, despite the alternative means for funding stem cell research, investigators must consider carefully whether they want to work in such a financially confusing (if scientifically exciting) field and, if so, where they should work. For instance, although few scientists have yet left the United States to pursue stem cell research abroad, other countries offer temptations to our scientists. The United Kingdom asked a parliamentary committee to determine what kind of research ought to be permitted and then issued guidelines that resemble the recommendations of the NIH's 1994 embryo research panel. Other European and some Asian countries have aggressively promoted stem cell research, sensing not only opportunities for discovery and medical progress but also a chance to move ahead of a confused American enterprise in this arena. This was most obviously the case in South Korea, where a large, well-supported team, headed by Professor Woo-Suk Hwang, reported having taken somatic cell nuclear transfer to the point of making embryonic stem cells with nuclei from patients with injuries and diseases that might be suitable candidates for cell therapies. Regrettably, much of Dr. Hwang's work is now acknowledged to have been fabricated, an admission that has significantly tarnished the reputation of the entire field.[17]

To me and to many of my colleagues, the way in which our government has handled the dramatic developments in research on embryos and stem cells reflects the undue influence of a few religious groups on the conduct of science in a diverse society. The opposition of the Catholic Church and other conservative Christians to this new scientific arena has been unremitting, and reflected in the positions taken by some leading members of the legislative and executive branches, including President Bush, Senator Sam Brownback, and Representative Dave Weldon, all of whom have proposed or endorsed highly restrictive legislation. Few arguments can seem as insulting to medical scientists as the claim that we are ethically irresponsible when we toil to extract stem cells from donated early human embryos, which would otherwise be destroyed, and use them for beneficial, potentially lifesaving purposes.

But there are reasons for optimism, too. The country has taken the debate about stem cells and cloning seriously, and most indicators point to increasing support for liberalization of existing policies. Second, the issues have further stimulated the public's interest in modern biology and its potential for medical benefit. Third, recent work in Japan and the United States offers grounds for optimism that cells closely resembling embryonic stem cells, iPS cells, can be produced by introducing a "genetic cocktail" into adult cells, thereby reprogramming them.*

If the study of cell reprogramming continues to deliver on its promise, human cells of the sort most desirable for research and treatment may eventually be obtainable without the use of embryos or nuclear transfer at all. This would fulfill a long-held dream of redeploying mature cells to behave like embryonic cells, then using those cells to treat patients from whom the cells were derived. For the foreseeable future, however, early human embryos and cells derived from them will be a staple of research, providing the "gold standards" against which reprogrammed cells must be compared. The absence of absolute prohibitions of embryo and stem cell research has allowed such research to proceed in this country, if not in an optimal fashion, despite restrictions on federal funding. Because of their promise, embryonic stem cells have become a useful political bellwether and have kept the promise of biomedical research at the forefront of public discourse. All in all, not bad outcomes.

---

* In the current early stages of development of these new means for reprogramming cells, the combination of introduced genes includes some with cancer-causing potential. Furthermore, the means of delivery are retroviruses, which insert proviruses into cell chromosomes, with potentially deleterious effects, as described in part 2. Efforts to find other ways to reprogram cells are now being strenuously pursued—with other genes, with other means of delivery, and with other chemical and physical signals to alter gene expression.

CHAPTER 14

Global Science and Global Health

—

Science can help to feed the hungry, heal the sick, protect the environ-
ment, provide dignity in work and create space for the joy of self-
expression. Yet . . . lack of opportunity to master science and the new
technologies will accentuate the divide between rich and poor.

—ISMAIL SERAGELDIN,
DIRECTOR, LIBRARY AT
ALEXANDRIA[1]

AS A MEDICAL STUDENT, I DEVELOPED AN INTEREST IN WHAT WAS
then called tropical medicine and worked in northern India for a few
months. I took a fourth-year elective at the Clara Swain mission hospital in Bareilly, a large town in Uttar Pradesh, about a hundred miles from
Delhi. My exposure to medicine in India overturned an earlier conviction that I might enjoy a career working as a physician in a poor country; I was also dismayed by some poor medical practices and occasionally
callous behavior. Although the experience persuaded me that I was better suited to other parts of the medical profession, it also ignited a long-
standing concern about the discrepancies between rich nations and
poor. When I arrived at the NIH as director many years later, my eyes
were opened to a much greater potential than I had recognized as a
medical student to the possibilities of using science, including science
performed in poor countries, to advance what is now more commonly
called global health.

Over the past few years, the world has given increasing attention to
the problems posed by disease in developing countries. Although still

operating far from the standards of medicine and science practiced in the wealthiest countries, even some of the least affluent nations can aspire to build effective health systems, promote wide use of vaccines, import modern drugs or manufacture their own generic pharmaceuticals, and participate in modern research to address regional diseases. We have come a long way from my generation's first view of the battle against disease in poor countries as sacrificial careers lived by missionaries working in ill-equipped clinics in the jungles of Africa, Asia, or South America.

There are a number of reasons for this change. A prominent one is the active and well-publicized interest in global health taken by philanthropic individuals and organizations, most obviously the foundation established by Bill and Melinda Gates. The endorsement of these efforts by famous figures in the entertainment world, such as Bono from U-2, has also been important. And economists, perhaps most prominently Jeffrey Sachs, the head of Columbia University's Earth Institute, have established the notion that improvements in health can promote economic development and that better health (and health care) should not be viewed merely as consequences of improved economies.

At more or less the same time, the worldwide epidemic of AIDS, the emergence of other novel infectious diseases (like Ebola and SARS), the recurrence and persistence of historically important diseases (like tuberculosis and malaria), and the threat of pandemics (like a repeat of the influenza epidemic of 1918) have concentrated the world's attention on the prospects for controlling these diseases as a matter of self-defense as well as altruism. Advances in medical science, offering the possibility of more effective prevention and treatment, have inspired hopes that science can successfully take on both new and old scourges.

Still, the pathways to better health in the developing world have not been carefully drawn. Nor have the responsibilities for achieving better health been clearly assigned to, or assumed by, the various players: the poor countries themselves (which generally devote surprisingly low percentages of their annual budgets to these issues, in the face of other, often staggering demands on limited resources); the advanced economies (which usually say that their primary concerns must be the problems that afflict their own citizens); or the nongovernmental agencies (which are often fully committed to these issues but, with the exception of the Gates

Foundation, don't have government-sized bank accounts). Efforts to promote greater attention to global health inevitably run into these explanations of neglect, reluctance, or limited action.

In this chapter, I discuss some of the efforts I've made to promote interest in global health and to expand the role of science in poor parts of the world. These activities are guided by a conviction that we can use the skills developed in wealthy countries and build scientific enterprises abroad to address the problems of the poor. My roles have been modest, sometimes embarrassingly so, in comparison with the monumental efforts devoted to this cause by some very remarkable people. Still, I hope that the perspective I bring to my limited efforts, and the perceptions I've taken away, will stimulate greater engagement by others in one of the great challenges of our time.

CONSIDERING MEDICAL SCIENCE IN AFRICA

When I arrived on the NIH campus in 1993, I was curious to learn what the agency was doing to improve international health and science. The place where I expected to find engagement with these issues was the Fogarty International Center (FIC), a unit of the NIH named for John E. Fogarty, a congressman devoted to growth of the NIH budget in the 1940s and 1950s. Unfortunately, the FIC's budget was paltry, in the range of 0.2 percent of the total NIH budget, and its small staff had little immediate responsibility for directing scientific programs. The FIC also had many administrative responsibilities—hosting foreign scientists on sabbatical at the NIH (mostly from advanced nations); procuring visas for thousands of foreign students and fellows at NIH (many of whom now hold prominent positions in a wide range of home countries[*]); funding fellowships to bring foreign scientists to our university labs; and fostering collaborations between scientists in the United States and abroad, usually as part of projects paid for by the other, larger institutes.

Thanks to the research support from other parts of the NIH, fund-

---

[*] I saw one of the benefits of the NIH training programs on my first night in Seoul in 1994 when I was greeted enthusiastically by hundreds of members of the Korean NIH Alumni Association who came to pay their respects to the new NIH director.

ing for international programs has generally been about five times greater than the budget for the FIC, although still a very modest portion of the entire NIH allotment. Of course, this simple arithmetic undervalues the contribution NIH makes to health in the developing world, since virtually all disorders studied with NIH funds occur in poor countries as well as in rich ones, and some (e.g., AIDS) may disproportionately affect poor countries. Nevertheless, I am persuaded, more and more with time, that the NIH should devote a greater portion of its resources specifically to global health.

The FIC did have the means to influence research abroad through its convening powers. One day in the summer of 1995, relatively early in my tenure as NIH director, the center sponsored a daylong meeting to discuss ways to promote biomedical science in Africa. This gathering attracted my attention for a number of reasons, especially my continuing concerns about our failure to bring science and health care in developing countries closer to the standards that now exist in the developed world. But I was also acutely conscious of the fact that much of the high-powered, expensive science that is supported by the NIH—work on genomes, protein structure, and signaling pathways—is much more likely to lead to benefits for patients in the world's advanced nations than for those in places like Africa in the next decade or two. Yet the world's greatest burden of disease remains in the poorest countries, where more than a billion people live on less than a dollar a day and where even routine care for common infections usually lies beyond reach of any but the affluent few. Furthermore, these countries usually have little or no capacity to perform the kinds of research that might help to combat the diseases most prevalent there—diseases that are often rare in wealthier economies, not major topics for research in scientifically advanced nations, and unattractive targets for drug and vaccine development by the established health industries.

FOCUSING ON MALARIA

I attended most of the talks and discussions at the FIC meeting on science in Africa, and I was pleased and surprised to find that several NIH institutes were already engaged in a diversity of projects in a number of

African countries. Of the various research topics discussed (including the genetics of chronic diseases and a multitude of infections), one stood out: malaria. This disease, once prevalent even in the temperate climates of Europe and North America, had been gradually coming under control in tropical zones after the Second World War, thanks to the widespread use of insecticides, such as DDT, and antimalarial drugs. But over the subsequent three decades, as the use of insecticides declined, malaria returned with a vengeance in large parts of Africa, Southeast Asia, and South America. The malarial parasite was becoming increasingly resistant to the cheapest, most commonly used drugs, and the insect "vector" that carried the parasite from patient to patient, the *Anopheles* mosquito, had developed resistance to many insecticides. By the 1990s, one to two million people, mostly young children, were dying of malaria each year, mainly in sub-Saharan Africa, with over three hundred million people infected worldwide, many chronically ill and unable to work.[2]

Because of its complex life cycle, assuming multiple forms and behaviors as it passes through mosquitoes and human beings, the malaria parasite offers many promising opportunities to interfere with its growth and development. By the 1990s, new methods in genetics, biochemistry, and cell biology had become available to attack the disease and its causative organism, but too few people and too few dollars had been engaged. Drug discovery and development of potential new agents had lagged because markets were considered to be too limited and too poor.

I suggested to the participants at the FIC meeting that we make an effort to expand research in Africa by focusing on this one disease—emphasizing its medical importance and the new opportunities for understanding the pathogen and its vector in greater detail, and building on the significant scientific foothold that had already been established. Some European funding agencies, such as Britain's Wellcome Trust and its Medical Research Council, had made investments to build laboratories performing malaria research in Africa, and they were interested in doing more. Some well-trained Africans had recently returned home after studies abroad to work on malaria in these labs and at a few African universities. The NIH itself had established a surprisingly good malaria research center in Bamako, Mali, staffed with Malian scientists who had trained in France and the United States, funded with NIH grants, and involved collaboratively with excellent American scientists at the NIH, Tulane, the University of Maryland, and elsewhere.

To discuss prospects for a more aggressive approach to malaria, the NIH organized a meeting of the relevant parties, including about fifty African investigators, in collaboration with the Pasteur Institute and several other organizations, in Dakar, Senegal, early in January 1997. This gathering was unusual. We arrived in Dakar with a pragmatic purpose— to propose coordinated actions that would improve the ways laboratories throughout Africa and the world studied malaria and applied their findings to prevention and treatment. Africans, Europeans, and Americans, grant makers and grant recipients, sat around tables together, spoke with similar levels of authority, and reached agreement on many issues. Before the meeting ended, essentially every participant strongly endorsed the formation of a research consortium, to be called the Multilateral Initiative on Malaria (MIM), that would coordinate research funded by many contributing agencies and conducted in many countries, especially Africa.[3]

Unfortunately, it was easier to define goals for malaria research in Africa than to find new support for any coordinated effort, especially one that would require the science funding agencies to give up some measure of autonomy and decision-making. Only the NIH and a couple of other organizations were willing to pledge funds to this international effort— in the aggregate, a few million dollars, a small fraction of the $50 to 100 million that would be needed for a major initiative. At a follow-up meeting in early July, just outside The Hague, in the Netherlands, most of the prospective European contributors balked at the idea of relinquishing control of even quite small sums to a centralized scientific advisory board. To my surprise, the NIH and I specifically were attacked as naïve interlopers on turf that belonged to European agencies that had more long-term ties to African countries. The NIH delegation was disappointed by the failure of other agencies to recognize the stature of our past efforts (one of the NIH institutes, the National Institute of Allergy and Infectious Diseases, was even then the world's largest funder of malaria research) and by the antagonism toward our ability to make specific spending proposals, without lengthy consultations with ministers at home or at the European Union headquarters in Brussels.[4]

Despite the relatively small size of the effort, MIM had enough money to offer some small grants, run workshops, and organize a small bureaucracy to coordinate its efforts. A decade later, MIM continues to survive as a respected convener of meetings and provider of small grants, but it has not commanded enough resources to reach its original ambitions. Nevertheless, it is one of the persistent symbols of the attention brought to the problem of malaria in the 1990s. This attention contributed to malaria's great prominence in recent years at the World Health Organization (WHO), the Gates Foundation, the Global Fund for AIDS, Tuberculosis, and Malaria, and a few drug companies. In 2008, the activities inspired by such advocacy have begun to show measurable rewards: the incidence and death rates for malaria have declined precipitously.[5] WHO has attributed these improvements mainly to the therapeutic effects of a relatively new and now widely used class of drug, the artemisinins, and to the preventive effects of insecticide-impregnated bed nets.

THE WHO COMMISSION ON MACROECONOMICS AND HEALTH

My experience during the founding of MIM taught me that good intentions and plans drawn up in an egalitarian fashion are not enough to elicit support for research that can improve health in poor countries. To be successful, proposals require a more sophisticated analysis of the costs and benefits and the backing of an international authority. For this reason, in 2000, soon after I left the NIH, I accepted an invitation from Gro Harlem Brundtland, then the head of the WHO, to join the Commission on Macroeconomics and Health, chaired by the economist Jeffrey Sachs, who was then at the Kennedy School at Harvard.

Sachs had become passionate about both the economic and the humanitarian reasons to improve the health of poor people in developing countries. When I first met him, strategically positioned on the landing of the major staircase at the World Economic Forum in Davos in January 1998, I was immediately impressed by his knowledge about poor-world diseases, including malaria; his enthusiasm for doing something about them; and his thoughtful analysis of the impact of illness on the economies of poor countries. A couple of years later, as leader of the commission, he skillfully guided a large research team to produce tally sheets of the major remediable threats to health, the costs of the remedies, and the embarrassingly small contributions to those costs made by donor nations. The United States, for example, comes in last among the twenty-two most advanced economies when foreign aid is ranked as a fraction of gross domestic product. And only one-eighth of our aid is devoted to health.

The commission's report was based on an argument that, despite its reasonableness, has only quite recently become accepted: better health drives economic productivity, not just the other way around.[6] The report makes concrete recommendations about the levels of funding that would be needed to make significant and rapid improvements in health in poor countries—from the roughly $6 billion of foreign assistance provided in 2001 to about $27 billion in 2007 and $38 billion in 2015, with corresponding new contributions from the recipient countries themselves. For each of the diseases on a relatively short list of major killers (AIDS, tuberculosis, malaria, maternal illnesses, tobacco-induced diseases, and common infections), we estimated the funds required to provide the improvements in care that would reduce the number of deaths, enhance work capacity, and improve economies. For example, a threefold increase in investment in health in poor countries was predicted to restore about 330 million years of disability-free life, and the increased capacity for useful work would in turn generate over $360 billion annually by 2015, a five- to tenfold return on the investment. The report also featured recommendations for research on global health, specific proposals for organizing health systems and delivering better care, and effective strategies for distributing additional funds for health.

Because the WHO is respected, the commission's report has been taken seriously by many countries, both rich and poor, and several, such as India and Malawi, have responded to the report's directive for countries to establish their own commissions on macroeconomics and health. These commissions tabulate regional health problems and make plans for solving them in ways appropriate to each country. The report is frequently cited by groups considering ways to build stronger systems for improving health in poor countries or to ameliorate the toll taken by one of the major threats to health studied by the commission. By emphasizing health systems rather than simply addressing single diseases like malaria, the report also anticipated a still-growing current interest in making fundamental changes in health care that are likely to have more long-standing effects on health in the developing world.

But the WHO is also strapped for cash. So developing countries committed to improving health conditions according to the plans we formulated must search elsewhere for donors or rearrange their own fiscal priorities. Or they must compete for the scarce dollars available from existing funding agencies or newly created international sources, such as the UN's Global Fund for AIDS, Tuberculosis, and Malaria.

A PROPOSAL FOR A GLOBAL SCIENCE CORPS

In December 2001, just three months after the terrorist attacks of September 11, I was scheduled to deliver the final talk at a scientific symposium in Stockholm, commemorating the centennial anniversary of the first Nobel Prizes in 1901. With the findings of the WHO commission and the specter of terrorism fresh on my mind, I decided to address the gulf between the sophisticated biomedical science the audience had been listening to and the deplorable health conditions in so much of the world. After all, Alfred Nobel had asked that his prizes be awarded to people whose scientific discoveries had made the greatest contributions to the betterment of mankind. Some Nobel Prizes in Physiology or Medicine, including some of the very first, had gone to those who had made major discoveries about malaria, tuberculosis, and other diseases common in poor countries. Why haven't the benefits been greater? Obviously many factors—political, educational, and financial—have contributed to the failures. But what can scientists do now to encourage greater progress?

I recommended several kinds of remedial initiatives—most of them obvious, a few original. One of the novel ideas, the creation of a Global Science Corps, attracted significant attention. The central notion was to encourage scientists in the more advanced countries to spend significant periods of time, say, one to two years, working in selected laboratories in poor countries, both to bring new technologies and perspectives and to learn about local problems, in health and other areas, that are amenable to scientific solutions. I envisioned several categories of scientists who might be willing to make such a commitment: younger people who had just finished their training but were not yet decided about how to use their skills; middle-aged faculty who were eligible for sabbaticals or leaves of absence and wanted to diversify their views of science; or scientists nearing or past retirement age who wished to consider working in a new environment in which their knowledge might have special benefits. A role model for someone in this last category was the famous British geneticist J. B. S. Haldane, who lived and worked at a genetics institute in rural India for several of the last years of his life.[7]

Of course, like all proposals to improve science and health, the corps would require administrative oversight and significant financial resources to pay for salaries, travel, living expenses, and research materials. Jim Wolfensohn, then the head of the World Bank, happened to be in Stockholm for the Nobel Prize festivities. While standing next to him in line for one of the events, I mentioned the proposal for the corps; in exchange, he told me about the Millennium Science Initiative (MSI), a not widely known effort to build scientific activity in less developed countries. Supported financially by the World Bank and administratively by a small team in Princeton, at the Institute for Advanced Study, where Wolfensohn was also chairman of the board, the MSI had organized competitions in developing countries, such as Mexico, Chile, and Brazil, to select scientific "centers of excellence" in various fields.[8]

It became apparent that MSI centers could serve as hosts for scientists from advanced countries who wished to become members of the Global Science Corps. To pursue this, after my return from Stockholm I met with Phillip Griffiths, then the director of the Institute for Advanced Study and still the leader of the MSI, to discuss our mutual interests in methods to improve science in science-poor countries. As a result, I have joined his team (now called the Science Initiatives Group, or SIG), and SIG has taken up the cause of the Global Science Corps. I have helped to oversee the MSI in Brazil and elsewhere and to initiate new MSI programs in Vietnam and a few African countries. In turn, SIG has launched an effort to make the GSC better known,[9] to identify science centers in poor and lower-middle income countries that would be attractive host institutions, to find scientists interested in serving in the corps, and to raise the significant funds (about $100,000 to $200,000 per year per person) that will be required to launch the first cohort. Finding willing hosts and motivated potential corps members has been easier than securing financial support for the project. So six years after making my proposal in Stockholm, the GSC remains only an attractive idea, with proponents but no performance.

THE GATES FOUNDATION AND ITS GRAND CHALLENGES IN GLOBAL HEALTH

With most governments responding sluggishly to pleas for altruism and most nongovernmental organizations chronically cash-poor, novel approaches to the medical problems of the poorest countries seem to depend increasingly on the good will of foundations established by a few extraordinarily wealthy people. The Bill and Melinda Gates Foundation, with an enormous endowment that recently rose to about $60 billion, thanks to a remarkable gift to the foundation by Warren Buffett, is prime among these. Its power to change the direction of science and health care is illustrated by one of its most notable projects, the Grand Challenges in Global Health—a program that has attracted new scientists to the field of global health, stimulated new ideas, and built research collaborations, by providing over $430 million to study some of the scientific and technical obstacles to improved health in the developing world.[10]

The Grand Challenges program is said to have been envisioned by Bill Gates himself, in conjunction with Rick Klausner, who was then the head the Global Health program at the Gates Foundation.* As Gates noted when he unveiled the initiative at the World Economics Forum in Davos in 2003, he and Klausner aimed to emulate David Hilbert's grand challenges to his fellow mathematicians one hundred years earlier. In 1900, Hilbert had defined what he thought were the twenty-three most important unsolved problems remaining in mathematics—and he did so in a way that captured the attention of the best mathematicians and led to the solution of all but a few of the grand challenges over the next several decades.[11]

---

* Klausner is a brilliant scientist and energetic leader who served as director of the National Cancer Institute during most of my time at the NIH.

The Gates Foundation's concept was similar to Hilbert's, although it ultimately required many more participants and entailed a more complex decision-making process. Rather than depend on one mathematical genius like Hilbert to identify the great problems left in mathematics, the Gates Foundation (in conjunction with the Foundation for the NIH) organized an effort to define the major scientific and technical obstacles that impede progress against diseases that disproportionately affect people living in poor countries. This involved extensive exchanges between the public health and scientific communities and a panel of assembled experts. And then, because biology and medicine are now much more expensive than old-style mathematics, large amounts of money and multiple review panels were needed to select and fund the most imaginative plans for confronting the new grand challenges.

Klausner asked me to chair an international board of senior scientists to solicit and select ideas that might become Grand Challenges and then oversee a process to award grants. The Grand Challenges concept quickly captured the attention of scientists throughout the world, including many who had not, until then, been working on diseases of the developing world. The seriousness of the commitment was represented by the initial announcement that $200 million would be available to fund the program; the number was later doubled by the Gates Foundation and further increased by funding from the Canadian Institutes for Health Research and the Wellcome Trust in the UK. The scientific board received over a thousand proposals of ideas for Grand Challenges, spent an exhausting weekend at the Airlie House conference center in Virginia in the late summer of 2003, trying to find the best ideas and then fashion them into stimulating challenges, which were organized in relation to major health goals. For example, to improve childhood vaccination programs, we challenged the scientific community to create vaccines that can be used in a single dose, administered without needles, or stored without refrigeration. Or to control insects that serve as vectors of infectious diseases, like malaria, we challenged scientists to come up with chemical or genetic strategies to reduce or incapacitate disease-transmitting insects.

In October, in a paper published in *Science* magazine,[12] we advertised the list of the fourteen Grand Challenges that we had selected, explained the selection process, and described the next steps for those seeking grants to address the challenges. The response was remarkable: about fifteen hundred teams of scientists, including many that were large, from several countries or from several institutions, both nonprofit and commercial, let us know that they were interested in tackling one of the Grand Challenges. We winnowed down these potential applicants to about four hundred, invited full applications from them, assembled about half a dozen review groups to evaluate the proposals, then reconvened the scientific board to make final decisions about funding. When all was settled, about forty-three awards were made, averaging about $10 million each.

In October 2007, the Grand Challenges grantees traveled to Cape Town, South Africa, for their third annual meeting. Gratifyingly, progress was evident on a variety of fronts. For instance, several grantees reported on new methods for delivering vaccines without needle injection, and others showed new ways to modify insect behavior with chemical odorants or with genetic manipulation. At this stage, very little was ready to be considered for widespread use, but the prospects for changing the practice of medicine and public health in poor countries seemed encouraging. Furthermore, the international teams formed to work on the Grand Challenges appeared to be doing well, and the multiple teams attacking the same problem had established strong channels of communication, a cooperative effort that counters the common conception of scientists as unduly competitive and secretive.

C. P. Snow's Predictions about Poverty

In his Rede Lecture on the two cultures, delivered some fifty years ago, C. P. Snow argued that only the culture of science and technology, not the culture of the arts, was equipped to repair what he saw as the greatest threat to the world's future: the growing disparities between the nations rich and the poor.[13] To fail to do so by the year 2000, he said in his British way, was "just not on." "Once the trick of getting rich is known, as it now is," he wrote, "the world can't survive half rich and half poor." Clearly, we haven't met his deadline; if anything, the gap has grown wider over the past fifty years, and it won't be easy to close it.

My occasional experiences of working to promote global health research during the past decade have convinced me that we can and should do more to support science in lower-income countries, especially science in the service of local problems. These problems affect essential features of life anywhere in the world: health, energy, the environment, and industrial development. Poor countries are sometimes penalized by conditions that inhibit their ability to respond to efforts to improve their science: civil war or other forms of political instability, graft in government, poor educational systems, and a loss of indigenous talent to more advanced nations. But in those several countries that have reduced obstacles to the development of scientific programs, there is often eager receptivity to ideas and people from abroad and a willingness to introduce science into a culture that may initially have a poor understanding of it.

I have seen this work most memorably in the Malaria Research and Training Center (MRTC) that the NIH and the U.S. Agency for International Development (USAID) set up in Bamako, the capital of Mali, more than a decade ago. Mali is one of the world's poorest nations, but strong national and tribal allegiances have brought several well-trained health workers, entomologists, and other scientists back to the country. This has happened, in part, because an excellent laboratory for clinical, insect, and parasite research, with modern instruments, Internet connections, governmental support, and even NIH grants and American collaborators, is available at the MRTC. The MRTC has become a focal point for research and training throughout Africa, holding scientific meetings and teaching courses in laboratory practice. When I visited Bamako after the malaria meeting in Dakar in 1997, I was impressed that Mali's President A. O. Konaré, himself an anthropologist, and the physician who led the National Assembly were well acquainted with the personnel and accomplishments of the center. They also recognized that the construction of research satellites in rural Mali was bringing better health care and knowledge about malaria to distant places that would otherwise not use the best practices to prevent and treat the disease.

GLOBALIZING SCIENCE AS AN ARM OF FOREIGN POLICY

In the example of the MRTC in Bamako, we can see an important means to enlarge and improve our relations with foreign countries. Science, and especially science related to health and other shared, beneficial goals, can be an effective arm of foreign policy. The methods and findings of science are inherently universal, and the manner of conducting science—in a common language, with common purpose and values, and with shared materials and information often provided through genuine collaborations—is conducive to improved relations.

One day in 1997, because of my recent visit to Mali, I was invited by the State Department to join several other members of the administration for lunch with President Konaré, who was visiting the United States. To my chagrin, the conversation was largely devoted to a discussion of some unfortunate irregularities in his recent election, marring Mali's record as an African nation that supports the principles of democracy. Wouldn't it have been more productive, especially with some scientist-administrators on hand, to devote part of the luncheon discussion to the possibilities of building other labs and training centers in Mali to complement the effort that has been made on malaria?

We should be making these efforts in other places as well. In Cuba, for instance, where relations with the United States remain chilly and stalemated, Havana has developed an excellent biotechnology center, staffed largely with people trained in Europe and North America. The center is a significant supplier of traditional vaccines to Central and South America and has even developed a novel vaccine against a form of meningitis. When I gave a series of lectures there, during a weeklong excursion to Cuba with Connie in January of 1993, I was amazed by the resilience of the center's scientists and by their eagerness to hear about developments in biology that might allow them to be more effective. Shouldn't we be encouraging connections between our scientists and those in Havana who are working against significant odds to improve health in their region?

Regrettably, in an age dominated by fears of terrorism and by a largely reactionary government led by George W. Bush, we have failed to seize many of the opportunities to use science to improve relations with other nations, including many of those who have traditionally been our allies, as well as those that have flaunted their hostility toward the United States. Our increasingly belligerent attitude towards immigrants, the laborious procedures required to obtain visas, a few high-profile instances in which we have denied visas to eminent scientists,* and the pitifully limited attention we have given to education, science, and technology in poor countries—all of these are undermining our position as a leader of a free world.

There has been one bright line in an otherwise unremitting litany of missed opportunities: the large investments that the Bush administration has made in the President's Emergency Program for AIDS Relief (PEPFAR) and in the Global Fund for AIDS, Tuberculosis, and Malaria.[15] But, unless we change our behavior in the near future, this one set of good deeds will be forgotten under the weight of misdeeds.

It has not been easy, even with more enlightened administrations, to provide the kind of financial and political support for health and science that is appropriate to the needs of poor countries. Even with a rapidly rising budget for the NIH in the final years of my time there, it would have been difficult to advocate a major redirection of funds toward the study of diseases that are rare in the United States but common in poor parts of the world. Because the budget of FIC, the one component of the NIH devoted entirely to international health and research, has been traditionally small, it was possible to accelerate its growth in the late 1990s, but that did not have a very significant effect on its resources and activities, in part because it lacked the staff required to build large and complex research programs.

The missed opportunities to make a more concerted effort to promote global health in the Clinton administration were not confined to the NIH. During those years, the USAID, traditionally charged to provide financial aid to many valuable programs in the developing world, had lost prestige and funding. For instance, to my astonishment, the agency had no senior experts on malaria and was unable to contribute intellectually or financially to our efforts to build the Multilateral Initiative on Malaria. And, despite a marked improvement in the U.S. economy in the late 1990s and despite an administration that professed sympathy toward

* The denial of a visa to Goverdham Mehta, the eminent Indian chemist in Bangalore, in February 2006, long after 9/11, was especially embarrassing, and incited many angry comments against the United States, even though the Immigration Service had improved some of its post-9/11 practices by then. When the State Department later attempted to issue a visa, the frustrated and humiliated Mehta refused to accept it.[14]

the developing world, no significant scale-up of humanitarian aid programs occurred.

In 1998, when the Clintons were preparing for their multinational
trip to Africa in the early spring, the president and Mrs. Clinton invited
me and Tony Fauci, the head of the National Institute of Allergy and
Infectious Diseases, to brief them informally on the status of health,
health care, and health research in Africa. We spoke with them, especially
the First Lady, at length about AIDS, tuberculosis, malaria, and other
infectious and noninfectious diseases, suggesting ways that the Clintons
could use their visit to encourage more attention to these issues, even in
very poor countries. When reports of their travels and speeches appeared
in the press, many topics were emphasized: tourism and trade, human
rights and democracy, environment, economics, and education, but not
health or science. The messages delivered and the trip itself were worthy,
and beneficial for our relationships with African nations. But I suspect
that the former president, now the head of the medically oriented Clinton Foundation, would agree that some important opportunities for promoting health and science were missed.

Attitudes in poor countries toward the leading powers have not been
helped by the rigid policies on drug pricing and intellectual property that
have been adopted by some (but certainly not all) of the major pharmaceutical companies. Although a few companies have recently devoted
efforts to the development of drugs that would be useful mainly in the
developing world, such enlightened approaches have been rare, for obvious economic reasons.* In response, many poor nations have viewed the
health industries and their wealthy host countries with suspicion when
proposals are made to study indigenous plants, animals, or microorganisms, as sources for useful compounds or even as parts of environmental

---

* I recall making a proposal to encourage more investment in drug development for treatment
of diseases prevalent in poor countries at an annual meeting of pharmaceutical leaders at the
luxurious Greenbrier resort in West Virginia in 1999. At the end of a speech about NIH policies, I suggested that the industry establish a tithing procedure by which all major companies
would devote a small portion of the profits from any blockbuster drugs to the purchase of
shares in a new company devoted to finding drugs for the developing world. At worst, a small
amount of money would be lost, but good feelings would be generated; at best, some profits
from new lifesaving medicines would be gained. The idea was greeted with derision, defen-
siveness, and silence.

or epidemiological surveys. Building greater trust between the rich and the poor will be required if health sciences are going to achieve the greatest possible benefits in poor countries.

Of course, missed opportunities to put the world's knowledge to better use have been common in human history. But, despite many failures, the opportunities persist, especially in a world that has been made smaller and more interactive by telecommunications, jet transport, and the Internet. Certainly, the possibilities for globalizing science, including the health sciences, go well beyond the few examples sketched out briefly in this chapter. In many parts of the world where science has been traditionally neglected or had an uneven record of accomplishment, there are signs of growth and interest. Biotechnology and information technology firms are proliferating in India; educational and scientific enterprises are being developed through collaborations between U.S. universities and rulers of some states in the Persian Gulf (Qatar, the Emirates, and Saudi Arabia); and facilities and funds for basic science are growing in parts of Asia (especially Korea, Singapore, and China) and even in some African countries (like South Africa and Rwanda). The traditionally strong scientific programs in Europe have been enhanced by additional funds from centralized sources, such as the European Union, with the result that countries with weaker programs, like Portugal and Greece, are doing better. In Cyprus, a country still torn by conflicts between Turkish and Greek elements, a new research university, the Cyprus Institute, is being created to serve the eastern region of the Mediterranean basin, with programs in energy, environment, economics, archaeology, and health.[16]

These are hopeful signs in a world beset with energy shortages, environmental degradation, climate change, persistent diseases, poor educational systems, and stubborn difficulties in supplying water and food to all its inhabitants. There are no easy fixes to these dilemmas. But any solutions are going to require a much broader pursuit and application of science. To achieve this, all parts of the world will need to participate in the adventures of science. In the process of globalizing science, the world is likely to become a better place, in part simply because its scientists are working together.

CHAPTER 15

Science Publishing and Science Libraries
in the Internet Age

—

I want a poor student to have the same means of indulging his learned
curiosity, of following his rational pursuits, of consulting the same
authorities, of fathoming the most intricate inquiry as the richest man
in the kingdom.

—ANTONIO PANIZZI,
THE FIRST LIBRARIAN OF
THE BRITISH MUSEUM,
1836

THE INTERNET AND THE DESKTOP COMPUTER HAVE TRANSFORMED THE
way science is practiced in virtually all fields, and the biomedical sciences
have not been exempt. Today most scientists obtain, use, and produce
information in ways that would have been unrecognizable twenty or thirty
years ago. These changes have profoundly and most contentiously affected
an aspect of science that is at the core of any scientist's life: the ways that
we publish, disseminate, read, store, and retrieve research papers.

In this chapter, I describe two of the most prominent features of this
still evolving landscape—public digital libraries and "open access"
publishing—both of which depend on an extraordinary feature of the
digital world: one copy of a text can suffice to provide it electronically,
instantaneously, and without further costs to anyone at any time and in
any place. The chapter will also reveal that I have been an enthusiastic
proponent of both the new libraries and the new publishing methods for

nearly a decade. As a result, this account will reflect my personal experiences and my passions for the subjects.

Public digital libraries of science are compendia of research articles, journals, and books; they constitute "databases" of published work that can be rapidly searched by anyone with an Internet connection. Unlike traditional public libraries, composed of paper copies of books and journals, their potential reach is infinite and thus threatening to publishers who depend on book sales and subscriptions. Because of this financial threat, we are still, despite recent progress, quite far from assembling open digital libraries that fulfill their potential as storehouses of knowledge.

The open access publishing movement seeks an even more radical change in the way scientific information is distributed. The goal is to deliver articles to all, immediately and freely, from an open access journal's website and from a public digital library. By making scientific information widely and swiftly available, open access publishers intend to be more useful than traditional publishers, who base their business on barriers to access, financing their journals with subscriptions for paper copies and for permission to view digital versions. Open access publishing, like subscription-based publishing, has real costs that must be paid—for reviewing, editing, producing, and formatting its journals. Because it abjures subscription barriers to access, open access publishing has adopted an alternative financial model. The costs are paid by the authors or, much more commonly, by the agencies that support the research.*

Viewed together, public digital libraries and open access publishing promise great benefits for science and society: equity, through universal and unfettered delivery of knowledge, mostly a product of public funding; more effective practice of science; and reduction in overall costs.

Everyone agrees that information technology is already fully capable of performing the tasks necessary to build extensive digital libraries of the existing biomedical literature and to convert publication practices to an open access mode. But, as this chapter will show, significant obstacles have slowed the development of these means for enhancing the use of scientific

---

* The formal definition and characteristics of open access publishing were agreed to at a meeting of the interested parties at the headquarters of the Howard Hughes Medical Institute, in Bethesda, Maryland, in the spring of 2003.[1]

texts. Traditional publishers have been concerned that digital libraries and a change in business models could entail a significant loss of revenues from subscriptions—reducing the profits for commercial publishers, whose margins now often exceed 30 percent, and affecting the ability of some scientific societies that publish journals to sponsor other worthwhile activities and meet staff payrolls. Many laboratory scientists have also resisted the new developments because of loyalties to existing journals, fears of disturbing a cultural environment that has supported their career growth, or misapprehensions about how open access publishing would work.

BECOMING AN ADVOCATE FOR NEW PRACTICES

Early in 1999, my final year as NIH director, I became a radical exponent of new methods for creating and using the scientific literature. Before my conversion, I was, like most of my colleagues, relatively unconcerned with the practices of scientific journals and the evolution of libraries of science. I hadn't thought much about how journals distributed the work they published, how they were paid or how much profit they made, or who owned the articles after publication. Like everyone in my field, I was gratified by the improvements that had occurred in ways to search the scientific literature. In particular, I learned to love PubMed, the website made freely available to everyone in the world by the National Library of Medicine at the NIH.[2]

PubMed is not a true library: it doesn't contain full texts. But it provides a very important library tool, a digital card catalog, that allows any user to seek lists of authors and titles, with abstracts for most of the entries, from most of the very extensive biomedical research literature. These lists are therefore remarkably convenient guides to published scientific or medical work, explaining why millions of people—and not just scientists and physicians—use PubMed every day. In addition, those who are privileged to work at institutions that have paid for subscriptions to the journals in which desired articles appeared can be linked to those journals through their institutional libraries and print out the full texts, if they exist in a digital form.*

* Only a few journals have digitized articles published before 1990; increasingly, these must be sought in library archives since most institutional libraries have dramatically reduced the

Before my eyes were opened to the potential for much wider electronic access to the scientific literature, I hadn't given much thought to how well the existing system served those who were not affiliated with major centers of learning and so could not get access to the full text of papers listed in PubMed. And I hadn't considered whether the computational advances that helped to create PubMed could be used to make yet more dramatic changes, so that systems for publishing, storing, and distributing scientific reports could be made more effective and more equitable.

I did, of course, recognize the enormous significance that journals have in the lives of all scientists. From my perspective as a laboratory scientist, I knew which journals were likely to publish papers I cared about—those with high academic standards, a strong reputation, and a focus on my special interests, such as virology, cancer genetics, or the biology of cancer cells. Those journals were, not surprisingly, the ones to which I turned weekly or monthly for new information, and the ones in which I usually aspired to have my own work appear. But I gave little thought to the fundamental principles on which the industry was based or to its operations.

This attitude was not simply self-serving. My colleagues and I had good reasons to respect our favorite journals for both the quality of the work they published and the rigor and aesthetics of the editing process. But our loyalty to these journals also had a self-serving aspect, one that discouraged us from thinking about how methods for publishing and distributing new papers might be improved. Gratitude to these journals for accepting our articles for publication, hopes for future acceptances, and a traditional notion of good citizenship in the scientific community made us willing to oblige the journals in various ways. For instance, like most of my colleagues, I turned the copyrights on my accepted papers over to the publishers without pause or complaint, and I freely donated my services and time to review and edit the work of other authors. I viewed these activities, which often took several hours or more each week, as dues to the scientific community—efforts that were also inher-

space they can assign to printed journals. Because most scientists now rarely bother with print versions, a large portion of our scientific legacy is consulted with decreasing frequency.

ently interesting or occasions for tutoring trainees about critical readings of new work. I don't think it ever occurred to me that I was also providing free labor to journals that were often making large earnings for stockholders (in the for-profit sector) or for scientific societies (in the nonprofit sector).

Occasionally, I lamented long delays in publication, high charges for color photographs or reprints, or high subscription fees (although many of those fees were paid by grants or institutional libraries). But I didn't develop a coherent point of view about how scientists publish their work and about how our institutions store and distribute published reports until the end of 1998, when a colleague at Stanford, Pat Brown, pushed me to think about some important questions: Was the scientific community taking adequate advantage of the Internet and new computational tools to improve publication practices and use of the literature? Could electronic public libraries provide much more than the titles and abstracts stored in the PubMed catalog—for instance, full texts of published reports? If information from DNA sequencing efforts, such as the Human Genome Project, was made freely and fully available on the Internet, couldn't we do the same for the scientific literature?

Following Pat Brown's lead, I soon learned about new publishing practices and about the prospects for building public digital libraries. While still serving as NIH director, I became a strong advocate for these new methods and helped to launch the first public digital library for the biomedical sciences, PubMed Central. Since then, I have become almost obsessive about the goals of expanding such libraries and creating open access journals. Now, more than eight years later, I continue to devote a significant portion of each week to advocacy for library and publishing practices that would make the world's scientific literature a more potent and accessible resource. In particular, I remain deeply engaged in the oversight of an organization called Public Library of Science (PLoS), a thriving open access publishing group that three of us founded more than seven years ago.[3]

In this chapter, I will describe how my conversion occurred, why the battles over publication practices have been virulent, and what PLoS is trying to achieve. But first I need to explain why this issue is so important to scientists and why it should matter to others as well.

How Scientists Are Affected by Publication Practices

Just as appropriated dollars are the "lifeblood" of a federal agency, so is publication the lifeblood in the career of a working scientist. Publication is the means by which an investigator tells his or her colleagues, the world in general, and posterity about what he or she has found in the course of doing experiments and how those findings might be interpreted in the light of preexisting knowledge. Through publication, an individual's (or, more commonly, a group's) experimental work and thought become part of the fabric of science, something to be talked about, contested, admired, built upon, criticized, or even neglected (but with the potential for redis-covery at a more opportune moment).

The written record is also crucial to the development of a scientist's career in deeply pragmatic terms. It is the most decisive means by which a scientist is evaluated by others at every stage—early in career develop-ment, when postdoctoral fellowships and first jobs are sought; in the midst of careers, when decisions are made about promotion and tenure; and later, when an investigator may become a candidate for prizes or for election to academies.

In an ideal world, all scientists would advance their knowledge by carefully reading the work of all other scientists, or at least the work of all those in the same field. That may once have been possible in the biomed-ical sciences, certainly before the twentieth century and even as recently as the 1960s, when the fields of biology and medicine were still relatively small by today's standards. But our scientific community has gotten very large, and the number of articles published each year in fields like genet-ics or developmental biology or oncology, let alone biomedical sciences in general, is far too large for any one person to do more than sample the offerings and hope to find what is most important and useful for his or her own work.

Under these circumstances, faced with the need to read selectively, we have all sought ways to improve the odds of reading productively. One time-honored way is *browsing*—looking through the tables of contents of those journals that we have learned from personal experience to be the most likely to contain papers we will value. These scans are intended to ensure that we encounter nearly everything of enormous importance to the broad expanse of biomedical research and most things of significance in our fields of special interest. Browsing is done most commonly by sub-scribing to perhaps a dozen selected journals—some wide in scope, oth-ers the leaders in a specialized field—and by reviewing the titles and authors of papers in every issue, reading relevant abstracts, and finally reading a few papers in full, carefully and critically.

Another way to approach the scientific literature is by *searching*—using whatever tools are available to survey a much larger set of journals sys-tematically for articles that address particular topics of interest. Twenty or thirty years ago this was done using the *Index Medicus*, a printed tome that listed all papers by topic and authors. People like me would regularly need to travel to our institutional libraries to consult the *Index* when wish-ing to learn the latest information about an unfamiliar topic or when needing to ensure that we weren't overlooking papers published on a familiar topic in unfamiliar journals. Now, of course, personal computers and digital databases have changed our habits. For at least the past decade, searching for articles in the biomedical research literature has been performed with much greater ease and thoroughness, by using (especially) PubMed, the NIH's online archive of titles, authors, and abstracts.

PubMed: Virtues and Limitations

The PubMed database compiles the titles, authors, and abstracts from all articles published in legitimate biomedical research journals over the past several decades, and it is used by millions of people, not just scientists, every day. (The others include students, teachers, journalists, observers of the biotech and pharmaceutical industries, science policy analysts, and patients, their families, and disease advocacy groups.) The method of use is simple: enter a couple of subject words or the name of an author or two, and the search engine will instantly deliver a long list of authors, titles, and journal citations, with an abstract available for most items.

The frustration comes when the user tries to see the entire papers, not just the abstracts. Until the start of 2000, access to the full text was possible only if the user had a personal subscription or worked at an institution that subscribed to the journal that published the article. Then he or she could link to the journal's website through the institution's library and view the complete paper. More recently, as I will describe in greater detail below, the situation has begun to improve, with the establishment of the NIH's full-text public digital archive called PubMed Central. Still, for most titles provided to most PubMed users, access to the full text will either be denied or permitted only after a fee is paid to the publisher (generally in the range of twenty to thirty dollars per article).

Not surprisingly, these barriers are irritants to many members of the public—especially to those who realize that much of the research was funded by their tax revenues, that the papers were written and reviewed at no charge by academic scientists, and that the charges and limitations on use are imposed by publishers to whom the authors have innocently relinquished copyright. Scientists at prestigious institutions may also become frustrated (and sympathetic with less well-connected individuals) when they find that they cannot gain access to articles when searching PubMed, at home or while traveling, from a computer terminal that does not belong to an academic institution's network.

WHY SCIENTISTS LOVE CERTAIN JOURNALS

Despite the importance and attractions of surveying the entire literature, nearly all of us maintain loyalties and subscriptions to certain journals that have traditionally contained articles of especially high interest and quality, particularly if those journals, such as *Science* and *Nature*, also contain essays, book reviews, political stories and commentary, obituaries, and other features. These allegiances to a few journals among the thousands of others in medical research also reflect established hierarchies of journals, based on the frequencies with which articles from them are cited. These rankings now have a profound and often invidious influence on the cultures of science and higher education. Publication in the most prominent and oft-cited journals is frequently taken as a goal and a virtue in itself, irrespective of the quality of individual papers. Status conferred by the acceptance of papers in journals like *Science*, *Cell*, and *Nature*, or even in subsidiary journals of these "flagship" periodicals (e.g., *Molecular Cell* or *Nature Biotechnology*) has an indisputable effect on the process of recruitment and promotion of faculty.

Keeping track of the alleged impact of journals, as gauged by the number of times their papers are cited, has itself become a minor industry, sometimes called bibliometrics. The most famous (or infamous) of its indicators, the "impact factor," is based on the average frequency at which a journal's papers are cited by all other papers each year. The excessive attention given to this pseudo-science, especially in Europe and other parts of the world, is having a noxious effect on evaluation of scientists for recruitment and promotion. Such indices are not independent of the overall quality of the journal, of course, but they are averages, so they don't apply to all papers. Furthermore, the numbers are influenced by other factors, including the number of papers published in an area of science. (If there are more papers in one specialized field than another, the number of citations of papers in that field is likely to be higher.)*

The tendency to look so favorably on those whose papers have appeared in certain journals—most famously *Nature, Science*, and *Cell*—has created an unhealthy compulsion among graduate students and postdoctoral fellows to attempt to publish in such journals, thereby reinforcing the hierarchy. Because of these pressures, other aspects of a journal that might contribute to its appropriateness (review processes and criteria, allowable length of articles, distribution and access policies, editing and presentation of figures) will be largely disregarded when a venue for publication is chosen. This can make it difficult for new journals, even those with more effective or more enlightened policies, including open access publication methods, to break into the upper echelons of the hierarchy.

* The best way to break the dominance of the journal hierarchy and impact factors is for institutional leaders to say that reviews of candidates for appointment and promotion must include critical reading of the candidates' best papers, not just an arithmetic accounting of the number of papers in "top journals." At MSKCC we now do this by asking those being proposed for our top faculty ranks to describe the significance of their five best scientific papers over the past several years and by requiring members of the promotion committees to read and evaluate those papers.

A BRIEF HISTORY OF SCIENCE PUBLISHING

How did things come to be this way? For over three hundred years—at least since the first issues of what was arguably the first real scientific journal, *Philosophical Transactions*, the Proceedings of the Royal Society of London, came rolling off the presses in 1665—the written record of science has been distributed on paper to paying subscribers and stored in private, academic, and public libraries. Compared with a system in which discoveries were usually announced and exhibited at elite gatherings of scholars and then written down in the form of large bound books by individual authors, the creation of the scientific journal as a compendium of relatively short articles, issued several times a year, was a major event that democratized science and fostered the communication of its findings. With the development of a process for reviewing contributions by fellow scientists ("peer review"), some control of quality was introduced. Payments for subscriptions sustained the journals published by scientific societies and eventually yielded profits for commercial publishers, especially as the number of scientists and research institutions grew.

This system worked reasonably well for a few hundred years, as long as the international scientific community was relatively small, the number of journals was few, and the segment of the population who wanted to read about recent discoveries had reasonable access to printed journals. Moreover, there was no obvious alternative. But we are now living in a very different world. Today there are over six thousand periodicals and numerous monographs in the biomedical sciences. Nearly all of them are produced by a few large, for-profit publishing companies, most of them international, or by a few dozen not-for-profit scientific societies and institutions. Science and medicine have assumed central roles in our society, and many people other than scientists and physicians want access to new information. Science is also increasingly a global activity, not just confined to academic institutions and industries in the most developed countries. So the traditional means of distributing information on paper are no longer adequate to the task of efficient distribution to potential readers. But, most important, our society's approach to the use and dissemination of information has been radically altered by computer science and the Internet, yet the impact of information technology on scientific publishing has only begun to be felt.

THE BUSINESS OF SCIENCE PUBLISHING

The economics of publishing scientific journals are unusual and differ from practices in other sectors of the publishing industry, in large part because the authors—scientists who write the articles at no cost to the publishers—seek fame but not money.* After writing their manuscripts and revising them in response to critical reviews (which are also normally provided to journals free of charge by other scientists), the author-scientists celebrate an acceptance notice, not by signing a contract for payment, as most professional writers would expect to do, but by transferring the copyright, which they should be entitled to keep, to the publishers. Moreover, quite a few publishers ask authors to defray the cost of publication in the form of "page charges" or payments for reprints or special features, like color photographs. Then the publishers sell the journals to individuals (mostly scientists, many of whom are also frequent authors) and to institutions (the places where the authors work and read), generally with high profit margins, often exceeding 30 percent. Most of these charges—the publication fees and institutional subscriptions in particular—are absorbed by the government and other funding agencies that have underwritten the scientific work. Taken together, this represents a major subsidy, now probably close to one billion dollars annually, of the publishing industry by the NIH—paid either directly through publication costs and subscription expenses charged to individual grants or indirectly through support of library subscriptions at research institutions. From the perspective of funding agencies, such costs are reasonable and necessary. They represent a relatively small fraction, a few percent, of the cost of doing research; and, unless it is published, scientific work remains unknown and hence irrelevant to the

---

* Although scientists are never paid for writing primary research reports, they are sometimes compensated for review articles or brief essays, and usually paid, sometimes handsomely, for writing books, especially textbooks that are widely used in high school or university classrooms. For instance, I certainly expect to be paid, modestly if not handsomely, for writing this book!

growth of knowledge. But it is also in the interests of the funders of research to control costs of publication and to enhance access to all published work.

Because each scientific report has its unique characteristics and unique findings, and because scientists publish the primary description of new findings only once, all scientific journals consist of articles that are not published elsewhere. In this sense, they are inherently monopolies—there can be no competing journal with the same material. Hence if the information is desirable and cannot be obtained elsewhere, the journal can demand high prices from subscribers, especially when those subscribers are academic research institutions that depend on their scientists to procure government grants and feel obliged to satisfy scientists' demand for the journals, even when they are extremely expensive. (At our own library at MSKCC, for instance, twenty journals that we purchase charge annual subscription fees of more than $5,000.) When large commercial publishers produce journals of uneven quality and desirability, they sometimes resort to "bundling" journal offerings, especially to institutions, so that the purchase of subscriptions to literally hundreds of indifferent journals, perhaps at a modest cost reduction, may be required to obtain one highly desirable product.*

Needless to say, this business can be very profitable for stockholders at large companies like Reed-Elsevier, the European conglomerate that attracts much of the ire of people like me. This company owns literally thousands of journals in the worlds of science, medicine, and engineering, some that are revered (such as *Cell* and its sister journals) and many that provide some service for highly specialized fields but are relatively humdrum and infrequently cited. By combining high institutional subscription rates, bundling strategies, and other business practices, the companies can produce those high profit margins that the investment firm Bear Stearns has characterized as "a stockholder's dream come true."[4]

Many scientific societies have also come to depend on journal subscription revenues that exceed the costs of production to support their

---

* In the past few years, academic protests against the use of this practice by Reed-Elsevier and others have sometimes improved the offered contracts, but the practice persists.

other good works, such as organizing meetings and helping with scientific careers. Some societies also claim that they attract new members by offering discounted subscription rates on their journals.* Most of the societies have been highly resistant to any movements toward greater access, even to the point of battling congressional directives to contribute to public libraries like PubMed Central, and hesitant to experiment with even those changes being contemplated by the private sector, like charging authors for an open access option. These inflexible policies have been largely championed by society staff, who (unlike the annually changing society officers from the scientific community) have long-term appointments, depend on society revenues for their salaries, know the financial plan that has worked historically, and often have an understandable allegiance to traditional features of their journals. Nevertheless, not all societies operate in this way. Some, like the American Society of Cell Biology, do not depend on their journals for income and receive most of their revenue from membership and meeting fees, allowing them to consider publication practices from the perspective of working scientists and the public.

The profits earned by publishers of scientific journals would be less objectionable if subscription fees did not severely limit access to those journals throughout the world. Even in the United States and other leading economies, where the scientific work has been performed, largely with public monies, it is not easy to view most of these journals without being a faculty member or trainee at a wealthy academic institution or employed by a large corporation that does scientific work. Outside the advanced countries, it is nearly impossible to obtain access to these journals, except for copies (usually out of date) that have been donated by scientists in rich countries or digital versions that some publishers offer for free to the very poorest countries, which have very few scientists.[5]

An unfortunate secondary consequence of price inflation for scientific journals has recently become evident in the academic sector, where the journals are in greatest demand and where scientists (who bring in most of the grant money) have a disproportionate influence on library

---

* Although this perk would disappear if societies converted to open access publishing, the societies could instead offer reduced authors' fees to members.

decision-making. Already strapped for cash, the libraries must compensate for the expenditures on scientific journals by reducing their purchases of journals and monographs in other fields—fields such as literature, history, and social sciences. As the historian and librarian Robert Darnton pointed out several years ago,[6] the loss of purchasing power at academic libraries affects the viability of university presses that publish scholarly work in the humanities and social sciences.

MY CONVERSION: THE MAKING OF A RADICAL

As recently as ten years ago, I was oblivious to the possibilities for transforming the ways in which scientific findings are disseminated. Like other scientists, I aspired to publish my work in what I considered to be the best journals; I subscribed to the journals I favored; and I worked at institutions that subscribed to most of the rest I might use. I applauded the electronic indices such as PubMed. (I was on hand, in my capacity as NIH director, when Vice-President Al Gore unveiled PubMed to the public in 1997.) And I was increasingly aware of the convenient digital forms of papers that some journals were providing to subscribers.

But my views broadened abruptly one morning in December of 1998 when I met Pat Brown for coffee, at the café that was formerly the famed Tassajara Bakery, on the corner of Cole and Parnassus, during a visit to San Francisco. Pat is an unusually brilliant medical scientist at Stanford who had worked with Mike Bishop and me in the 1980s, demonstrating for the first time that retroviruses could correctly integrate their DNA into another molecule of DNA in a test tube, not just in an intact cell.*

A few weeks before our coffee, Pat had learned about the methods being used by the physicist Paul Ginsparg and his colleagues at Los Alamos to allow physicists and mathematicians to share their work with one another over the Internet. They were posting "preprints" (articles not yet submitted or accepted for publication) at a publicly accessible

---

* Later, on his own at Stanford, Pat Brown developed some of the first methods for assessing thousands of genes for their activity (being read out to form messenger RNA) in selected cell types or tissues. These so-called high throughput arrays have revolutionized the practice of molecular biology, and Pat has been justly honored for his imaginative work in a variety of ways.

website (called LanX or arXiv)[7] for anyone to read and critique. Pat had presented these practices to his own laboratory group. The subsequent discussions prompted him to think about the possibilities for publishing work in the biomedical sciences on the Internet, recognizing that the large size of our field and its many cultural differences from physics would probably require other kinds of models than the one the physicists had used.

Initially, I could only listen. But I knew enough about the advantages of presenting papers in a digital format, the virtues of searching a database of complete articles, and the costs of publishing to recognize that Pat's ideas deserved a lot more attention. When I returned to my office at the NIH, I looked at Ginsparg's website, continued my conversation with Pat by email, and started thinking about how Internet-based distribution and storage of biomedical research articles could dramatically alter the way we worked.

TAKING ON THE PROBLEM: E-BIOMED

The more I thought about this, the more I was convinced that a radical restructuring of methods for publishing, transmitting, storing, and using biomedical research reports might be possible and beneficial. In a spirit of enthusiasm and political innocence, I wrote a lengthy manifesto, proposing the creation of an NIH-supported online system, called E-biomed.[8]

The main goal was to create a central repository of scientific reports that would be immediately available to all Internet users for digital searches or browsing. Many of these articles would simply be online versions of existing journals, accepted for publication after traditional peer review by established editorial boards. Some would be articles submitted to and reviewed by the editorial boards of new online journals formed to publish within the E-biomed system. But E-biomed would also display, in a separate section, reports that were not peer-reviewed in the traditional manner, including papers that might normally not be published at all, such as those describing a new method or idea, or those reporting negative results from experiments or clinical trials. The costs of building and maintaining the electronic platform and software would be paid by the

NIH, but the costs of reviewing, editing, and publishing would be covered by the editorial boards and the organizations that assembled them. An international governing board would oversee the operations and set the rules.

After showing my E-biomed document to some friends and the NIH institute directors, I was emboldened to send it to many scientists and reporters and to post it on the NIH director's website in early May of 1999. It did get attention: several dozen articles appeared in major newspapers and the leading science magazines, and I received hundreds of responses from scientists and other commentators from around the world. While there were many encouraging comments, there were at least as many criticisms, concerns, and troubled questions. I tried to respond to these about six weeks later by posting an addendum to the original E-biomed manifesto.[9] Some were easy to answer: the NIH was not trying to take over the publishing industry, the material that was not peer-reviewed would be clearly delineated from articles that were reviewed by traditional methods, the contents would be properly archived, and so forth. But other issues were harder to deal with. Most importantly, I had not explained how a journal's costs of publication would be met in a system that would surely reduce, if not eliminate, paid subscriptions to the journals.

In retrospect, I see that I failed to propose a clear plan to finance what we would now call open access publishing. I had presumed that scientists had a strong allegiance to publication on paper, and I was trying to convince them of the virtues of digital publication by proposing an appealing transformation of science publishing, one that promoted greater access and utility. In fact, however, most scientists were more protective of their favorite journals than of paper itself, and they sought a gentler transition to an increasingly electronic world, a transition that would not threaten the viability of those journals. Others in the scientific community, including some who were receptive to the underlying concepts, worried that E-biomed might undermine peer review, that the multihued hierarchy of distinctive journals might be replaced by a gray monolith of government reports, that the NIH (and thus the federal government) would control all aspects of science publication, and that their professional societies and traditionally favored journals might be destroyed by this cyberjuggernaut.

Some of these concerns were answerable; others led me to modify the proposal in style or substance.

The most shrill opposition came, disappointingly, from the staffs of many respected scientific and medical societies, including some (like the American Society of Biochemistry and Molecular Biology) that had been in the vanguard of electronic formatting of scientific articles in their own journals (such as the *Journal of Biological Chemistry*). They said I was demeaning their past and current efforts to improve publication practices and threatening to undermine their means of support for other beneficial activities. Other societies welcomed the new ideas for disseminating scientific work; the American Society of Cell Biology, in particular, eventually made its journal, *Molecular Biology of the Cell*, into one that is virtually open access.

The for-profit publishing houses were also unhappy, and sent their lead lobbyist, the former congresswoman Pat Schroeder, to Capitol Hill to talk to members of my appropriations subcommittees. Even my strongest supporter in Congress, John Porter, was sufficiently concerned by her visit to ask me to come to his office to explain what I was trying to do, in a chat that was uncomfortable for both of us. According to him, Schroeder claimed that I was trying to undermine the free enterprise system by turning the NIH into a federal publishing company. Some of the warnings raised by Schroeder and others were designed to appeal to his belief in the free market, although I was not proposing to eliminate publishers or the competition for readers and authors. Admittedly, if E-biomed had been adopted in its original form, many of the participating journals would have lost revenues; the proposal lacked a credible business plan. But at that stage there was also no obligation to participate.

How E-biomed Became a Public Library: The Birth of PubMed Central

Despite continuing opposition to E-biomed from several quarters, by the end of 1999, as I was departing the NIH for MSKCC, I did have one important achievement to point to: the opening of a full-text public digital library of biomedical reports. Throughout the discussions of the E-biomed proposal and the subsequent modifications, I had received sensible and highly informed advice from David Lipman, the leader of NIH's computer science programs at the National Library of Medicine and the genius behind PubMed. David recognized, more acutely than I did, that the most compelling and achievable feature of the E-biomed proposal was not its complex scheme for web-based publishing. Changes in publication practices would need much more debate, preferably outside the domain of the NIH, to be accepted by the scientific community.

But David saw that another aspect of E-biomed, one that entailed the creation of a full-text public digital library, was within reach. He realized that a repository of this kind could be created, despite anticipated resistance from the publishers, if the deposition of articles occurred several months after the date of publication, so that the subscription base of existing journals would not be significantly eroded.*

By late August of 1999, largely through David's efforts, we promulgated an announcement of "an NIH-operated site for electronic distribution of life sciences research reports" called PubMed Central. As envisioned in the August announcement, PubMed Central would be less ambitious than E-biomed. It would have no role, not even an indirect one, in producing journals. But the new repository would be organized along the lines of the repository in the original E-biomed proposal, including a category of reports that were "screened but not formally peer-reviewed." When PubMed Central was launched at the end of December, however, that still contentious part of the proposal was also eliminated.

What remained in the PubMed Central plan seemed practical and achievable. The new digital library would make accessible to all Internet users the peer-reviewed articles voluntarily provided, preferably within six months of publication, by any journals, new or established, that were listed in PubMed. Importantly, PubMed Central would be conveniently integrated with PubMed, an NIH service that was already respected and time-tested. Copyrights could be retained by the journals, and did not need to be held by the authors as proposed for E-biomed (as is now prescribed for open access publishing).

---

* Library research had shown that most subscribers browse their journals for only a couple of months after publication; after that, they find articles of interest by searches. So a delay of six months before articles become freely Internet accessible would deter all but a few readers from canceling subscriptions.

We naïvely thought that many journals would willingly participate. The interval between publication and deposition would protect their subscription base. Making articles more easily available would enhance reputations and serve the public. And scientists would appreciate the enhanced access that others would have to their work and that they would have to the work of others. Yet, initially, PubMed Central was nearly empty. David, Pat Brown, and I persuaded a few journals to donate their material as an experiment—the *Proceedings of the National Academy of Sciences* was our most prestigious success—but nearly all subscription-based journals were nervous, if not antagonistic, fearing the proverbial slippery slope: shorter intervals between publication and submission, followed by declines in subscribers. An innovative commercial publisher in London, Vitek Tracz, was sufficiently convinced about the virtues of making scientific reports freely available that he founded a new organization, called BioMed Central,[10] to create open access journals—digital journals that derive income from authors' fees and from advertising. The name was clearly an homage to PubMed Central, and BioMed Central articles, placed in the digital library at the time of publication, constituted a significant fraction of PubMed Central's content in the early days.

For PubMed Central to thrive and for scientists to experience its advantages, more of the existing journals—especially the most prominent ones—had to make their articles available. The suggested interval between publication and deposition in the library was extended from six months to a year, in hopes of increasing the number of participating journals. By then, in 2000, I was no longer director of the NIH, and had been asked by the National Library of Medicine to serve as a member of PubMed Central's advisory board, along with Pat Brown and Paul Ginsparg (the inventor of the online archive of physics preprints). Those of us who were strong advocates for the new public library regarded the reluctance of publishers to participate as unacceptable obstructionism. After all, the publishers depended on the free services of publicly-funded scientists to produce their journals, but were unwilling to improve public access to the work of those scientists, even on terms— a one-year delay before submission—that would not materially affect their subscription rolls.

THE ORIGINS OF PLoS: FROM ADVOCACY TO OPEN ACCESS PUBLISHING

Pat and I decided to take political action. In doing so, we were joined by Mike Eisen, a young and exceptionally smart computational biologist who had been recruited recently to the faculty of UC Berkeley after working with Pat during postdoctoral studies at Stanford. Late in 2000, Pat, Mike, and I wrote a short declaration of purpose—we called it a pledge, publishers called it a boycott—in which we said that, one year hence, the signatories would no longer submit articles, provide reviewing or editing services, or purchase individual subscriptions to journals that had not agreed to deposit their articles with PubMed Central.[11] We called our advocacy effort the Public Library of Science (PLoS) to denote our goal of building a science library that would be open to all.

More than thirty thousand scientists from over one hundred countries signed the pledge. The campaign attracted attention in the science press and spurred discussion among my colleagues. But, during the ensuing year, fewer than one hundred journals of the roughly six thousand in biomedical sciences agreed to participate, and not many of these ranked among the most prominent. The poor level of participation made the pledge hard to carry out, since both trainees and full-fledged scientists have an understandable need to publish their best work in the most prestigious journals for career advancement and appropriate dissemination of important work. Only a few of the most committed signatories (and, of course, those of us who wrote it) felt obliged to honor their commitment to the letter. Even for us, this position created difficulties when other members of our labs and our research collaborators wanted to publish jointly authored work in noncompliant journals.

Despite its slow start, PubMed Central has steadily grown over the past few years, so that by the middle of 2007 it contained nearly a million full articles. By then, nearly three hundred journals were participating, and some—including prominent ones, like the *Proceedings of the National Academy of Science* and several journals published by the American Society of Microbiology—provided many years of content, even back to the founding of some journals. Still, this represents only about 5 percent of the journals in our field, and many journals that have refused to participate are among the most prominent and most frequently cited.*

PLoS Becomes a Publisher of Open Access Journals

By 2002, Pat, Mike Eisen, and I realized that even widespread endorsement of the PLoS pledge was not going to persuade most publishers to participate in PubMed Central. So we sought stronger measures to transform science publishing and demonstrate the virtues of enhanced access, and decided to publish open access journals ourselves. Of course, we were not the first to do this—BioMed Central was publishing quite a few, and some traditionally subscription-based journals, like the *Journal of Clinical Investigation*, were making their content freely available on their own websites—but we envisioned something more dramatic.

We aspired to produce open access journals of the very highest caliber—journals that could compete for exciting articles with the traditional powerhouses, like *Cell* or the *New England Journal of Medicine*; journals that would generate high-impact factors to attract high-end authors; and journals that would prove to a still skeptical scientific community that greater access, even true open access, was a practical goal, not just sophomoric idealism.

To do this, we drew up a prospectus for an open access, online publishing house that retained the name of our advocacy group, PLoS, and we persuaded the trustees of the Gordon and Betty Moore Foundation to support the idea. Once we had developed a reasonable business plan, the foundation gave us enough money—nine million dollars—to fund a publishing project that could, in principle, make us self-supporting in five years.** The essential feature of the financial proposal was the use of authors' fees to cover publication costs, which we estimated to range between one and three thousand dollars. We viewed such costs as reason-

---

* As will be evident near the end of this chapter, this situation has been dramatically changed by a congressional directive in the 2008 appropriations bill requiring deposition of papers by NIH-supported authors at PubMed Central.

** Now, just over five years after beginning to publish, and with the help of some additional philanthropy from the Sandler Foundation and others, our budget projections indicate that we are about two years away from self-sufficiency. Not a bad record for a "start-up."

able; they would represent about 1 percent of the average cost of doing the NIH-sponsored research required for one manuscript. Furthermore, we thought the publication fees should be considered a part of the cost of doing research; the work would be worth very little if it were not published.

At the heart of our plan was the creation of two outstanding, so-called flagship, journals, *PLoS Biology* and *PLoS Medicine*, which would be both broad in scope and sufficiently selective and prestigious to compete with the very best traditional, subscription-based journals in those large fields. Shortly thereafter, we would use the credentialed name PLoS to build a collection of journals dedicated to some of the most important disciplines in these fields, such as genetics, global health, computational biology, infectious diseases, and so forth. Finally, we would establish a broad, encyclopedic publishing site for all kinds of reports in biology and medicine that met a credible technical standard, regardless of perceived importance. This final step would be essential for two reasons. First, the high volume of publishing, with low editorial costs, would help to pay for the more selective, prestigious, and expensive journals. Second, this expansive repository would become the platform for many kinds of experiments in electronic publishing, including the use of postpublication exchanges between readers and authors.

The principal source of revenues would be publishing fees, paid by authors, usually from their grants, once their papers had been peer-reviewed and accepted.* We also expected to sell advertising space on the journals' websites and to solicit various kinds of philanthropic support. These might include foundation grants, such as the one given to us by the Moores; institutional and individual memberships, of the type offered by National Public Radio for not dissimilar services; and donations from friends of open access publishing, both scientists and nonscientists.

Because the world of traditional publishing employs a lot of very talented scientist-editors who are disaffected with the current system, we were able to hire several well-known editors from some of the most

---

* From the start, we recognized that some authors might not be able to afford these charges, and decided that no favorably reviewed paper would be turned away for this reason. In practice, over 90 percent of PLoS authors have paid their fees.

highly regarded journals, such as *Cell, Nature,* and *Lancet.* These acts of editorial rebellion immediately alerted many leading scientists to our efforts. We and our new editors then assembled a technical staff, rented offices in San Francisco and in Cambridge, UK, recruited boards of academic editors to help with reviews of manuscripts, and persuaded about ten outstanding people—including Paul Ginsparg, the creator of the physics preprint website, LanX; Larry Lessig, the founder of Creative Commons; and Allan Golston, then the chief financial officer of the Gates Foundation—to join the board of directors. With all these people in place, we were able to launch our first journal, *PLoS Biology*—covering, as we liked to say, "all of biology, from molecules to ecosystems"—in October 2003.

Right from the first issue, which featured a report of a brain stimulator to control movements of mechanical limb,[12] *PLoS Biology* has been highly successful, with many outstanding articles, frequent coverage in the press, and enormous numbers of visitors to the journal's website. The journal has scored well from the first measurement of that problematic, but closely watched, indicator, the impact factor. The high score has doubtless contributed significantly to the number of submissions, which has grown to more than two hundred manuscripts per month.*

The success of *PLoS Biology* has also influenced, and been influenced by, other signs of acceptance of open access publishing: support by many funding organizations; the continued growth of Vitek Tracz's BMC journals; and the introduction of an "open access option" for individual articles in a few prominent subscription-based journals, especially the *Proceedings of the National Academy of Sciences.* At the same time, PLoS itself has expanded in accord with the original plans, launching *PLoS Medicine* in October 2004, followed by community journals (*PLoS Pathogens, PLoS Computational Biology, PLoS Genetics, PLoS Neglected Tropical Diseases*), then the encyclopedic, high volume publishing site, called *PLoS ONE.***

We anticipate that *PLoS ONE* will become a novel platform for convening groups of scientists and others interested in specific aspects of science for continuing conversations after publication. In one model, PLoS

---

* Since *PLoS Biology* generally publishes fewer than twenty articles per month, the rejection rate is high; this factor both ensures prestige and drives expenses up, since well-paid professional editors must monitor the review process for rejected as well as accepted papers.

** All of these journals can, of course, be seen and used by anyone, anytime, at www.plos.org.

would cooperate with groups that have a special interest—a disease or a subdiscipline or a biological phenomenon—to build "hubs" or "portals" that contain up-to-date catalogs of relevant, publicly accessible articles, information about public events, links to serious blogs and other websites, and open conversations. We imagine a time when most people interested in an area of science would begin their day by logging onto one or more PLoS hubs to learn what is new—interactive publishing at its best.

PLoS has done these things and continues to thrive, while retaining its idealism. In less than five years, it has became a highly regarded scientific publishing house. At the same time, as an open access publisher and an advocate for public libraries, it has expanded the public's access to the scientific literature

SUPPORT FOR PUBLIC ACCESS FROM THOSE WHO FUND RESEARCH

A turn of the political and cultural tide in favor of expanded public access to the scientific literature in just the past year or two encourages confidence in the future of PLoS, open access journals in general, and public digital libraries. This shift reflects an alliance of common interests. Funders of research, both government agencies and nonprofit institutions, want to know that publications emerging from the work they support have the greatest possible distribution and impact; that can occur only if access to those papers is as easy as possible. Librarians, strapped for cash by the rising prices of institutional subscriptions, which can range up to $20,000 or more for journals that publish only once or twice a month, want more journals to be available through open access methods or digital public libraries. And many scientists have begun to appreciate the benefits of enhanced access, including the motivating prospect of being read and cited more frequently themselves.

Statements and actions from those who fund research have been especially important, because they get the attention of the scientists whom they support even more than do the journals that publish the scientists' work. The prestigious Howard Hughes Medical Institute (HHMI) was among the first to offer support, encouraging its investigators to publish in open access journals, providing them with supplementary funds to cover authors' fees, and, more recently (in the summer of 2007), insisting that all their work appear in PubMed Central within six months after publication. In taking this recent step, the HHMI was following the lead of the Wellcome Trust, the largest funder of medical research in the United Kingdom, which instructed its grantees in 2006 that they were permitted to use grant funds to pay authors' fees at open access journals and that, in any case, their work had to appear in a public digital library within six months of publication. Thus encouraged, and further stimulated by a favorable report about open access from the UK House of Commons[13] and supportive statements by the UK Research Councils and other funders, a group of British institutions established the world's second public digital library for life sciences research, UK-PubMed Central. This event was both symbolically important, as a sign of the international spirit of the movement toward greater access, and pragmatically reassuring, as evidence that electronic libraries had backup features in case of technical failures or fiscal uncertainty. Other European funding sources—in France, Germany, and elsewhere, and most recently the European Research Council—have also voiced enthusiastic support for enhanced public access. And, early in 2008, the Faculty of Arts and Sciences at Harvard University voted unanimously to require its members to provide all of their scholarly papers for posting on an openly accessible university website.[14*]

Although in 1999 the NIH was the first to set up a public digital library, recently the United States has yielded leadership of the drive toward greater access to the United Kingdom and other European countries. Although some members of Congress were persuaded that federally supported research articles should appear in PubMed Central, the first legislative effort to encourage this was largely abortive. In 2005, a statement in its appropriation bill directed the NIH to develop a so-called

---

* This policy requires that authors negotiate with journals to allow a license to be given to the university, a step that some journals may be unwilling to take. To avoid penalizing faculty who insist on publishing in such journals, the policy also provides an "opt-out" clause. But Harvard faculty must recognize how much the journals need them; the claim by Pat Schroeder that "some journals will be less than enthused about publishing Harvard faculty" is an empty threat.[15]

public access policy. However, under pressure from publishers, the formulated policy was inherently weak—"requesting," rather than mandating (or even encouraging), grantees to deposit NIH-supported articles in PubMed Central within a year after publication. Some recalcitrant society publishers, such as the American Society of Hematology and the American Association for Cancer Research, told their members and authors that they were not obligated to fulfill the request, that the deposition process might be difficult, that the societies would not help, and that papers posted in PubMed Central might differ from versions published in the society's journals.[16] Not surprisingly, compliance with the policy was poor—only about 4 percent of NIH-supported reports were deposited by investigators (in addition to those published in the 5 percent of journals that already provided their contents to the digital library).

In response to this ineffective showing, in 2007 a coalition of concerned members of Congress, librarians, open access publishers (including PLoS), and some scientific leaders worked to put a stronger policy in place, one that would mandate the deposition of all reports of NIH-funded research in PubMed Central. Although strong resistance from commercial and society publishers managed to extend the maximum delay from six months to one year after publication, the new measure survived scrutiny and remained in the appropriations bill through protracted debates.

On December 26, 2007, when President Bush signed the highly contentious appropriations bill for fiscal year 2008, the new NIH public access policy became the law of the land, and the policy was put in place by the NIH on April 7, 2008. This was a momentous occasion for the open access movement, for PLoS, for PubMed Central, for the NIH—and for me personally.[17] All journals must now accept the idea that at least some of their articles, those describing work supported by the NIH, will appear in the public library. If they don't comply, the journals will run the unacceptable risk of not attracting manuscripts from anyone whose work is supported by the NIH. The expansion of PubMed Central is likely to build enthusiasm for it, most journals will lose very few, if any, subscribers, and journals may even recognize the benefits—to them and the public—of placing all their content, including old issues, in a public library. The general movement toward public access is also likely to increase the attractions of true open access journals, which routinely place their papers in a digital public library at the time of publication.

A FINAL WORD ABOUT PUBLICATION PRACTICES

From the time of my fateful conversation with Pat Brown in a San Francisco café, enormous progress has been made toward a more equitable, more efficient, and more useful means of publishing and distributing reports of scientific work. Despite impressions that might be created by this personal account, movement towards greater access did not originate with us, nor would it have occurred without many thousands of people who have taken up the cause. Some of these people have come from the rank and file of the scientific community—investigators who want their work to be readily found, easily read, and frequently used and cited. Some have come from funding agencies that have learned that current practices may impede access to the work the agencies have paid for in the public interest.* More scientific allies have come from less well-endowed academic institutions, small commercial laboratories, lower-income countries, and other places where the lack of funds to buy subscriptions to journals limits access to published work that the public has largely paid for.** And many more supporters have come from groups of nonscientists—health care workers, patients and their advocates, teachers and students, reporters and their readers—frustrated by the obstacles to material they want to see and, as tax-paying citizens, feel a right to see.

Nor would it be correct to conclude that the battles have been won. Open access publishing is now accepted, but it is not yet nearly as widespread as it deserves to be. Public digital libraries are well established and rapidly growing. But, even with the new edicts from funders and the new

* In one important epiphany, the then new head of the Wellcome Trust, Mark Walport, found that he could not gain access to an electronic copy of a published paper describing work that was financed by his own agency, while using his personal computer on a trip. Such moments produce converts.

** Imagine being a scientist in one of these places and recognizing that your colleagues at rich institutions have access to all of the most desirable journals in your field, placing you at a distinct disadvantage in a competitive field.

NIH public access policy, a significant amount of current work will not be included. Furthermore, most older work, a legacy of many billions of dollars worth of research supported by federal and other funding agencies, has not been deposited in digital libraries and remains under copyright restrictions in its original, paperbound, and now largely warehoused journals.

I know about this deficiency from personal experience. One night, preparing for a class on the history of modern cancer research, I tried to get an electronic copy of the 1976 paper in *Nature* that describes our discovery of the c-src gene,[18] the work that was cited as the basis for our Nobel Prize in 1989. I searched PubMed and found only the authors and title, not even an abstract. The article was not deposited in PubMed Central. I eventually found a copy only by searching with Google Scholar. A professor in the Midwest had provided a poorly scanned copy to his class, and that copy made its way into the pages searched by Google. Surely, this is not the way to treat our scientific heritage. Increasing the world's access to the legacy we have and the legacy we are building will be an important project for a very long time.

EPILOGUE

A Life in Science

—

Science . . . cannot exist without a community of scientists. . . .

—JOSHUA LEDERBERG,
SCIENCE, TECHNOLOGY,
AND GOVERNMENT FOR A
CHANGING WORLD[1]

SCIENCE IS AN INHERENTLY PARADOXICAL ACTIVITY. NEARLY ALL GREAT ideas come from individual minds, and they are often first tested experimentally by a single person. But validation and acceptance of new information requires communication, convening, and consensus building—activities that involve a community. In many ways, it is this balance between the imagination of the individual and the conviction of the community that makes science particularly interesting and gratifying. Scientists may work and compete as individuals, but the competitive efforts are ultimately directed to the construction of a common edifice, knowledge of the natural world. There are few other fields in which such fierce independence serves the public good in such a transparently shared fashion.

Readers of these pages will have learned about my proclivities for communal activities. From my youthful adventures with the Amherst College newspaper to my more recent pleasures as a leader of the NIH, MSKCC, and the Public Library of Science, I have enjoyed doing things as part of a group. My scientific work, too, has been a shared enterprise—initially with Perlman and Pastan, later with Bishop, Vogt, and the West Coast Tumor Virus Consortium, more recently with the Lung Cancer

Oncogenome Group, and always with students, postdocs, and technicians. And some of my most passionately held positions on the politics of science have also been communal in character: developing better means for sharing scientific information, fostering the growth of science abroad, and advocating federal policies—on funding or stem cells—that advance the cause of biomedical research and the scientific community more generally.

These recurrent themes document my concern for community, but ultimately all of us must also be scientists privately, too, each in our own way, with our own history of engagement with science and our own convictions about its powers and joys. Although I define myself, here and elsewhere, as a scientist, I have never believed that I was destined, genetically or culturally, to be one. I happen to possess traits that are useful for a scientist—intellectual aptitude, an attraction to quantitative approaches, a skeptical frame of mind. But these qualities would also have helped me in other fields: journalism, business, policy studies.

There is, nevertheless, a widespread belief that scientists are born, not made, and that the determinants of success in science are mainly inherited. New friends often express surprise when they learn that my two sons are involved in the arts—jazz trumpet for Jacob, theater and writing for Christopher—and often comment that they must have gotten their mother's genes (Connie is a journalist and horticulturist).

I hope to have dispelled some of this misguided thinking in the course of describing how I became a scientist. The tolerance we enjoy in America for delayed career decisions allowed me to explore more possibilities than might have been allowed elsewhere. Then a few fortunate collisions with inspiring people and ideas oriented me increasingly toward basic research on viruses and genes. In telling a story that may now seem to have a certain logic, I do not mean to disguise the degree to which serendipity influenced the outcome.

I wanted this text to illustrate what I take a scientist to be, and to reflect my attitudes toward science—both its strengths and its limitations. In its broadest terms, science is a process that allows us to know things —and sometimes to understand them—by making observations, by testing hypotheses with experiments, and by thinking logically about the findings. I consider these principles to apply to virtually all fields of learning, including the humanities and social sciences, not just the natural sciences for which the term "science" is often reserved.

We live in an age of unprecedented technology. Since advances in the natural sciences generally depend on the development of more powerful means of measurement, it is not surprising that we have such a remarkable knowledge of the natural world and that the kinds of questions we can legitimately ask continue to expand. What we have done and can soon do as scientists would have been unimaginable even a generation ago.

Still, science is inevitably an incomplete process, and our knowledge of nearly all aspects of the natural world remains very far from complete. In the study of cancers, for example, we have yet to learn the full repertoire of events that drive a normal cell to adopt a malignant behavior or to identify the changes in most cancer cells that are optimal targets for intervention. Furthermore, our knowledge does not improve the societies in which we live unless other kinds of actions, both political and pragmatic, are taken. This means, in the case of cancer research, that our discoveries about cancer-causing mechanisms have little significance for the public unless we can find more effective ways to treat and prevent the disease and can deliver new benefits in an equitable manner.

Finally, some of man's deepest questions—about the origins of the universe or the purpose of life—remain beyond the grasp of science and are currently addressed only by the beliefs that belong to religions. Despite their undeniable cultural importance, religions for me do not provide a path to understanding or a basis for conviction. I admit that I am mystified by the universe, amazed that life has arisen even once, and immensely gratified that it has developed into the often delightful form it has taken for me. Jacques Monod, the French geneticist and philosopher who pioneered the study of gene regulation through his work with François Jacob on the lac operon, expressed the bafflement that all of us, scientists and nonscientists, are likely to experience when looking for explanations of our origins: "[L]ike the man who has just won a million, we still feel the strangeness of our condition."[2]

Given the circumstances of our existence in a universe without apparent purpose, I am surprised when human powers of observation and deduction actually tell us something profound about these grand topics. In my own lifetime, the most powerful and aesthetically satisfying examples of such revelatory science have come from two disciplines. Astrophysics has described the size, characteristics, and age of our universe. And molecular biology has shown that all forms of life on earth make use of the same basic rules for encoding and transmitting information, implying that these forms arose from a single, happy chance. Of course, neither set of findings tells us about the purposes of the universe or of life on earth. But it is extraordinary to have such dimensions to our knowledge. Doing science to learn these things is the best way I know to live with an incomprehensible universe.

Notes

—

PREFACE

1. C. P. Snow, *The Two Cultures* (Cambridge and New York: Cambridge University Press, 1998).
2. François Jacob, *The Statue Within: An Autobiography*, trans. Franklin Philip (New York: Basic Books, 1988).

INTRODUCTION

1. American Cancer Society, "Cancer Statistics 2006 Presentation," http://www.cancer.org/docroot/PRO/content/PRO_1_1_Cancer_Statistics_2006_Presentation.asp.
2. H. Varmus, "The new era in cancer research," *Science* 312 (26 May 2006): 1162–65.

CHAPTER 1: ORIGINS AND BEGINNINGS

1. Oliver Sacks, *Uncle Tungsten: Memories of a Chemical Boyhood* (New York: Alfred A. Knopf, 2001).
2. I. A. Richards, *Practical Criticism: A Study of Literary Judgment* (New York: Harcourt, Brace, 1929).
3. Zhores Medvedev, *The Rise and Fall of Trofim D. Lysenko*, trans. I. M. Lerner (New York: Columbia University Press, 1969).
4. James D. Watson, *The Molecular Biology of the Gene* (New York: W. A. Benjamin, 1965); B. Alberts, A. Johnson, J. Lewis, M. Raff, K. Roberts, and P. Walter, *The Molecular Biology of the Cell*, 5th ed. (New York: Garland Science, 2007).
5. J. D. Watson and F. H. Crick, "Molecular structure of nucleic acids: A structure for deoxyribose nucleic acid," *Nature* 171 (15 April 1953): 737–38.
6. O. T. Avery, C. M. MacLeod, and M. McCarty, "Studies on the chemical nature

of the substance inducing transformation of pneumococcal types: Induction of transformation by a desoxyribonucleic acid fraction isolated from Pneumococcus type III" (1944), reprinted in *Molecular Medicine* I (May 1995): 344–65; A. D. Hershey and M. Chase, "Independent functions of viral protein and nucleic acid in growth of bacteriophage," *Journal of General Physiology* 36 (May 1952): 39–56.

7. Horace F. Judson, *The Eighth Day of Creation: Makers of the Revolution in Biology* (New York: Simon and Schuster, 1979).

8. See note 5 above.

9. M. W. Nirenberg and J. H. Matthaei, "The dependence of cell-free protein synthesis in E. coli upon naturally occurring or synthetic polyribonucleotides," *Proceedings of the National Academy of Sciences* 47 (Oct. 1961): 588–602; P. Leder, B. F. Clark, W. S. Sly, S. Pestka, and M. W. Nirenberg, "Cell-free peptide synthesis dependent upon synthetic oligodeoxynucleotides," ibid., 50 (Dec. 1963): 1135–43; P. Lengyel, J. F. Speyer, and S. Ochoa, "Synthetic polynucleotides and the amino acid code," ibid., 47 (Dec. 1961): 1936–42.

CHAPTER 2: FROM LITERATURE TO MEDICINE TO SCIENCE

1. Douglas Bush, *English Literature in the Earlier Seventeenth Century, 1600–1660* (New York: Oxford University Press, 1945).

2. R. L. Perlman and I. Pastan, "Cyclic 3′5′-AMP: Stimulation of beta-galactosidase and tryptophanase induction in E. coli," *Biochemical and Biophysical Research Communications* 30 (27 March 1968): 656–64.

3. F. Jacob and J. Monod, "Genetic regulatory mechanisms in the synthesis of proteins," *Journal of Molecular Biology* 3 (June 1961): 318–56.

4. http://nobelprize.org/nobel_prizes/medicine/laureates/1965/jacob-lecture.pdf.

5. http://nobelprize.org/nobel_prizes/medicine/laureates/1965/monod-lecture .pdf.

6. http://nobelprize.org/nobel_prizes/medicine/laureates/1971/sutherland-lecture .pdf.

7. R. L. Perlman and I. Pastan, "Regulation of beta-galactosidase synthesis in *Escherichia coli* by cyclic adenosine 3′5′-monophosphate," *Journal of Biological Chemistry* 243 (Oct. 1968): 5420–27.

CHAPTER 3: THE FIRST TASTE OF SCIENTIFIC SUCCESS

1. Harvard University Commencement Address (1996), http://www.mskcc.org/ mskcc/html/1802.cfm.

2. D. Gillespie and S. Spiegelman, "A quantitative assay for DNA-RNA hybrids with DNA immobilized on a membrane," *Journal of Molecular Biology* 12 (July 1965): 829–42.

3. H. E. Varmus, R. L. Perlman, and I. Pastan, "Regulation of *lac* messenger

ribonucleic acid synthesis by cyclic adenosine 3′,5′-monophosphate and glucose," *Journal of Biological Chemistry* 245 (May 1970): 2259.

4. M. Emmer, B. deCrombrugghe, I. Pastan, and R. Perlman, "Cyclic AMP receptor protein of E. coli: Its role in the synthesis of inducible enzymes," *Proceedings of the National Academy of Sciences USA* 66 (June 1970): 480–87; L. Eron, R. Arditti, G. Zubay, S. Connaway, and J. R. Beckwith, "An adenosine 3′,5′-cyclic monophosphate-binding protein that acts on the transcription process," ibid., 68 (Jan. 1971): 215–18.

5. Gunther S. Stent, *The Coming of the Golden Age: A View of the End of Progress* (Garden City, N.Y.: Natural History Press, 1969).

6. L. Gross, *Oncogenic Viruses*, 2nd ed. (Oxford and New York: Pergamon Press, 1970).

7. J. M. Coffin, S. H. Hughes, and H. E. Varmus, eds., *Retroviruses* (Cold Spring Harbor, N.Y.: Cold Spring Harbor Laboratory Press, 1997).

8. H. M. Temin, "The effects of actinomycin D on growth of Rous sarcoma virus in vitro," *Virology* 20 (Aug. 1963): 577–82; "The participation of DNA in Rous sarcoma virus production," ibid., 23 (Aug. 1964): 486–94.

9. J. P. Bader, "Metabolic requirements for infection by Rous sarcoma virus, I: The transient requirement for DNA synthesis," *Virology* 29 (July 1966): 444–51.

10. F. Crick, "Central dogma of molecular biology," *Nature* 227 (8 Aug. 1970): 561–63.

CHAPTER 4: RETROVIRUSES AND THEIR REPLICATION CYCLE

1. H. M. Temin, "Homology between RNA from Rous sarcoma virus and DNA from Rous sarcoma virus-infected cells, *Proceedings of the National Academy of Science USA* 52 (Aug. 1964): 323–29; "The Participation of DNA in Rous sarcoma virus production," *Virology* 23 (Aug. 1964): 486–94.

2. http://nobelprize.org/nobel_prizes/medicine/laureates/1989/presentation-speech.html.

3. P. Rous, "Transmission of a malignant new growth by means of a cell-free filtrate," *Journal of the American Medical Association* 56 (1911): 198.

4. P. Rous in Report of the Director of the Laboratories to the Rockefeller Institute for Medical Research (April 1910), p. 265.

5. Ibid. (Jan. 1911), pp. 297–98.

6. P. Rous and W. F. Friedewald, "The Carcinogenic effect of methylcholanthrene and of tar on rabbit papillomas due to a virus," *Science* 94 (21 Nov. 1941): 495–96.

7. P. Rous, "Surmise and fact on the nature of cancer," *Nature* 183 (16 May 1959) 1357; http://nobelprize.org/nobel_prizes/medicine/laureates/1966/rous-lecture.html.

8. H. M. Temin and H. Rubin, "Characteristics of an assay for Rous sarcoma virus and Rous sarcoma cells in tissue culture," *Virology* 6 (Dec. 1958): 669–88.

9. H. M. Temin, "The DNA provirus hypothesis: The establishment and implications of RNA-directed DNA synthesis," *Science* 192 (4 June 1976): 1075–80.

10. H. M. Temin and S. Mizutani, "RNA-dependent DNA polymerase in virions of Rous sarcoma virus," *Nature* 226 (27 June 1970): 1211–13; D. Baltimore, "Viral RNA-dependent DNA polymerase," ibid., 1209–11.

11. D. Baltimore, A. S. Huang, and M. Stampfer, "Ribonucleic acid synthesis of vesicular stomatitis virus, II: An RNA polymerase in the virion," *Proceedings of the National Academy of Sciences USA* 66 (June 1970): 572–76.

12. J. Sambrook, H. Westphal, P. R. Srinivasan, and R. Dulbecco, "The integrated state of viral DNA in SV40-transformed cells," *Proceedings of the National Academy of Science USA* 60 (Aug. 1968): 1288–95.

13. F. H. Crick, "Central Dogma of Molecular Biology," *Nature* 227 (8 Aug. 1970): 561–63; News and Views, "Central Dogma Reversed," ibid., 226 (27 June 1970): 1198–99.

14. J. D. Boeke and J. P. Stoye, "Retrotransposons, endogenous retroviruses, and the evolution of retroelements," in *Retroviruses*, ed. J. M. Coffin et al. (Cold Spring Harbor, N.Y.: Cold Spring Harbor Laboratory Press, 1997), 343–436.

15. Ibid.

16. Ibid.

17. H. E. Varmus, P. K. Vogt, and J. M. Bishop, "Integration of deoxyribonucleic acid specific for Rous sarcoma virus after infection of permissive and nonpermissive hosts," *Proceedings of the National Academy of Sciences USA* 70 (Nov. 1973): 3067.

18. H. E. Varmus and P. O. Brown, "Retroviruses," in *Mobile DNA*, ed. M. Howe and D. Berg (Washington, D.C.: American Society for Microbiology, 1989); H. E. Varmus, "Retroviruses," *Science* 240 (10 June 1988): 1427–35.

19. S. Hughes, P. K. Vogt, P. R. Shank, D. Spector, H. J. Kung, M. L. Breitman, J. M. Bishop, and H. E. Varmus, "Proviruses of avian sarcoma virus are terminally redundant, co-extensive with unintegrated linear DNA, and integrated at many sites in rat cell DNA," *Cell* 15 (1978): 1397; P. R. Shank, S. Hughes, H. J. Kung, J. Majors, N. Quintrell, R. V. Guntaka, J. M. Bishop, and H. E. Varmus, "Mapping unintegrated avian sarcoma virus DNA: Termini of linear DNA bear 300 nucleotides present once or twice in two species of circular DNA," ibid., 1383.

20. See note 18 above.

21. P. O. Brown, B. Bowerman, H. E. Varmus, and J. M. Bishop, "Correct integration of retroviral DNA in vitro," *Cell* 49 (1987): 347.

22. P. O. Brown, "Integration," in *Retroviruses*, ed. Coffin et al., pp. 161–204.

23. E. A. Emini and H. Y. Fan, "Immunological and pharmacological approaches to the control of retroviral infections," in *Retroviruses*, ed. Coffin et al., pp. 637–706.

24. http://www.hivandhepatitis.com/recent/2007/1101607_a.html.

CHAPTER 5: THE RSV ONCOGENE AND ITS PROGENITOR

1. W. Cooper, *The Struggles of Albert Woods* (London: Jonathan Cape, 1952).

2. D. Hanahan and R. Weinberg, "The Hallmarks of Cancer," *Cell* 100 (2000): 57–70.

3. A. Knudson, "Mutation and cancer: Statistical study of retinoblastoma," *Proceedings of the National Academy of Sciences USA* 68 (April 1971): 820–23; R. A. Weinberg, *The Biology of Cancer* (New York: Garland Science, 2006).

4. P. C. Nowell and D. A. Hungerford, "Chromosome studies on normal and leukemic human leukocytes," *Journal of the National Cancer Institute* 25 (1960): 85–109.

5. S. Yoshinaga, K. Mabuchi, A. J. Sigurdson, M. M. Doody, and E. Ron, "Cancer risks among radiologists and radiologic technologists: Review of epidemiologic studies," *Radiology* 233 (2004): 313–21.

6. B. N. Ames, W. E. Durston, E. Yamasaki, and F. D. Lee, "Carcinogens are mutagens: A simple test system combining liver homogenates for activation and bacteria for detection," *Proceedings of the National Academy of Sciences USA* 70 (Aug. 1973): 2281–85; J. McCann, E. Choi, E. Yamasaki, and B. N. "Detection of carcinogens as mutagens in the Salmonella/microsome test: Assay of 300 chemicals," ibid., 72 (Dec. 1975): 5135–39.

7. http://cancergenome.nih.gov.

8. G. S. Martin, "Rous sarcoma virus: A function required for the maintenance of the transformed state," *Nature* 227 (5 Sept. 1970): 1021–23.

9. R. J. Huebner and G. J. Todaro, "Oncogenes of RNA tumor viruses as determinants of cancer," *Proceedings of the National Academy of Sciences USA* 64 (Nov. 1969): 1087–94.

10. P. E. Neiman, S. E. Wright, C. McMillin, and D. MacDonnell, "Nucleotide sequence relationships of avian RNA tumor viruses: Measurement of the deletion in a transformation-defective mutant of Rous sarcoma virus," *Journal of Virology* 13 (April 1974): 837–46.

11. K. Toyoshima, R. R. Friis, and P. K. Vogt, "The reproductive and cell-transforming capacities of avian sarcoma virus B77: Inactivation with UV light," *Virology* 42 (Sept. 1970): 163–70; P. H. Duesberg and P. K. Vogt, "Differences between the ribonucleic acids of transforming and nontransforming avian tumor viruses," *Proceedings of the National Academy of Sciences USA* 67 (Dec. 1970): 1673–80.

12. A. Bernstein, R. MacCormick, and G. S. Martin, "Transformation-defective mutants of avian sarcoma viruses: The genetic relationship between conditional and nonconditional mutants," *Virology* 70 (March 1976): 206–9.

13. D. Stehelin, R. V. Guntaka, H. E. Varmus, and J. M. Bishop, "Purification of

DNA complementary to nucleotide sequence required for neoplastic transformation of fibroblasts by avian sarcoma viruses," *Journal of Molecular Biology* 101 (1976): 349.

14. D. Stehelin, H. E. Varmus, J. M. Bishop, and P. K.Vogt, "DNA related to the transforming gene(s) of avian sarcoma viruses is present in normal avian DNA," *Nature* 260 (11 March 1976): 170.

15. D. H. Spector, H. E. Varmus, and J. M. Bishop, "Nucleotide sequences related to the transforming gene of avian sarcoma virus are present in the DNA of uninfected vertebrates," *Proceedings of the National Academy of Sciences USA* 75 (1978): 4102.

16. N. Rosenberg and P. Jolicoeur, "Retroviral Pathogenesis," in *Retroviruses*, ed. J. M. Coffin et al. (Cold Spring Harbor, N.Y.: Cold Spring Harbor Laboratory Press, 1997), chap. 10.

17. T. Padgett, E. Stubblefield, and H. E. Varmus, "Chicken macrochromosomes contain an endogenous provirus and microchromosomes contain sequences related to the transforming gene of ASV," *Cell* 10 (1977): 649; A. P. Czernilofsky, A. D. Levinson, H. E. Varmus, J. J. Bishop, E. Tischer, and H. M. Goodman, "The oncogene of an avian sarcoma virus (*src*): Nucleotide sequence of the gene and proposed amino acid sequence for gene product," *Nature* 287 (18 Sept. 1980): 198; R. C. Parker, H. E. Varmus, and J. M. Bishop, "The cellular homologue (c-src) of the transforming gene of Rous sarcoma virus: Isolation, mapping, and transcriptional analysis of c-src and flanking regions," *Proceedings of the National Academy of Sciences USA* 78 (1981): 5842.

18. S. H. Hughes, P. K. Vogt, J. M. Bishop, and H. E. Varmus, "Endogenous proviruses of random-bred chickens and ring-necked pheasants: Analysis with restriction endonucleases," *Virology* 108 (Jan. 1981): 222; B. Baker, H. Robinson, H. E. Varmus, and J. M. Bishop, "Analysis of endogenous avian retroviruses DNA and RNA: Viral and cellular determinants of retrovirus gene expression," *Virology* 114 (Oct. 1981): 8.

19. See note 14 above.

20. D. Spector, K. Smith, T. Padgett, P. McCombe, D. Roulland-Dussoix, C. Moscovici, H. E. Varmus, and J. M. Bishop, "Uninfected avian cells contain RNA related to the transforming gene of avian sarcoma viruses," *Cell* 3 (1978): 371.

21. See note 2 above.

22. See note 16 above.

23. J. S. Brugge and R. L. Erikson, "Identification of a transformation-specific antigen induced by an avian sarcoma virus," *Nature* 269 (22 Sept. 1977): 346–48.

24. M. S. Collett and R. L. Erikson, "Protein kinase activity associated with the avian sarcoma virus src gene product," *Proceedings of the National Academy of Sciences USA* 75 (April 1978): 2021–24; A. Levinson, H. Oppermann, L. Levintow, H. E. Varmus, and J. M. Bishop, "Evidence that the transforming gene of avian sarcoma virus encodes a protein kinase associated with a phosphoprotein," *Cell* 15 (1978): 561.

25. Rosenberg and Jolicoeur, "Retroviral Pathogenesis."

26. T. Hunter and B. M. Sefton, "Transforming gene product of Rous sarcoma virus phosphorylates tyrosine," *Proceedings of the National Academy of Sciences USA* 77 (March 1980): 1311–15; O. N. Witte, A. Dasgupta, and D. Baltimore, "Abelson murine leukaemia virus protein is phosphorylated *in vitro* to form phosphotyrosine," *Nature* 283 (28 Feb. 1980): 826–31.

CHAPTER 6: HOW PROTO-ONCOGENES PARTICIPATE IN CANCER

1. R. Weiss, "The search for human RNA tumor viruses," in *RNA Tumor Viruses*, pt. 3 of *Molecular Biology of Tumor Viruses*, 2nd ed., ed. R. Weiss et al. (Cold Spring Harbor, N.Y.: Cold Spring Harbor Laboratory, 1982), 1205–1281.

2. B. J. Poiesz, F. W. Ruscetti, A. F. Gazdar, P. A. Bunn, J. D. Minna, and R. C. Gallo, "Detection and isolation of type C retrovirus particles from fresh and cultured lymphocytes of a patient with cutaneous T-cell lymphoma," *Proceedings of the National Academy of Sciences USA* 77 (Dec. 1980): 7415–19; M. Yoshida, I. Miyoshi, and Y. Hinuma, "Isolation and characterization of retrovirus (ATLV) from cell lines of human adult T-cell leukemia and its implication in the diseases," ibid., 79 (March 1982): 2031–35.

3. H. E. Varmus, N. Quintrell, and J. Wyke, "Revertants of an ASV-transformed rat cell line have lost the complete provirus or sustained mutations in *src*," *Virology* 108 (1981): 28–46.

4. G. S. Payne, S. A. Courtneidge, L. B. Crittenden, A. M. Fadly, J. M. Bishop, and H. E. Varmus, "Analyses of avian leukosis virus DNA and RNA in bursal tumors: Viral gene expression is not required for maintenance of the tumor state," *Cell* 23 (1981): 311.

5. W. S. Hayward, B. G. Neel, and S. M. Astrin, "Activation of a cellular onc gene by promoter insertion in ALV-induced lymphoid leukosis," *Nature* 290 (9 April 1981): 475–80.

6. D. Sheiness and J. M. Bishop, "DNA and RNA from uninfected vertebrate cells contain nucleotide sequences related to the putative transforming gene of avian myelocytomatosis virus," *Journal of Virology* 31 (Aug. 1979): 514–21.

7. G. S. Payne, J. M. Bishop, and H. E. Varmus, "Multiple arrangements of viral DNA and an activated host oncogene in bursal lymphomas," *Nature* 295 (21 Jan. 1982): 209–14.

8. R. Nusse and H. E. Varmus, "Many tumors induced by the mouse mammary tumor virus contain a provirus integrated in the same region of the host genome," *Cell* 31 (1982): 99.

9. R. Nusse and H. E. Varmus, "*Wnt* genes," *Cell* 69 (1992): 1073–88; the Wnt Homepage, maintained by R. Nusse, can be found at http://www.stanford.edu/~rnusse/wntwindow.html.

10. F. Rijsewijk, M. Schuermann, E. Wagenaar, P. Parren, D. Weigel, and R. Nusse,

"The Drosophila homolog of the mouse mammary oncogene int-1 is identical to the segment polarity gene wingless," *Cell* 50 (1987): 649–57; C. Nüsslein-Volhard and E. Wieschaus, "Mutations affecting segment number and polarity in Drosophila," *Nature* 287 (30 Oct. 1980): 795–801.

11. K. R. Thomas and M. R. Capecchi, "Targeted disruption of the murine int-1 proto-oncogene resulting in severe abnormalities in midbrain and cerebellar development," *Nature* 346 (30 Aug. 1990): 847–50.

12. T. Reya, A. W. Duncan, L. Ailles, J. Domen, D. C. Scherer, K. Willert, L. Hintz, R. Nusse, and I. L. Weissman, "A role for Wnt signalling in self-renewal of haematopoietic stem cells," *Nature* 423 (22 May 2003): 409–14.

13. R. Taub, C. Moulding, J. Battey, W. Murphy, T. Vasicek, G. M. Lenoir, and P. Leder, "Activation and somatic mutation of the translocated c-myc gene in burkitt lymphoma cells," *Cell* 36 (1984): 339–48.

14. N. E. Kohl, N. Kanda, R. R. Schreck, G. Bruns, S. A. Latt, F. Gilbert, and F. W. Alt, "Transposition and amplification of oncogene-related sequences in human neuroblastomas," *Cell* 35, no. 1, pt. 1 (1983): 359–67; M. Schwab, K. Alitalo, K. H. Klempnauer, H. E. Varmus, J. M. Bishop, F. Gilbert, G. Brodeur, M. Goldstein, and J. Trent, "Amplified DNA with limited homology to *myc* cellular oncogene is shared by human neuroblastoma cell lines and a neuroblastoma tumour," *Nature* 305 (15 Sept. 1983): 245–48.

15. P. C. Nowell and D. A. Hungerford, "Chromosome studies on normal and leukemic human leukocytes," *Journal of the National Cancer Institute* 25 (1960): 85–109.

16. J. D. Rowley, "A new consistent chromosomal abnormality in chronic myelogenous leukaemia identified by quinacrine fluorescence and Giemsa staining," *Nature* 243 (1 June 1973): 290–93.

17. J. Groffen, J. R. Stephenson, N. Heisterkamp, A. de Klein, C. R. Bartram, and G. Grosveld, "Philadelphia chromosomal breakpoints are clustered within a limited region, bcr, on chromosome 22," *Cell* 36 (1984): 93–99; E. Shtivelman, B. Lifshitz, R. P. Gale, and E. Canaani, "Fused transcript of abl and bcr genes in chronic myelogenous leukaemia," *Nature* 315 (13 June 1985): 550–54.

18. Y. Ben-Neriah, G. Q. Daley, A. M. Mes-Masson, O. N. Witte, and D. Baltimore, "The chronic myelogenous leukemia-specific P210 protein is the product of the bcr/abl hybrid gene," *Science* 233 (11 July 1986): 212–14.

19. http://www.sanger.ac.uk/genetics/CGP/cosmic; http://cancergenome.nih.gov.

20. O. T. Avery, C. M. MacLeod, and M. McCarty, "Studies on the chemical nature of the substance inducing transformation of pneumococcal types: Induction of transformation by a desoxyribonucleic acid fraction isolated from Pneumococcus type III" (1944), reprinted in *Molecular Medicine* 1, no. 4 (May 1995): 344–65.

21. C. Shih, B. Z. Shilo, M. P. Goldfarb, A. Dannenberg, and R. A. Weinberg, "Passage of phenotypes of chemically transformed cells via transfection of DNA and chromatin," *Proceedings of the National Academy of Sciences USA* 76 (Nov. 1979): 5714–18.

22. C. J. Der, T. G. Krontiris, and G. M. Cooper, "Transforming genes of human bladder and lung carcinoma cell lines are homologous to the ras genes of Harvey and Kirsten sarcoma viruses," *Proceedings of the National Academy of Sciences USA* 79 (June 1982): 3637–40; L. F. Parada, C. J. Tabin, C. Shih, and R. A. Weinberg, "Human EJ bladder carcinoma oncogene is homologue of Harvey sarcoma virus ras gene," *Nature* 297 (10 June 1982): 474–48; M. Goldfarb, K. Shimizu, M. Perucho, and M. Wigler, "Isolation and preliminary characterization of a human transforming gene from T24 bladder carcinoma cells," ibid., 296 (1 April 1982): 404–9; E. Santos, S. R. Tronick, S. A. Aaronson, S. Pulciani, and M. Barbacid, "T24 human bladder carcinoma oncogene is an activated form of the normal human homologue of BALB- and Harvey-MSV transforming genes," ibid., 298 (22 July 1982): 343–47.

23. J. L. Bos, "Ras oncogenes in human cancer: A review," *Cancer Research* 49 (1 Sept. 1989): 4682–89; http://www.sanger.ac.uk/genetics/CGP/cosmic; http://cancergenome.nih.gov.

24. B. Rubinfeld, B. Souza, I. Albert, O. Müller, S. H. Chamberlain, F. R. Masiarz, S. Munemitsu, and P. Polakis, "Association of the APC gene product with beta-catenin," *Science* 262 (10 Dec. 1993): 1731–34; L. K. Su, B. Vogelstein, and K. W. Kinzler, "Association of the APC tumor suppressor protein with catenins," ibid., 1734–37; H. Clevers, "Wnt/beta-catenin signaling in development and disease," *Cell* 127 (2006): 469–80; http://www.sanger.ac.uk/genetics/CGP/cosmic; http://cancergenome.nih.gov.

CHAPTER 7: TARGETED THERAPIES FOR HUMAN CANCERS

1. D. J. Slamon, B. Leyland-Jones, S. Shak, H. Fuchs, V. Paton, A. Bajamonde, T. Fleming, W. Eiermann, J. Wolter, M. Pegram, J. Baselga, and L. Norton, "Use of chemotherapy plus a monoclonal antibody against HER2 for metastatic breast cancer that overexpresses HER2," *New England Journal of Medicine* 344 (15 March 2001): 783–92.

2. C. L. Sawyers, L. Timson, E. S. Kawasaki, S. S. Clark, O. N. Witte, and R. Champlin, "Molecular relapse in chronic myelogenous leukemia patients after bone marrow transplantation detected by polymerase chain reaction," *Proceedings of the National Academy of Sciences USA* 87 (Jan. 1990): 563–67.

3. D. Sidransky, T. Tokino, S. R. Hamilton, K. W. Kinzler, B. Levin, P. Frost, and B. Vogelstein, "Identification of ras oncogene mutations in the stool of patients with curable colorectal tumors," *Science* 256 (3 April 1992): 102–5.

4. Daniel Vasella and Robert Slater, *Magic Cancer Bullet: How a Tiny Orange Pill May Rewrite Medical History* (New York: HarperCollins, 2003); T. Hunter, "Treatment for chronic myelogenous leukemia: The long road to imatinib," *Journal of Clinical Investigation* 117 (Aug. 2007): 2036–43.

5. B. J. Druker, M. Talpaz, D. J. Resta, B. Peng, E. Buchdunger, J. M. Ford, N. B.

Lydon, H. Kantarjian, R. Capdeville, S. Ohno-Jones, and C. L. Sawyers, "Efficacy and safety of a specific inhibitor of the BCR-ABL tyrosine kinase in chronic myeloid leukemia," *New England Journal of Medicine* 344 (5 April 2001): 1031–37.

6. http://www.cancer.gov/newscenter/gleevecpressrelease.

7. G. D. Demetri, M. von Mehren, C. D. Blanke, A. D. Van den Abbeele, B. Eisenberg, P. J. Roberts, M. C. Heinrich, D. A. Tuveson, S. Singer, M. Janicek, J. A. Fletcher, S. G. Silverman, S. L. Silberman, R. Capdeville, B. Kiese, B. Peng, S. Dimitrijevic, B. J. Druker, C. Corless, C. D. Fletcher, and H. Joensuu, "Efficacy and safety of imatinib mesylate in advanced gastrointestinal stromal tumors," *New England Journal of Medicine* 347 (15 Aug. 2002): 472–80.

8. N. P. Shah, J. M. Nicoll, B. Nagar, M. E. Gorre, R. L. Paquette, J. Kuriyan, and C. L. Sawyers, "Multiple BCR-ABL kinase domain mutations confer polyclonal resistance to the tyrosine kinase inhibitor imatinib (STI571) in chronic phase and blast crisis chronic myeloid leukemia," *Cancer Cell* 2, no. 2 (Aug. 2002): 117–25.

9. M. Talpaz, N. P. Shah, H. Kantarjian, N. Donato, J. Nicoll, R. Paquette, J. Cortes, S. O'Brien, C. Nicaise, E. Bleickardt, M. A. Blackwood-Chirchir, V. Iyer, T. T. Chen, F. Huang, A. P. Decillis, and C. L. Sawyers, "Dasatinib in imatinib-resistant Philadelphia chromosome-positive leukemias," *New England Journal of Medicine* 354 (15 June 2006): 2531–41; H. Kantarjian, F. Giles, L. Wunderle, K. Bhalla, S. O'Brien, B. Wassmann, C. Tanaka, P. Manley, P. Rae, W. Mietlowski, K. Bochinski, A. Hochhaus, J. D. Griffin, D. Hoelzer, M. Albitar, M. Dugan, J. Cortes, L. Alland, and O. G. Ottmann, "Nilotinib in imatinib-resistant CML and Philadelphia chromosome-positive ALL," ibid., 2542–51.

10. See note 7 above.

11. C. L. Sawyers, "Making progress through molecular attacks on cancer," *Cold Spring Harbor Symposia on Quantitative Biology* 70 (2005): 479–82.

12. D. J. Slamon, E. H. Romond, E. A. Perez, and CME Consultants, Inc., "Advances in adjuvant therapy for breast cancer," *Clinical Advances in Hematology and Oncology* 4, no. 3, suppl. 1 (March 2006): 4–9.

13. C. I. Bargmann, M. C. Hung, and R. A. Weinberg, "The neu oncogene encodes an epidermal growth factor receptor-related protein," *Nature* 319 (16 Jan. 1986): 226–30.

14. H. Varmus, W. Pao, K. Politi, K. Podsypanina, and Y.-C.N. Du, "Oncogenes come of age," *Cold Spring Harbor Symposia on Quantitative Biology* 70 (2005): 1–9; B. Weinstein, "Addiction to oncogenes—the Achilles heel of cancer," *Science* 297 (5 July 2002): 63–64.

15. D. W. Felsher and J. M. Bishop, "Reversible tumorigenesis by MYC in hematopoietic lineages," *Molecular Cell* 4, no. 2 (Aug. 1999): 199–207.

16. L. Chin, A. Tam, J. Pomerantz, M. Wong, J. Holash, N. Bardeesy, Q. Shen, R. O'Hagan, J. Pantginis, H. Zhou, J. W. Horner II, C. Cordon-Cardo, C. D. Yancopoulos, and R. A. DePinho, "Essential role for oncogenic Ras in tumour maintenance," *Nature* 400 (29 July 1999): 468–72.

17. C. S. Huettner, P. Zhang, R. A. Van Etten, and D. G. Tenen, "Reversibility of acute B-cell leukaemia induced by BCR-ABL1," *Nature Genetics* 24, no. 1 (Jan. 2000): 57–60.

18. H. Varmus, "The new era in cancer research," *Science* 312 (26 May 2006): 1162–65.

19. G. H. Fisher, S. H. Wellen, D. Klimstra, J. M. Lenczowski, J. W. Tichelaar, M. J. Lizak, J. A. Whitsett, A. Koretsky, and H. E. Varmus, "Induction and apoptotic regression of lung adenocarcinomas by regulation of a K-Ras transgene in the presence and absence of tumor suppressor genes," *Genes and Development* 15 (2001): 3249–62.

20. V. A. Miller, M. G. Kris, N. Shah, J. Patel, C. Azzoli, J. Gomez, L. M. Krug, W. Pao, N. Rizvi, B. Pizzo, L. Tyson, E. Venkatraman, L. Ben-Porat, N. Memoli, M. Zakowski, V. Rusch, and R. T. Heelan, "Bronchioloalveolar pathologic subtype and smoking history predict sensitivity to gefitinib in advanced non-small-cell lung cancer," *Journal of Clinical Oncology* 22 (15 March 2004): 1103–9.

21. B. Vennström and J. M. Bishop, "Isolation and characterization of chicken DNA homologous to the two putative oncogenes of avian erythroblastosis virus," *Cell* 28 (1982): 135–43.

22. T. J. Lynch, D. W. Bell, R. Sordella, S. Gurubhagavatula, R. A. Okimoto, B. W. Brannigan, P. L. Harris, S. M. Haserlat, J. G. Supko, F. G. Haluska, D. N. Louis, D. C. Christiani, J. Settleman, and D. A. Haber, "Activating mutations in the epidermal growth factor receptor underlying responsiveness of non-small-cell lung cancer to gefitinib," *New England Journal of Medicine* 350 (20 May 2004): 2129–39; J. G. Paez, P. A. Jänne, J. C. Lee, S. Tracy, H. Greulich, S. Gabriel, P. Herman, F. J. Kaye, N. Lindeman, T. J. Boggon, K. Naoki, H. Sasaki, Y. Fujii, M. J. Eck, W. R. Sellers, B. E. Johnson, and M. Meyerson, "EGFR mutations in lung cancer: Correlation with clinical response to gefitinib therapy," *Science* 304 (4 June 2004): 1497–500.

23. W. Pao, V. Miller, M. Zakowski, J. Doherty, K. Politi, I. Sarkaria, B. Singh, B. Heelan, V. Rusch, L. Fulton, E. Mardis, D. Kupfer, R. Wilson, M. Kris, and H. E. Varmus, "EGF receptor gene mutations are common in lung cancers from 'never smokers' and are associated with sensitivity of tumors to gefitinib and erlotinib," *Proceedings of the National Academy of Sciences USA* 101 (Sept. 2004): 13306–11.

24. W. Pao, T. Y. Wang, G. J. Riely, V. A. Miller, Q. Pan, M. Ladanyi, M. F. Zakowski, R. T. Heelan, M. G. Kris, and H. E. Varmus, "KRAS mutations and primary resistance of lung adenocarcinomas for gefitinib or erlotinib," *PLoS Medicine* 2, no. 1 (2005): e17.

25. K. Politi, M. F. Zakowski, P. Fan, E. A. Schonfeld, W. Pao, and H. E. Varmus, "Lung adenocarcinomas induced in mice by mutant EGF receptors found in human lung cancers respond to a tyrosine kinase inhibitor or to down-regulation of the receptors," *Genes and Development* 20 (2006): 1496–510.

26. W. Pao, V. A. Miller, K. Politi, G. J. Riely, R. Somwar, M. F. Zakowski, M. G. Kris, and H. E. Varmus, "Acquired resistance of lung adenocarcinomas to gefitinib or erlotinib is associated with a second mutation in the EGFR kinase domain," *PLoS Medicine* 2, no. 3 (2005): e73.

CHAPTER 8: PARTNERSHIPS IN SCIENCE

1. Frederic Lawrence Holmes, *Meselson, Stahl, and the Replication of DNA: A History of "The Most Beautiful Experiment in Biology"* (New Haven: Yale University Press, 2001).

2. John Jenkin, *William and Lawrence Bragg, Father and Son: The Most Extraordinary Collaboration in Science* (Oxford: Oxford University Press, 2007).

3. David H. Hubel and Torsten N. Wiesel, *Brain and Visual Perception: The Story of a 25-Year Collaboration* (New York: Oxford University Press, 2005).

4. W. B. Yeats, *The Bounty of Sweden: A Meditation, and a Lecture, Delivered before the Royal Swedish Academy, and Certain Notes* (Dublin: Cuala Press, 1925).

5. http://nobelprize.org/nobel_prizes/medicine/laureates/1989/varmus-speech .html.

CHAPTER 9: THE ROAD TO BUILDING ONE

1. Harriet Zuckerman, *Scientific Elite: Nobel Laureates in the United States* (New York: Free Press, 1979).

2. M. Singer and D. Soll, "Guidelines for DNA hybrid molecules," *Science* 181 (21 Sept. 1973): 1114.

3. P. Berg, D. Baltimore, S. Brenner, R. O. Roblin, and M. F. Singer, "Asilomar conference on recombinant DNA molecules," *Science* 188 (6 June 1975): 991–94; P. Berg and M. F. Singer, "The recombinant DNA controversy: Twenty years later," *Proceedings of the National Academy of Sciences USA* 92 (Sept. 1995): 9011–13.

4. http://www4.od.nih.gov/oba/RAC/guidelines_02/NIH_Guidelines_Apr_ 02.htm.

5. J. Coffin, A. Haase, J. A. Levy, L. Montagnier, S. Oroszlan, N. Teich, H. Temin, K. Toyoshima, H. Varmus, P. Vogt, et al., "What to call the AIDS virus?" *Nature* 321 (1 May 1986): 10; H. E. Varmus, "Naming the AIDS Virus," in *The Meaning of Aids: Implications for Medical Science, Clinical Practice, and Public Health Policy,* ed. E. T. Juengst and B. A. Koenig (New York: Praeger, 1989), 3–11.

6. http://www.cshlpress.com/default.tpl?cart=120920971280173009&--eqsku datarq=347; http://www.accessexcellence.org/RC/AB/WYW/wkbooks.

7. John H. Trattner, *The 1992 Prune Book: 50 Jobs That Can Change America* (Washington, D.C.: Council for Excellence in Government, 1992).

CHAPTER 10: BEING NIH DIRECTOR

1. http://www.nih.gov/about/almanac/historical/legislative_chronology.htm; S. P. Strickland, *The Story of the NIH Grants Programs* (Lanham, Md.: University Press of America, 1989.

2. H. Varmus, "Shattuck Lecture: Biomedical research enters the steady state," *New England Journal of Medicine* 333 (21 Sept. 1995): 811–15.

3. G. J. Nabel, "Challenges and opportunities for development of an AIDS vaccine," *Nature* 410 (19 April 2001): 1002–7.

4. L. K. Altman and A. Pollack, "Failure of vaccine test is setback in AIDS fight," *New York Times*, 22 Sept. 2007.

5. J. Sulston and G. Ferry, *The Common Thread: A Story of Science, Politics, Ethics and the Human Genome* (Washington, D.C.: Joseph Henry Press, 2002); J. C. Venter, *A Life Decoded: My Genome, My Life* (New York: Viking Penguin, 2007).

6. D. G. Nathan and H. E. Varmus, "The National Institutes of Health and clinical research: A progress report," *Nature Medicine* 6 (Nov. 2000): 1201–4.

7. J. Cohen, "Is NIH's crown jewel losing luster?" *Science* 261 (27 Aug. 1993): 1120–27.

8. "Intramural Research Program: Report of the External Advisory Committee of the Director's Advisory Committee and Implementation Plan and Progress Report" (NIH, 1994, unpublished; available at the NIH Library, Bethesda, Md.).

9. D. Willman, "Stealth merger: Drug companies and government medical research," *Los Angeles Times*, 7 Dec. 2003; R. Steinbrook, "Financial conflicts of interest and the NIH," *New England Journal of Medicine* 350 (22 Jan. 2004): 327–30.

10. J. Kaiser, "Varmus backs some limits on NIH's consulting policy," *Science* 303 (19 March 2004): 1749.

CHAPTER 11: PRIORITY SETTING

1. Hearing before the Subcommittee on Health and the Environment of the Committee on Commerce, House of Representatives, *New Developments in Medical Research: NIH and Patient Groups*, 26 March 1998.

2. National Institutes of Health, *Setting Research Priorities at the National Institutes of Health*, Sept. 1997; http://www.nih.gov/about/researchplanning.htm.

3. Committee on the NIH Research Priority-Setting Process, Institute of Medicine, *Scientific Opportunities and Public Needs: Improving Priority Setting and Public Input at the National Institutes of Health* (Washington, D.C.: National Academy Press, 1998), http://www.nap.edu/openbook.php?isbn=030906130X.

4. H. Varmus, "Proliferation of National Institutes of Health," *Science* 291 (9 March 2001): 1903–5.

5. Committee on the Organizational Structure of the NIH, National Research Council, *Enhancing the Vitality of the National Institutes of Health: Organizational Change to Meet New Challenges* (Washington, D.C.: National Academy Press, 2003).

6. http://www.nih.gov/about/reauthorization/HR6164EnrolledVersion.pdf; http://www.nih.gov/about/reauthorization.

CHAPTER 12: BAD TIMES AND GOOD TIMES AS NIH DIRECTOR

1. Hearings before the Subcommittee on Oversight and Investigations of the Committee on Energy and Commerce, House of Representatives, *Scientific Misconduct in Breast Cancer Research*, 13 April and 15 June 1994.

2. Hearing before the Subcommittee on Oversight and Investigations of the Committee on Commerce, House of Representatives, *Continued Management Concerns at the NIH*, 19 June 1997.

3. National Institute for Occupational Safety and Health 1996, *National Occupational Research Agenda* (Publication No. 96-115).

4. Steering Committee for the Workshop on Work-Related Musculoskeletal Injuries: The Research Base, Committee on Human Factors, National Research Council, *Work-Related Musculoskeletal Disorders: A Review of the Evidence* (Washington, D.C.: National Academies Press, 1998).

5. S. G. Stolberg, "Clinton decides not to finance needle program," *New York Times*, 21 April 1998.

6. M. Schoofs and R. Zimmerman, "Clinton says he regrets decisions against needle-exchange program," *Wall Street Journal*, 12 July 2002.

7. Harvard University Commencement Address, 1996, http://www.mskcc.org/mskcc/html/1802.cfm.

8. http://www.answers.com/topic/family-and-medical-leave-act-of-1993.

9. W. J. Clinton, *My Life* (New York: Alfred A. Knopf, 2004).

CHAPTER 13: EMBRYOS, CLONING, STEM CELLS, AND THE PROMISE OF REPROGRAMMING

1. R. G. Edwards, B. D. Bavister, and P. C. Steptoe, "Early stages of fertilization in vitro of human oocytes matured in vitro," *Nature* 221 (15 Feb. 1969): 632–35; P. C. Steptoe and R. G. Edwards, "Birth after the reimplantation of a human embryo," *Lancet* 312 (12 Aug. 1978): 366.

2. http://www.history.nih.gov/01Docs/historical/documents/PL103-43.pdf.

3. R. D. Palmiter and R. L. Brinster, "Transgenic mice," *Cell* 41 (1985): 343–45.

4. M. R. Capecchi, "Gene targeting in mice: Functional analysis of the mammalian

genome for the twenty-first century," *Nature Reviews Genetics* 6 (June 2005): 507–12.

5. National Institutes of Health, *Report of the Human Embryo Research Panel* (27 Sept. 1994).

6. J. B. Gurdon, R. A. Laskey, and O. R. Reeves, "The developmental capacity of nuclear transplanted from keratinized skin cells of adult frogs," *Journal of Embryology and Experimental Morphology* 34, no. 1 (Aug. 1975): 93–112.

7. Stephen S. Hall, *Merchants of Immortality: Chasing the Dream of Human Life Extension* (New York: Houghton Mifflin, 2003), 104–22.

8. G. Kolata, "Scientist reports first cloning ever of adult mammal," *New York Times* 23 Feb. 1997, p. A1; I. Wilmut, A. E. Schnieke, J. McWhir, A. J. Kind, and K. H. Campbell, "Viable offspring derived from fetal and adult mammalian cells," *Nature* 385 (27 Feb. 1997): 810–13.

9. Hearings before the Subcommittee on the Departments of Labor, Health and Human Services, Education, and Related Agencies, Committee on Appropriations, House of Representatives, 26 Feb. 1997, pp. 13–18.

10. K. Hochedlinger and R. Jaenisch, "Nuclear transplantation, embryonic stem cells, and the potential for cell therapy," *New England Journal of Medicine* 349 (17 July 2003): 275–86.

11. Hearings before the Subcommittee on Public Health and Safety, Senate Labor and Human Resources Committee, Biomedical Research, 1 May 1997.

12. S. Castle, "Europe fails to endorse milk and meat from clones," *New York Times,* 25 July 2008.

13. K. Takahashi, K. Tanabe, M. Ohnuki, M. Narita, T. Ichisaka, K. Tomoda, and S. Yamanaka, "Induction of pluripotent stem cells from adult human fibroblasts by defined factors," *Cell* 131 (2007): 861–72; K. Okita, T. Ichisaka, and S. Yamanaka, "Generation of germline-competent induced pluripotent stem cells," *Nature* 448 (19 July 2007): 313–17; J. Yu, M. A. Vodyanik, K. Smuga-Otto, J. Antosiewicz-Bourget, J. L. Frane, S. Tian, J. Nie, G. A. Jonsdottir, V. Ruotti, R. Stewart, I. I. Slukvin, and J. A. Thomson, "Induced pluripotent stem cell lines derived from human somatic cells," *Science* 318 (21 Dec. 2007): 1917–20.

14. J. A. Thomson, J. Itskovitz-Eldor, S. S. Shapiro, M. A. Waknitz, J. J. Swiergiel, V. S. Marshall, J. M. Jones, "Embryonic stem cell lines derived from human blastocysts," *Science* 282 (6 Nov. 1998): 1145–47.

15. J. A. Thomson, J. Kalishman, T. G. Golos, M. Durning, C. P. Harris, R. A. Becker, and J. P. Hearn, "Isolation of a primate embryonic stem cell line," *Proceedings of the National Academy of Sciences USA* 92 (Aug. 1995): 7844–48.

16. Memorandum from Harriet S. Rabb to Harold Varmus, M.D., Director, NIH, 15 Jan. 1999; E. Marshall, "Ruling may free NIH to fund stem cell studies," *Science* 283 (19 Jan. 1999), http://sciencenow.sciencemag.org/cgi/content/full/1999/119/2; J. A. Johnson and B. A. Jackson, Stem Cell Research, Congres-

sional Research Service, 19 Sept. 2000, http://www.law.umaryland.edu/marshall/
crsreports/crsdocuments/RS20523.pdf.

17. W. S. Hwang, S. I. Roh, B. C. Lee, S. K. Kang, D. K. Kwon, S. Kim, S. J. Kim,
S. W. Park, H. S. Kwon, C. K. Lee, J. B. Lee, J. M. Kim, C. Ahn, S. H. Paek, S. S.
Chang, J. J. Koo, H. S. Yoon, J. H. Hwang, Y. Y. Hwang, Y. S. Park, S. K. Oh,
H. S. Kim, J. H. Park, S. Y. Moon, and G. Schatten, "Patient-specific embryonic
stem cells derived from human SCNT blastocysts," *Science* 308 (17 June 2005):
1777–83; Erratum in *Science* 310 (16 Dec. 2005): 1769; Retraction by D.
Kennedy, in *Science* 311 (20 Jan. 2006): 335; N. Wade and C. Sang-Hun,
"Researcher faked evidence of human cloning, Koreans report," *New York Times*,
10 Jan. 2006.

CHAPTER 14: GLOBAL SCIENCE AND GLOBAL HEALTH

1. I. Serageldin, "World poverty and hunger—the challenge for science, *Science* 296
(5 April 2002): 54–58.1.

2. R. M. Packard, *The Making of a Tropical Disease: A Short History of Malaria* (Baltimore:
Johns Hopkins University Press, 2007).

3. http://www.mimalaria.org/eng/aboutmim.asp.

4. D. Butler, "Malaria meeting charts rocky path ahead," *Nature* 338 (17 July 1997):
219.

5. D. G. McNeil, "Nets and new drug make inroads against malaria," *New York Times*,
1 Feb. 2008.

6. Commission on Macroeconomics and Health, *Macroeconomics and Health: Investing
in Health for Economic Development* (Geneva: World Health Organization, 2001),
http://whqlibdoc.who.int/publications/2001/924154550X.pdf.

7. R. W. Clark, *JBS: The Life and Work of JBS Haldane* (New York: Coward-McCann, 1969).

8. http://www.msi-sig.org.

9. http://www.msi-sig.org/scicorp.html; H. Varmus, "Building a global culture of
science," *Lancet* 360, suppl. (Medicine and Conflict) (21 Dec. 2002): s1–s4.

10. http://www.gcgh.org/about/Pages/Overview.aspx.

11. J. J. Gray, *The Hilbert Challenge* (Oxford: Oxford University Press, 2000).

12. H. Varmus, R. Klausner, E. Zerhouni, T. Acharya, A. S. Daar, and P. A. Singer,
"Grand Challenges in Global Health," *Science* 302 (17 Oct. 2003): 398–99.

13. C. P. Snow, *The Two Cultures* (Cambridge and New York: Cambridge University
Press, 1998).

14. S. Vendantam, "Scientist's visa denial sparks outrage in India," *Washington Post*, 23
Feb. 2006.

15. S. G. Stolberg, "In global battle on AIDS, Bush creates legacy," *New York Times*, 5
Jan. 2008.

16. http://www.cyi.ac.cy.

CHAPTER 15: SCIENCE PUBLISHING AND
SCIENCE LIBRARIES IN THE INTERNET AGE

1. Bethesda statement on open-access publishing, 20 June 2003, http://www.earlham.edu/~peters/fos/bethesda.htm.
2. http://www.ncbi.nlm.nih.gov/sites/entrez?cmd=search&db=pubmed.
3. http://www.plos.org; P. O. Brown, M. B. Eisen, and H. E. Varmus, "Why PLoS became a publisher," *PLoS Biology* 1, no. 1 (Oct. 2003): e36.
4. Bear Stearns, "European Equity Research Report on Reed Elsevier" (29 Sept. 2003).
5. http://www.who.int/hinari/about/en.
6. R. Darnton, "The new age of the book," *New York Review of Books*, 18 March 1999.
7. http://arxiv.org.
8. H. Varmus, "E-biomed: A proposal for electronic publication in the biomedical sciences" (NIH preprint 04.99doc; Bethesda, Md.: National Institutes of Health, 19 April 1999).
9. http://www.nih.gov/about/director/pubmedcentral/ebiomedarch.htm.
10. http://www.biomedcentral.com.
11. http://www.plos.org/about/letter.html.
12. J. M. Carmena, M. A. Lebedev, R. E. Crist, J. E. O'Doherty, D. M. Santucci, et al., "Learning to control a brain–machine interface for reaching and grasping by primates," *PLoS Biology* 1, no. 2 (2003): e42.
13. Science and Technology Committee, UK House of Commons. *Scientific Publications: Free for All?* (London: Stationery Office, 20 July 2004).
14. http://www.news.harvard.edu/gazette/2008/02.14/99-fasvote.html.
15. A. Lawler, "Harvard faculty votes to make open access its default mode," *Science* 319 (22 Feb. 2008): 1025.
16. http://www.hematology.org/policy/statements/nih_policy.cfm.
17. H. Varmus, "Progress toward public access to science," *PLoS Biology* 6, no. 4 (2008): e101.
18. D. Stehelin, H. E. Varmus, J. M. Bishop, and P. K. Vogt, "DNA related to the transforming gene(s) of avian sarcoma viruses is present in normal avian DNA," *Nature* 260 (11 March 1976): 170; see also above, chap. 5, n. 14.

EPILOGUE: A LIFE IN SCIENCE

1. J. Lederberg, in *Science, Technology, and Government for a Changing World* (New York: Carnegie Commission on Science, Technology, and Government, 1993).
2. Jacques Monod, *Chance and Necessity: An Essay on the Natural Philosophy of Modern Biology*, trans. Austryn Wainhouse (New York: Alfred A. Knopf, 1971).

Glossary

–

ATP. A nucleotide that serves as the principal source of energy in cells and is usually the source of phosphate that protein kinases (including tyrosine kinases) add to proteins.

BACTERIOPHAGE. A virus that infects and grows in bacteria.

BASE. A component of nucleotides and hence of RNA and DNA; four types are found in DNA and abbreviated A, C, G, and T.

BLASTOCYST. An early form of the embryo, containing many pluripotent cells in the inner cell mass.

CARCINOMA. A cancer arising from epithelial cells, such as the predominant cells in the lung, skin, kidney, pancreas, breast, and colon.

CENTRAL DOGMA. The term used to denote a major tenet of molecular biology: that genetic information flows from DNA to RNA to protein.

CLONE. A collection of entities—DNA molecules, cells, organisms—derived from and identical to a single progenitor and hence identical to each other.

CLONING. The act of making a clone of DNA, cells, organisms (or other things), usually requiring a number of related, but independent, sequential steps, such as somatic cell nuclear transfer for the cloning of organisms.

CLONING, REPRODUCTIVE. The act of cloning organisms with the intent to generate individuals that can mature into full-fledged adults.

CLONING, THERAPEUTIC. The act of cloning organisms with the intent to develop early embryos (blastocysts) from which human pluripotent cells can be derived.

CYCLIC AMP. A derivative of ATP that conveys signals in cells.

DNA. The hereditary material of cells and many viruses, formed of a chain of nucleosides derived from "deoxynucleotide" building blocks. DNA is usually present in cells as chromosomes in a double-stranded form (a double helix), but it can also exist in a single-stranded form.

EMBRYO. A developing organism in its relatively early phases, including the zygote, blastocyst, preimplantation, and postimplantation phases.

EMBRYO, PREIMPLANTATION. A mammalian embryo before it has implanted (or would normally implant) in the wall of the uterus; in human beings, this phase normally lasts about fourteen days.

ENDOCRINOLOGY. The study of hormones and the glands that produce them.

FETUS. A developing organism in its relatively late phases; the boundary between embryonic and fetal stages is arbitrarily assigned for different organisms. In human beings, this phase is usually considered to consist of the final two-thirds (six months) of gestation.

GENE. A functional component of a nucleic acid (DNA or RNA) that performs a defined function (such as encoding a protein) and is the hereditary unit of organisms, cells, and viruses.

GENETIC CODE. The correspondence between three bases in DNA or RNA and actions of the protein-synthetic machinery; each three-base "word" signals start, stop, or the addition of a specific amino acid to a growing protein chain.

GENOME. The complete set of genetic material (DNA in cells; DNA or RNA in viruses) in any biological entity.

HEMATOLOGY. The study of blood-forming organs and blood.

IMMUNOLOGY. The study of the immune system and its cell types.

INTEGRATION. The insertion of DNA (for instance, retroviral DNA) into a cell chromosome by cutting the chromosome and joining the two ends of incoming DNA to the cut ends of the chromosome.

LAC OPERON. The constellation of three bacterial genes that encode three proteins required to metabolize lactose.

LEUKEMIA. A cancer of blood cells, with the appearance of the cancer cells in the bloodstream.

LTR. The long terminal repeats at the ends of newly synthesized and integrated retroviral DNA; a signature of proviruses.

LYMPHOMA. A cancer of blood cells in the so-called lymphocyte lineage, usually without the appearance of cancer cells in the bloodstream.

MOLECULAR HYBRIDIZATION. The association of two strands of nucleic acid (DNA-DNA, DNA-RNA, or RNA-RNA) by base-pairing between complementary sequences.

NUCLEIC ACID. DNA or RNA.

NUCLEOTIDE. Small molecules that serve as building blocks for DNA and RNA, composed of one of four bases, a sugar, and some phosphate.

NUCLEUS. A portion of "eukaryotic" cells that consists of all of the cell's chromosomes and many proteins and other substances enclosed by a bilayered membrane. The nucleus thus contains all of the cell's genetic information (its genome) other than the small amount of DNA present in another organelle, the mitochondria.

ONCOGENE. A gene (viral or cellular) that makes a functional contribution to the conversion of a normal cell to a cancer cell.

PROTEIN. A major constituent of cells, composed of a chain of amino acids.

PROTEIN KINASE. An enzyme (also a protein) that takes phosphate from ATP and adds it to proteins, usually on the amino acids serine or threonine, more rarely on the amino acid tyrosine.

PROTO-ONCOGENE. A normal cellular version of a gene that can be converted to an oncogene by mutation or changes in gene expression.

PROVIRUS. The integrated form of retroviral DNA, which is synthesized after infection by reverse transcriptase.

PROVIRUS, ENDOGENOUS. A provirus that is genetically transmitted and is found in all cells of an organism; established by earlier (sometimes ancient) infections of germ cells by a retrovirus.

RIBOSOME. A biochemical machine formed of RNA and protein that synthesizes protein according to instructions (the genetic code) found in messenger RNA.

RETROVIRUS. A virus (such as RSV or HIV) that converts its RNA genome into a DNA form (provirus) early in infection.

RNA. A chain of nucleic acid, formed of ribonucleotide building blocks, normally found as a single chain, sometimes as a double-stranded form. RNA comprises the genome of some viruses (such as retroviruses) but is most commonly encountered as the "message" that carries information stored in DNA to the protein-synthesizing machinery.

SARCOMA. A cancer of connective tissue, such as bone, muscle, fibrous tissue, or fat.

SOMATIC. The property of belonging to cell lineages that do not participate in reproduction and hence do not transfer their genes to progeny organisms.

SOMATIC CELL NUCLEAR TRANSFER (OR "NUCLEAR TRANSFER"). The relocation of a nucleus, with its chromosomes, from a somatic cell to an egg. The egg is usually one from which the original, germinal nucleus has been removed with a needle. The transfer itself is commonly accomplished by fusing the relatively small somatic cell with the large enucleated egg.

STEM CELLS. Immature cells capable of dividing to give rise to daughter cells that are identical in potential to the stem cell (replacement or "self-renewal") and destined to mature into more highly differentiated members of one or more cell lineages.

STEM CELLS, ADULT. Cells that meet the criteria of stem cells but are isolated specifically from fully formed individuals and likely to generate mature cells that belong to only a single lineage or organ type (e.g., blood-forming stem cells or neuronal stem cells).

STEM CELLS, EMBRYONIC. Immature cells derived from the inner cell mass of blastocysts (early embryos), with pluripotent potential.

STEM CELLS, INDUCED PLURIPOTENT. Cells with the characteristics of pluripotent embryonic stem cells, but derived from more mature (or differentiated) cells that have been subjected to an "inducing agent" such as introduced genes.

STEM CELLS, PLURIPOTENT. Stem cells (e.g., those derived from blastocysts) able to generate progeny that give rise to more than one cell type or organ.

TRANSCRIPTION. The synthesis of RNA from a DNA template (or, vice versa, reverse transcription); the RNA is complementary to its DNA template (one strand of duplex DNA).

TRANSLATION. The synthesis of protein according to instructions in messenger RNA; performed by ribosomes.

TYROSINE KINASE. A protein kinase (such as the kinases encoded by src or abl genes) that transfers phosphate from ATP to the amino acid tyrosine in proteins.

VIRUS. A package of nucleic acid (DNA or RNA) wrapped up in protein that multiplies only after infecting cells.

ZYGOTE. The single-cell product of fertilization (the fusion of an egg and a sperm), with the potential to give rise to a complete organism through embryogenesis and fetal development.

References

—

GENERAL REFERENCES

Alberts, B., A. Johnson, J. Lewis, M. Raff, K. Roberts, and P. Walter, *The Molecular Biology of the Cell*, 5th ed., New York: Garland Science, 2007.

Bishop, J. Michael, *How to Win the Nobel Prize: An Unexpected Life in Science*, Cambridge: Harvard University Press, 2003.

Bush, Vannevar, *Science: The Endless Frontier*, Washington, D.C.: United States Office of Scientific Research and Development, 1946.

Cairns, John, Gunther S. Stent, and James D. Watson, eds., *Phage and the Origins of Molecular Biology, The Centennial Edition*, Cold Spring Harbor, N.Y.: Cold Spring Harbor Laboratory Press, 2007.

Coffin, John M., Stephen E. Hughes, and Harold Varmus, eds., *Retroviruses*, Cold Spring Harbor, N.Y.: Cold Spring Harbor Laboratory Press, 1997.

Crick, Francis, *What Mad Pursuit: A Personal View of Scientific Discovery*, New York: Basic Books, 1988.

Gross, Ludwik, *Oncogenic Viruses*, 2nd ed., Oxford: Pergamon Press, 1970.

Judson, Horace F., *The Eighth Day of Creation: Makers of the Revolution in Biology*, New York: Simon and Schuster, 1979; *25th Anniversary Edition*, Cold Spring Harbor, N.Y.: Cold Spring Harbor Laboratory Press, 1996.

Varmus, Harold, and Arnold J. Levine, eds., *Readings in Tumor Virology*, Cold Spring Harbor, N.Y.: Cold Spring Harbor Laboratory Press, 1983.

Varmus, Harold, and Robert A Weinberg, *Genes and the Biology of Cancer*, New York: Scientific American Books, 1992.

Watson, James D., *The Double Helix*, New York: Simon and Schuster, 1968.

———, *The Molecular Biology of the Gene*, New York: W. A. Benjamin, 1965.

Weinberg, Robert A., *The Biology of Cancer*, New York: Garland Science, 2006.

ACCESS TO AUTHOR'S SPEECHES AND PAPERS

MSKCC President's Pages (contains major speeches and testimony since 1993 and current activities): http://www.mskcc.org/mskcc/html/515.cfm.

The Harold Varmus Papers at the National Library of Medicine: http://profiles.nlm.nih.gov/MV.

Materials about the 1989 Nobel Prize in Physiology or Medicine: *Les Prix Nobel 1989*, Stockholm: Edita Norstedts Tryckeri, 1990: http://nobelprize.org/nobel_prizes/medicine/laureates/1989.

Acknowledgments

—

I AM INDEBTED TO TWO SETS OF PEOPLE WHO PLAYED DIFFERENT SORTS of roles in making this volume happen: the several people who assisted me with the Norton Lectures in 2004 and with the production of the book that evolved from them, and the much larger group of people who have been important to me in the phases of my life and career that are described here.

This book would not exist if Jean Strouse had not invited me to give the Norton Lectures, and it would be a lesser book if she had not advised and encouraged me, and edited my texts generously, during their preparation and over the subsequent four years of dilatory expansion to book length. I appreciate the help I have received from several people at W. W. Norton, especially its president and my editor, Drake McFeely, who made essential suggestions about the book's organization and style; his assistant, Kyle Frisina, who helped to assemble the photo illustrations; and Otto Sonntag, who improved the text by scrupulous copyediting. Sue Weil at MSKCC and Jamie Simon at the Salk Institute drew cartoons that are embedded in the text, and Marc Smolonsky in the NIH Director's Legislative Office and Renee Mastrocco at the Rockefeller University Archives provided access to documents that would otherwise have been difficult to obtain. Finally, I am greatly indebted to my friend and college classmate, Peter Berek, who was willing to read the entire manuscript in its penultimate phase, quickly and on short notice, and then offered astute comments that inspired the writing of an epilogue.

It is impossible to acknowledge formally all of those who have offered guidance, help, and friendship during a life that—while hopefully far from over—has already been long and complex. The list is headed by my beloved wife, Constance Casey; I hope that I have exercised the narrative restraint necessary to satisfy her critical mantra: "Keep them begging for more!" My sons, Jacob and Christopher, have given me perspective by their good humor and talents in the arts. The members of my first nuclear family—my parents, Bea and Frank, and my sister, Ellen—have influenced my life in many ways, especially by their strong social values.

My days at Amherst College were enriched by close relationships with many classmates and faculty members. Among these, Bill Pritchard, Ben DeMott, and Roger Sale were the teachers of literature who inspired me to consider a new direction professionally, and Peter Berek and Steve Arkin were fellow students who became lifelong friends in that other profession. I am grateful to my classmate Art Landy for inviting me to come along on his well-earned trip to Moscow and peer into the future of science. My brief time at Harvard Graduate School was made tolerable by the attentions of some great teachers, especially the late Bill Alfred and Anne Ferry, and by the antics of my roommates, Peter Berek and Bob Hirsch. At medical school, my redirection from literature and psychiatry to academic medicine and science was fostered by the teachings of Paul Marks, the late Don Tapley, and many others, and an important long-term friendship evolved from my close association with my classmate George Stewart.

At the NIH in the late 1960s, my introduction to scientific life was greatly influenced by the guidance I received from Ira Pastan, his colleagues (especially Bob Perlman and Benoit DeCrumbrugghe), and his wife, Linda.

My twenty-three years at UCSF began with an essential invitation from Mike Bishop, Leon Levintow, and Warren Levinson to join their group and would have been profoundly different without the intellectual stimulation and material benefits of my long-standing partnership with Mike. The years were also productive and enjoyable because of close interactions with too many others—faculty, fellows, students, and research associates—to laud each as they deserve. But a few warrant special mention: the two other faculty members of the Gang of Four, Marc Kirschner and Bruce Alberts, who nurtured my interest in the politics of science; my running partner and sounding board, Zach Hall; those trainees, including (especially, but in no special order) Titia DeLange, Tyler Jacks, Roel Nusse, Peter Pryciak, Greg Payne, Art Levinson, Steve Hughes, Ron Swanstrom, John Majors, Don Ganem, John Young, Pat Brown, and the late Richard Parker, who kept in touch and remained good friends, while becoming valued colleagues, after incubation at UCSF; and some laboratory staff whose steadfast work over many years was essential to the success of the Bishop-Varmus enterprise: Suzanne Ortiz, Nancy Quintrell, Jean Jackson, Karen Smith, and the late Lois Fanshier and Lois Serxner.

Life as the NIH director threw me together with a host of remarkably talented people, only a few of whom can be mentioned here. Donna Shalala offered me the job and treated me extraordinarily well. My daily life was dependent on the hard work of Vida Beaven, who served as my life organizer, and Ruth Kirschstein, who as deputy director did many unpleasant things that would otherwise have fallen to me. The various members of my "small staff" and the directors of the many institutes and centers were crucial for whatever success my tenure enjoyed; some of their achievements, but certainly not all, are noted in the text. The labors of Suzanne Ortiz, Pam Schwartzberg, Eric Holland, and others allowed my laboratory work to continue under difficult circumstances.

At Memorial Sloan-Kettering, I have enjoyed a supportive relationship with an extraordinary board, headed by Sandy Warner, Lou Gerstner, and Dick Beattie; the talents of the three other major leaders of the Center, Tom Kelly, Bob Wittes, and John Gunn; and the continued, essential attentions of Suzanne Ortiz and Vida Beaven to my lab and office.

Throughout my scientific career, I have been fortunate to have marvelous colleagues at other institutions who were willing to collaborate, write, edit, or simply talk with me; an incomplete list must include Peter Vogt, Bob Weinberg, David Baltimore, the late Howard Temin, Irv Weissman, Eric Lander, Mike Fried, John Wyke, Steve and Gail Martin, Robin Weiss, Arnold Levine, Inder Verma, John Coffin, Steve Hughes, Howard Schachman, David Hirsch, David Kessler (who suggested that I include a section on scientific partnerships after hearing me talk about them at Mike Bishop's recent birthday celebration), and Elias Zerhouni (my successor at the NIH). My colleagues at the Public Library of Science (especially the other co-founders, Pat Brown and Mike Eisen),

David Lipman at the National Library of Medicine and PubMed Central, Philip Griffiths and Arlen Hastings at the Science Initiatives Group, and Jeff Sachs at the Commission on Macroeconomics and Health are among those who have made my extracurricular activities especially fruitful.

Like many authors before me, I want to emphasize that any deficiencies in this text or the career it describes cannot be attributed to any of those named here, only to your narrator.

Illustration Credits

—

Index

—

"Insert" refers to the photo insert following page 146.